KOSHER INVESTIGATOR

How Rabbi Berel Levy built the OK and transformed the world of kosher supervision

Dovid Zaklikowski

With an epilogue by
Rabbi Menachem Hacohen

HASIDIC ARCHIVES   *New York*

Kosher Investigator © 2017 Dovid Zaklikowski

All rights reserved, including the right to
reproduce this book or portions thereof,
in any form, without prior permission,
in writing, from Hasidic Archives

www.HasidicArchives.com
HasidicArchives@gmail.com

ISBN 978-1-944875-04-6

Design by Hasidic Archives Studios

Printed in Hong Kong

בס"ד

*Dedicated to the
kosher consumer*

Contents

New Face on the Block   1

The Beginnings   12
American in Poland   25
War   40
Laying the Foundation   52

Day School Movement   60
A Mission   65
Lakewood   70
Elizabeth   73
National Education   80

The Investigator   116
Kosher Complications   135

Symbol Trouble	148
Sour Grapes	160

Ambassador — 176
In The USSR — 192

How Did He Do It? — 238

Rabbi Levy Explains — 244
Dairy Bread	244
Glatt Kosher	245
Bishul Akum	249
Foods from Israel	251
Blood Spots	254
Challah	256
Kitniyos	258
Cheese	261
Dark Chocolate	263

The Final Article — 266

T.U. Correspondence — 276

Bibliography	**284**
Acknowledgments	**288**
Index	**291**

PROLOGUE

NEW FACE ON THE BLOCK

When Rabbi Berel (Bernard) Levy assumed leadership of the Organized Kashruth "OK" Laboratories (the "Circle K") in 1968, some in the business speculated that he would be easy to push around. After all, the rabbi was relatively new to the growing and highly competitive field of kosher supervision.

OK Labs already certified products from major brands such as General Mills and Carvel, and under Rabbi Levy's direction, the list of companies began to grow. Soon he found himself in need of more supervisors, *mashgichim*, who would work onsite in factories to ensure that companies followed the complex kosher laws.

That was when Rabbi Chaim Yehudah "Yudel" Hurwitz, secretary-manager of the Kashruth Supervisors Union Local 621, saw an opportunity. Until then, the "Mashgiach Union" had represented only individual supervisors who worked at specific restaurants or wedding halls. If he could convince Rabbi Levy to hire his workers for agency jobs, the union's power would be substantially increased.

Rabbi Hurwitz was seen as a hero when he established the union in the early 1930s to protect mashgichim who supervised caterers at Jewish events. At that time, many caterers felt that giving the supervisor some leftover food was payment enough for his work.

"Everyone [should] take care [to eat at a caterer] that the supervision is 100 percent Union Made [sic]," read a 1945 union press release. According to the Indianapolis *Jewish Post,* the union alleged that "these men [the supervisors] were underpaid, and were often afraid to oppose the manager on matters of principle relating to dietary laws. So unionization will help religion."

In 1970, New York Governor Nelson Rockefeller praised Rabbi Hurwitz at the Jewish National Fund's 31st annual Maccabean Festival Dinner as one of "a few men who have been able to be both a servant to G-d and a statesman of labor, and to serve both causes completely."

Notwithstanding his success in making the supervisor's life more bearable, Rabbi Hurwitz at times engaged in nefarious actions, bullying catering halls and eateries into hiring union members. In this spirit, he contacted the new head of OK Labs and requested a meeting. Always courteous, Rabbi Levy agreed.

At the appointed time, Rabbi Hurwitz swaggered into the rabbi's office and, before any words were exchanged, took a handgun out of his pocket and placed it on the desk. His message was clear: he was prepared to back up the union's demands with force.

Rabbi Levy took one look at the gun and said, "If you want to use the gun, use it. Get it over with. Otherwise, place your gun in your car."

Rabbi Hurwitz replied that he could not leave the gun in the car, but Rabbi Levy was already walking toward the door. "Go put the gun in the car, or this meeting has just been canceled," he said. "I am not going to sit here while the gun is out on the table."

Rabbi Hurwitz protested, but Rabbi Levy was implacable. The gun was returned to the car.

The two discussed the pros and cons of using supervisors from the union; however, Rabbi Levy felt that he could not trust supervisors on someone else's recommendation. The OK symbol was his responsibility, and he needed to choose his mashgichim himself.

Occupation Change

Before entering the field of kosher supervision, Rabbi Levy had dedicated himself to Jewish education for more than two decades. At different times he had been involved in almost every aspect: running schools, fundraising, and heading development for a national educational organization.

In 1968, Rabbi Berel Levy was relatively new to the world of kosher supervision, and some in the business thought they could take advantage of him; however, that perception quickly changed. Courtesy of OK Kosher

As a good educator, he was always ready to ask questions, and it was his curiosity about how foods were made that led him to the OK. Asked how Rabbi Levy got involved in kosher supervision, his wife, Thelma Levy, replied, "*Kashrus* in his life, no matter how you looked at it, was, as we say in Yiddish, *geknipte ungebunden*. It was always related."

In the late 1940s, Rabbi Levy, who was then living in New Haven, Connecticut, met and befriended Dr. Pinchas Hacohen Peli, Connecticut representative of Hapoel Hamizrachi, whose mission was to fundraise for the organization's institutions in the newly established state of Israel.

Dr. Peli would later become renowned as a scholar, prolific writer and editor of the Israeli newspaper *Panim-el-Panim*, among other publications. Over the years, the friendship grew to include Dr. Peli's two brothers and their extended family.

Dr. Peli's uncle and father-in-law, Rabbi Hersch Kohn, known as the "Maxwell House Rabbi," gave kosher certification to a handful of companies that produced pantry staples, including Domino Sugar. Rabbi Kohn chose not to supervise poultry and dairy, because he felt they were too complicated to oversee.

When Rabbi Kohn needed assistance, Dr. Peli suggested his friend Rabbi Levy. Over the years, Rabbi Kohn asked Rabbi Levy to supervise plants from time to time, which he did after hours and during vacation from his day jobs. At one point, when Rabbi Kohn was eager to quit the business and retire to Israel, he told Rabbi Levy, "If I had someone like you to buy it, I would sell the supervision."

In 1965, Rabbi Levy's tenure as director of development at Torah Umesorah, the National Society for Hebrew Day Schools, was drawing to a close. He accepted Rabbi Kohn's offer and purchased the supervision, though it remained a part-time job. Three years later, he acquired the OK and became a full-time player in the kosher world.

The Chemist

No one could be involved in kosher supervision in America without being aware of Organized Kashruth Laboratories, which was celebrating its 30th year in 1965. The OK was founded by chemist Abraham Goldstein, who had been the first director of the Orthodox Union's kosher certification.

Mr. Goldstein immigrated to America after receiving his chemistry degree, and began working in kosher in 1917. His first project was to get companies to produce kosher rennet, allowing people to make kosher cheese at home. He also convinced a company to produce certified ko-

Rabbi Levy entered the world of kosher supervision at the request of Rabbi Kohn, who was known as the Maxwell House Rabbi. This ad notes that the coffee is kosher for Passover under Rabbi Kohn's supervision.

sher crackers, something that was unheard of at the time.

In the early 1920s, the Orthodox Union's women's division formed the Kosher Certification Service (KCS) in an effort to promote observance of the kosher laws, and hired Mr. Goldstein to head it. The chemist took his job seriously, meeting with companies, reviewing lists of ingredients and working with a board of rabbis to ensure that food was fit for kosher consumption.

"Through the tireless efforts of Mr. Abraham Goldstein of our Executive Committee, a large number of firms are applying to us for our supervision and endorsement for *kashruth*," the Orthodox Union's president, Rabbi Herbert S. Goldstein, said in a November 1927 speech. "In addition to the kosher crackers of the Loose-Wiles Sunshine Biscuit Company, we have persuaded Heinz (of 57 Varieties fame) to place on the

Chemist Abraham Goldstein, a pioneer of kosher production in the United States, with his three daughters. Courtesy of Ezra and Monica Friedman

labels of such of their products, twenty-six in number, as do not contain animal fat, and which are periodically inspected by us, the letter U in the letter O, indicating Orthodox Union."

In 1931, a rabbi sent rennet produced by the Junket Company to Mr. Goldstein to be tested for its kosher status. He ruled that it was not kosher, but when presented with this ruling, the company produced a kosher approval from Rabbi Shmuel Aaron Pardes, a member of the Orthodox Union's rabbinical board. A very public disagreement about the standards for kosher certification ensued between Rabbi Pardes and Mr. Goldstein, with the OU's board siding with Rabbi Pardes. The two sides publicly belittled one another, and in 1935 Mr. Goldstein left the OU to start the OK.

Mr. Goldstein passed away in 1944, and his son George, who had worked closely with his father, replaced him. At the time, the OK was focused on publishing the *Kosher Food Guide*, which at one point was printing over 120,000 copies and was widely distributed in the United States. The *Guide* fought fiercely for the kosher consumer, taking on major companies by debunking claims that their products were kosher.

Several companies were putting non-kosher animal gelatin in food products and denying that they were doing it. True to their name, OK Labs would put products through chemical tests that revealed the presence of the gelatin. When that happened, the products would become the subjects of fiery articles in the *Guide*.

When George Goldstein (pictured) wanted to retire, his son Arthur had no interest in taking over the OK, and introduced his father to Rabbi Levy. Courtesy of the Goldstein family

Despite fierce opposition from the OU and others, the OK's supervision began to grow. With the power of the *Guide* behind it, at one point the OK was the largest kosher supervision agency in the United States.

In the 1960s, George Goldstein wanted to retire. His son, Arthur, was not interested in taking over the business because of the amount of travel involved, so the search for a buyer began.

Down the block from Arthur Goldstein's home in the Borough Park neighborhood of Brooklyn was the iconic Lubavitch synagogue Ahavas Achim Tzemach Tzedek. Arthur would occasionally pray there on Shabbat morning, and there he met Rabbi Levy, who was a regular. With a shared interest in the kosher food world, the two soon became friendly.

One day, when father and son were discussing the future of the OK, Arthur suggested that Rabbi Levy would be the perfect person to take over the business. Like the Goldsteins, Rabbi Levy was a straight shooter and a man of principle. For a price tag of $50,000, ownership of the OK was transferred to Rabbi Levy.

In the final issue of the *Guide* in July 1968, a "special announcement" appeared on page 25:

> This issue of the Kosher Food Guide will be the last one published. After 34 years of publication, the Kosher Food Guide will be succeeded by an entirely new publication, the *Jewish Homemaker*.

There was no mention of the sale. That was left for the first issue of the *Homemaker*, where, above ads for Jennil bouillon cubes and Red Star yeast, a headline proclaimed: "O.K. Laboratories Under New Leadership."

A group of "rabbinic and lay leaders vitally concerned with the advancement of strict kosher supervision and observance have, after prolonged negotiations, assumed direction of the O.K. Laboratories and responsibility for the registered OK emblem and the Kosher Food Guide," the article announced.

Readers were assured that the OK would not only be involved in kosher supervision, but would also continue to promote awareness and observance of the laws of kosher. The article outlined three main principles by which the organization would be governed:

> 1. A rabbinical court *(bais din)* of accepted Torah authorities will

approve every certified product *(hechsher)*, and will resolve all questions pertaining thereto.

2. All supervising rabbis *(rabbaonim)* and supervisors *(mashgichim)* are men who respect and accept the direction and the opinion of the great Jewish decisors *(gedolei Yisroel)* and whose personal lives and synagogues are in strict accordance with Jewish law.

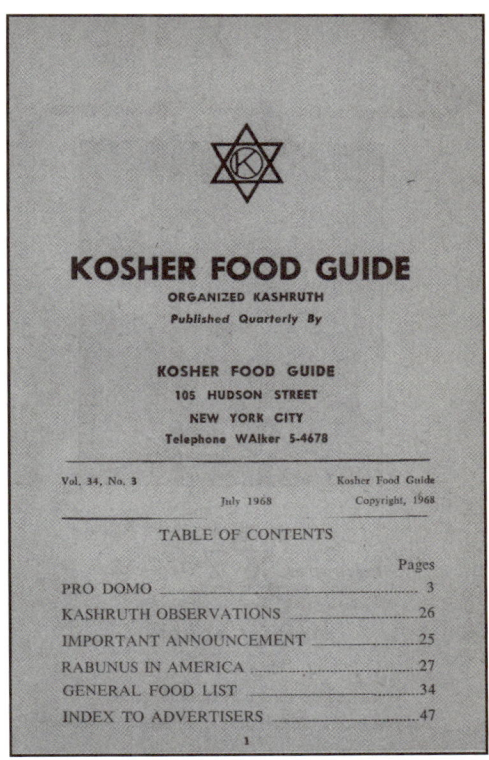

The Goldsteins used the Kosher Food Guide to educate the public and expose companies who were falsely claiming their products were kosher. The "important announcement" in this last issue of the guide heralded Rabbi Levy's new Jewish Homemaker publication. Courtesy of OK Kosher

3. A member of the staff who is both a recognized Torah scholar and an eminent scientist with extensive background in food chemistry will review questions involving scientific determinations.

Despite the use of a rabbinic board, from the beginning Rabbi Levy made it clear that the OK would not fall prey to the controversies and infighting that plagued other supervising agencies. "With OK Operations, the only authority and set of standards will be those of Rabbi Levy."

If a mashgiach on the road encountered a question or problem, he would immediately call Rabbi Levy. Rabbi Levy took every question seriously, when necessary visiting the factory himself.

"I remember having been awakened countless times by my father," his son and successor, Rabbi Don Yoel Levy, said, "and him telling me that he couldn't sleep all night because he was worrying about how to tackle a kashrus problem. Either he or I would catch the first plane available and go immediately to resolve the issue."

A 1979 article in the *New York Times* described how Rabbi Levy entered the kosher business by helping Rabbi Kohn. "Before you knew it, I got involved in it," he told the paper, "and this became my main occupation."

Noting that the OK was then certifying Barricini candy, Grape-Nuts cereal, Maxwell House coffee, Kraft margarine, Philadelphia cream cheese, Log Cabin syrup and Sam's knishes, among many other products, the reporter concluded, "Before anyone else knew it, he became a conglomerate."

The OK has come a long way since 1968, when its headquarters consisted of a desk in the Levy home. Today, a visitor to their large building in the Crown Heights neighborhood of Brooklyn will find dozens of offices buzzing with scholarly discussion and camaraderie. It is the largest independent kosher services agency, with 600,000 products under its supervision in 90 countries.

RABBI BERNARD LEVY

IF YOU DON'T ASK

There's an old, somewhat cynical, Yiddish folk saying: "Az m'fregt a shayla s'iz treif." If you ask a question of a Rav on a point of Kashrus it will most probably turn out to be *treif*. In these days of modern technology and chemical research, however, the formula might almost be reversed: "Az m'fregt *nit* kein shayla s'iz treif." If the conscientious Jewish Homemaker does not make proper inquiries, the chances are that a surprising number of items she takes into her home may not only be of questionable Kashrus, but may be out and out *treif*.

Whereas in former years the role of the Rav as a "posek"—an arbiter of Jewish law—demanded of him mainly a thorough knowledge of Shulchan Aruch and the later halachic literature on the subject of Kashrus, today's constantly changing conditions make it almost imperative for him to have, besides this knowledge, a tremendous amount of expertise in modern methods of food production.

The fact is that most foods brought into the average American household today go through some sort of processing and packaging. Every major company in the industry has a laboratory and a research department. These companies are constantly looking for ways to improve their products and to lengthen their shelf life. As a result, new ingredients, additives and preservatives are being perfected and put into use every day. In order to ascertain the Kashrus of any given product it is necessary to know the sources of these ingredients.

A good deal of the confusion in Kashrus is also due to the listing of ingredients on product labels. Many homemakers, seriously interested in maintaining Kosher homes are in the habit of reading these labels and, relying on their limited knowledge of ingredients, accepting the products as Kosher. Everyone knows that there are laws requiring these listings and that there are penalties for fraud. But what is not common knowledge is that these laws are limited in their requirements. A first-hand knowledge of these limitations is necessary in order to be able to determine whether the label, even accepted at its face value, is a guarantee of Kashrus.

The purpose of this column is to clarify these and similar questions related to modern Kashrus observance. For the past five years, in the course of my work in the Kashrus certification of a wide variety of food products, I have spent a great deal of time visiting a variety of food processing plants, and have gained quite a bit of first-hand information in this field which I intend to share with you. In the coming issues of the Jewish Homemaker I hope to answer the following questions:

Do all processed products require rabbinical supervision?
Are all vegetable oils and shortenings kosher?
Do natural and artificial flavors contain non-kosher ingredients?
Are kosher glycerines available?
Are there kosher gelatines available?
Are all semi-sweet chocolates pareve?
Are there any shaylos with dry cereals?
What is glatt kosher?
Are all chocolates kosher?
Can one rely upon the lists of ingredients listed on labels?

Perhaps you have a question of your own. By all means send it in. We shall try to answer in this column those questions which are, in our opinion, of universal interest.

An information gap in this area has led to quite a bit of confusion in Kashrus observance. The purpose of this column will be to share our knowledge with you in order to make it easier and more pleasurable for you, the Jewish Homemaker, to keep a kosher home.

JANUARY-FEBRUARY 1969

Rabbi Levy envisioned a magazine that would cover not only issues related to kosher, but also topics of general Jewish interest. The most controversial section, however, was his column, titled in the initial 1969 issue "If You Don't Ask." Courtesy of OK Kosher

PART ONE

THE BEGINNINGS

Berel Levy's strength of character was evident from his childhood. Born in The Bronx, New York, on November 18, 1921, to Louis (Eliezer) and Lillian (Liba) Levy, he was the youngest of three children. In Belarus, their family name was Lev; however, when they arrived in the United States, it was changed to Levy on the whim of an immigration agent.

His parents had both been raised in observant Jewish families, but they were no longer religious by the time Berel was born. He excelled in his studies, and his parents encouraged him to become a doctor. The young man had other ideas, however. He was attracted to the ways of his grandparents, about whom his parents had told him stories.

Berel Sussman, his maternal grandfather, who lived in the city of Ilya, in what today is Belarus, had been a fiery follower of the Chabad-Lubavitch movement. He used to say, "In the womb I was already a Lubavitcher." Young Berel heard how his grandfather once chastised the local slaughterer in his small Lithuanian town for the vulgar way he dressed. His zeal was a little too much for the members of his synagogue, and he was asked to leave the congregation. He did not want to join the other non-Chassidic synagogue in town, so he stood at the synagogue's

From an early age Berel, photographed here as a baby, followed his convictions.
Courtesy of Thelma Levy

window to pray, until finally he was permitted inside again.

Berel's parents lived in The Bronx for much of his childhood. There, as a young boy, he met his maternal great-uncle, Rabbi Avraham Dov Ber Levine. Rabbi Levine had arrived in the United States in 1923, shortly after Berel was born. Known as the *Malach* (angel), he was a fervent Chabad chassid and a great Talmudic scholar.

Rabbi Levine took a hard line against any connection with materialism and the non-Jewish world. He had photos of himself destroyed, and refused to receive visitors on American holidays. The young Berel was deeply impressed with his uncle's devotion to Torah, and with his insistence that American Jewish communities should emulate those in Europe, rather than conforming to secular American culture.

Under his uncle's influence, Berel announced that he wanted to

Berel's uncle, Rabbi Levine, known as the Malach (the Angel), did not allow himself to be photographed. In the 1960s a photograph of him on vacation (sitting, right) was discovered, and Rabbi Levy cherished it. Courtesy of Thelma Levy

leave public school and attend Yeshivah Torah Vodaath in Williamsburg, Brooklyn. His father reluctantly agreed, but his mother was not pleased with the move, putting them at odds for many years. "My grandmother was a strong-minded woman," recalled Fruma Gartenhaus, Rabbi Levy's eldest daughter. "My grandfather was a soft-spoken and kind person, who maintained a very close relationship with our family."

Around that time the Levy family moved to Connecticut, and at the age of 10, Berel moved into his uncle's house and began making the long commute from The Bronx to Williamsburg by trolley each day.

On the train, he often met Rabbi Weiler, who encouraged him to persevere in his studies. "Never give up," he told him, explaining how important it was to master one piece of the Talmud before continuing to the next one. "There were no shortcuts in those days," Rabbi Levy later said. "Either you learned hard and succeeded; or you didn't, and you would struggle in understanding the basics."

At times, when there was no room at the Levine home, Berel would sleep in a local synagogue or in someone's guesthouse. He never severed ties with his parents, however, and would occasionally visit them in Connecticut, though his commitment to a religious life never wavered.

Eventually, Liba Levy made peace with the path her son had chosen. Years later she would recall that when she was pregnant with Berel, she was in a car accident on a trip to the Catskills, and severely injured her neck. She was told that she would lose her child, but dismissed the doctor's words and continued with the pregnancy, hoping for the best.

Berel was born healthy, and the doctors told her that it was a miracle. "They said according to the medical books we both should not have survived," she remembered.

Before she left the hospital, one doctor told her that the miracle must have happened because "your baby is a spiritual child."

"You see," she once told her daughter, "he was spiritual since he was born."

Chassidic Influence

Founded in 1918, Torah Vodaath was among the first religious day schools in America. It was established by a group of Orthodox parents who hoped to avoid the temptations and the pressure to conform that had led so many Jewish children to abandon observance in public schools. The school would provide a quality Torah education coupled with secular studies. The first year, ninety children attended classes from preschool through sixth grade.

In 1922, Rabbi Shraga Feivel Mendlowitz was hired to teach eighth grade, and when the principal suddenly left in the middle of the year, he was asked to lead the school. While most of the students were American boys whose parents had abandoned traditional Jewish dress, Rabbi Mendlowitz stood out with a big beard and sidelocks. The new principal blended a love for study with an enthusiastic Chassidic outlook. He created the unique educational philosophy that Torah Vodaath uses to this day.

That philosophy was some years in the making, however. During the first decade of his leadership, Rabbi Mendlowitz confronted challenges from two charismatic Chassidic rabbis who had, in his mind, a negative influence on his students.

The first was Rabbi Yisroel Jacobson. Rabbi Jacobson followed his parents from the Soviet Union to America in 1923, with his wife and three young children. The move was made possible by his family connections, who vouched that the Chassidic man would be able to support his family in the new country.

A staunch Chabad chassid, Rabbi Jacobson had been involved in many of the covert Chabad activities in the Soviet Union. He was a scholar and activist, and it was his mission to arrange for the immigration of other Chabad followers to the United States. Unfortunately, the 1924 Immigration Act made this mission extremely difficult.

The Jacobsons moved to the "Jerusalem of America," the bustling neighborhood of Brownsville, Brooklyn. There the dynamic speaker was hired to be the rabbi of Anshei Babroisk, a congregation that had its roots in Chabad. Rabbi Jacobson became an integral part of the Chabad leadership in America.

In the early 1930s, he was delivering classes and conducting Chassidic gatherings at his home and in the synagogue. Many of the students of Torah Vodaath attended.

"Rabbi Jacobson's weekly gatherings were associated with warmth, congeniality and an awe-inspiring depth of Torah study," former student Rabbi Avraham Hecht wrote in his autobiography. "Relaxed by the informal stance of this learned individual, the teenagers and young men would share their thoughts, questions and quandaries with one whom they knew could be trusted. With an unusual amount of patience and understanding, Rabbi Jacobson resolved their problems and cleared up their confusion."

Rabbi Mendlowitz had a less favorable impression of Rabbi Jacobson's influence on his students. The school administrator respected Chabad teachings, but had misgivings about the sixth Chabad Rebbe, Rabbi Yosef Yitzchak Schneersohn, known as the Rebbe Rayatz. Rabbi Mendlowitz balked at the idea of Torah Vodaath students being in the thrall of one of the Rayatz's followers.

Rabbi Shraga Feivel Mendlowitz (pictured) wanted more than just Talmudic studies for his students, and arranged for older students to study Tanya with Rabbi Levine. Courtesy of Torah Umesorah

Clearly, the students needed more than just Talmudic study; they needed the warmth of Chassidic philosophy. The yeshivah began offering classes in Jewish philosophy and Chassidic texts. In addition, he sought a personality who could replace Rabbi Jacobson as a leader and source of inspiration for the students. He found it in Rabbi Levine, the Malach, whom he had known for years.

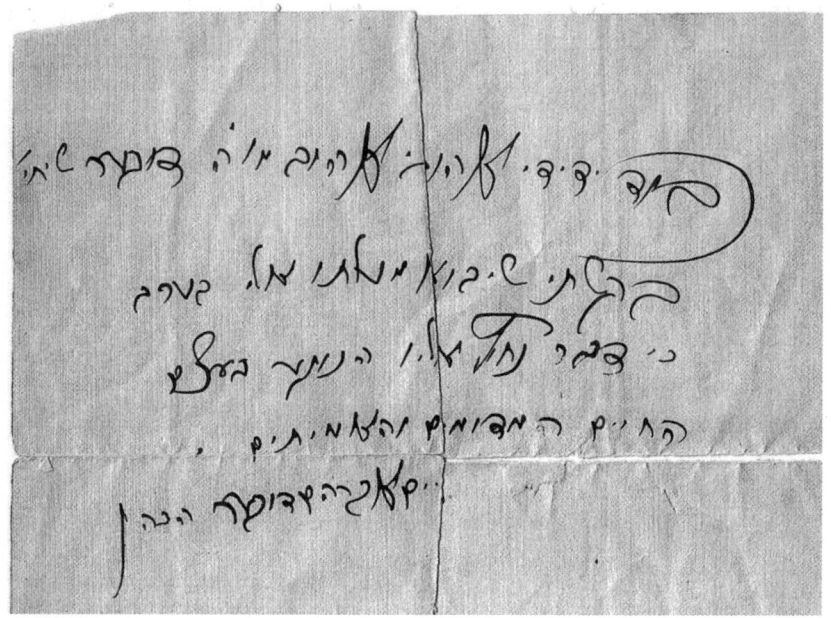

Rabbi Levine was not happy when he heard that Berel was studying secular subjects. With this note he summoned him for a one-on-one discussion about it.
Courtesy of Thelma Levy

By the time he arrived in the United States, Rabbi Levine didn't want anything to do with the current Chabad-Lubavitch leadership. Rather, he described himself as the student of the first three Chabad rebbes: Rabbi Schneur Zalman of Liadi (the author of *Tanya* and *Shulchan Aruch Harav*), Rabbi Dovber, and Rabbi Menachem Mendel (known as the Tzemach Tzedek). Rabbi Levine's rejection of the Rebbe Rayatz made him an attractive choice for Rabbi Mendlowitz.

Many Torah Vodaath students were indeed greatly influenced by Rabbi Levine, but not in the way Rabbi Mendlowitz had hoped. Rabbi Levine's young followers did away with their dress shirts, fedora hats and short jackets. They began to wear the dress of Chassidic Jews in Poland – long frocks, their tzitzit on top of their shirts, and felt hats without "pinches."

Rabbi Levine also taught the students to only use the Slavita and Zhitomer prints of the Talmud, and not the one that was favored at the school. He told them that Torah Vodaath itself was not a desirable place to study, because they taught secular subjects, and even had some disparaging words for Rabbi Mendlowitz.

Rabbi Levine was soon at odds with the school administration, and his most devoted followers were expelled. Shortly afterwards, he established his own yeshivah.

The young Berel was among the group of students, known as the Malachim (the angels), who followed his uncle to the new yeshivah, Nesivos Olam.

During this period, Berel's parents urged him strongly to continue with his secular studies, and he obliged them by studying math and history at night.

One day he received a note from Rabbi Levine: "I ask that your honor come this evening, for I have something crucial to discuss with you that is relevant to the essence – the imaginative and the real – part of life."

According to Rabbi Levine's biography, *Hamalach*, when Berel arrived that night, his uncle told him, "You learned about George Washington, your first president. I want to tell you something that you may not know about him. He was a drunk."

Berel got the message: the heroes of American history were not necessarily admirable people by Jewish standards.

Meeting in the Street

In the mid-1930s, brothers Leibel and Zalman Posner had just arrived in Brooklyn from Linden, New Jersey, to study at Torah Vodaath. One Friday evening, the two young boys, still before their bar mitzvahs, were walking on Lee Avenue in Williamsburg when they met Berel. "He was dressed like the Malachim," recalled Rabbi Leibel Posner. "I still re-

When it became difficult for Rabbi Levine to talk, he sent his students to study Tanya with Rabbi Yisroel Jacobson (left). Berel was greatly influenced by the rabbi and the friends he met there, among them Rabbi Shlomo Zalman Hecht (right). Also in the photo (center) is Rabbi Jacobson's father, Yaakov Leib. Courtesy of Yisroel Hecht/Lubavitch Archives

call very vividly his appearance. He had a round hat, *kapote* [frock] and curled *payos* [sidelocks]. His beard hadn't even started to grow."

For no apparent reason, Berel stopped them to talk, welcomed them and offered some words of inspiration. "It's close to 80 years since we first met that Friday night on Lee Avenue, but the little spark of warmth he struck in the heart of a lonely little out-of-town kid is still burning in the heart of a grandfather," said Rabbi Posner.

Another Mentor

Rabbi Yisroel Jacobson's parents lived in The Bronx, and when he first arrived in the United States, he and his father attended the synagogue where Rabbi Levine was the rabbi. A staunch follower of the Rebbe Rayatz, Rabbi Jacobson wanted nothing to do with Rabbi Levine. In synagogue, however, he was cordial to the rabbi.

Rabbi Levine ignored the fact that the Jacobsons and some others in his congregation were followers of the Rayatz, and took a liking to the younger Rabbi Jacobson. Shortly after he arrived, Rabbi Levine asked him to teach a Chabad discourse to his congregation, and afterwards he complimented Rabbi Jacobson on his delivery.

Thus began an unlikely friendship that would have many repercussions. When his

When Rabbi Levine died, the Jacobson family (pictured) welcomed Berel into their home. From left to right: Rochel (Altein), Shaina, Chaya (Hecht), Eva (Hartheimer) and Rabbi Jacobson. Courtesy of Agudas Chasidei Chabad Library

chain-smoking of Turkish cigars caught up with him, affecting his throat and making it difficult for him to teach, Rabbi Levine guided many of his students to go to Rabbi Jacobson to study *Tanya*, the fundamental text of Chabad. "Remember that you are going there to learn *Tanya*. Disregard anything he tells you about the Rayatz," he told his faithful students.

That was how Berel Levy came to meet Rabbi Jacobson. Within a few months he became close with the rabbi and, without his uncle's knowledge, secretly began attending Rabbi Jacobson's gatherings and those of other Chassidic luminaries who visited the United States.

By the time Rabbi Levine passed away in 1938, the 17-year-old was well on his way to becoming a full-fledged Chabad chassid. The Jacobsons welcomed the now homeless Berel into their home, where he slept in the kitchen on two chairs pushed together. Rabbi Jacobson treated him like a son and became one of the most influential people in his life.

Study Abroad?

In 1938, Berel's close friend Shlomo Zalman Hecht, whom he had met at Rabbi Jacobson's gatherings, became engaged to Rabbi Jacobson's daughter Chaya Sora. The groom had one condition, however. He requested that after the wedding his wife should accompany him to Otwock, Poland, where the main Chabad yeshivah, Tomchei Tmimim Lubavitch, was then located. The young woman agreed.

The idealistic young Hecht prevailed on Berel and another friend, Avraham Barnetsky, to follow him to Otwock. Berel was hesitant. "The distance between Bridgeport, Connecticut, and the town of Otwock," he wrote later, describing his qualms, "seemed much greater [than it was] in the eyes of that 17-year-old boy."

The Rebbe Rayatz himself had doubts about American students coming to study in Poland. At the time the financial situation of the yeshivah was, to say the least, not good. The students lived on rationed food, and the dormitories were far below the standard of living that Americans were used to.

"It is surely a good idea for them to come," the rebbe told his aide Reb Chatche Feigin. "However, we need to figure out the situation with the food. Will they be able to manage in yeshivah life with the other students? Or perhaps they could finance their own lodging and meals."

Berel was not deterred by a lack of material comforts. If anything, the hard life in Otwock was an inducement to go. He had learned how to live frugally from his uncle—from the time he had moved in with Rabbi Levine, he had received very little financial support from his parents. He

From a young age, Berel made do with very little in order to follow his dream of studying Torah. This 1938 passport photo was taken before his trip to Poland.
Courtesy of Thelma Levy

decided that to Poland he would go. The question was, how?

Steamer tickets to Poland were expensive. Berel's parents would not pay for the trip, and he was penniless. Rabbi Jacobson wrote a letter encouraging people to assist the young man in realizing his dreams, and Berel went around collecting money. The rabbi also asked those in his community to help purchase the tickets.

The date of departure neared, and only a small portion of the required funds had been collected. Berel was very pained that he had not succeeded in raising the money he needed. At the last minute, Rabbi Jacobson decided to foot the rest of the bill.

Irving Block, who attended Talmud Torah with Berel in Connecticut, remembered his friend's excitement about his upcoming trip. "I can see

At first, Rabbi Yosef Yitzchak Schneersohn, the sixth Chabad Rebbe, doubted whether the Americans would be able to handle the primitive conditions in the yeshivah in Otwock, Poland, but Berel proved that they could. Rabbi Schneersohn is seen here in Otwock around the time Berel arrived. Courtesy of Lubavitch Archives

myself walking one afternoon with your dad," he wrote to Rabbi Levy's son in 1994. "He was telling me that he is going to study in [Poland]."

Rabbi Jacobson wrote to inform the Rayatz that the students would be departing for Otwock, noting that "the second student, Berel Levy, is seventeen years old. He has many capabilities. He is the nephew of Rabbi Levine, and he studied by him. It is several months since he became close [to Chabad], and he is capable of, G-d willing, being a superb [student]."

AMERICAN IN POLAND

In November 1938, Berel Levy and Avraham Barnetsky boarded the famed *Queen Mary* in New York, bound for Poland. Berel's parents and siblings came to see him off, as did many of his friends from yeshivah and Rabbi Jacobson's classes.

His recently issued passport, which described him as 5'10" with brown eyes and black hair, was stamped with a warning from the State Department: "American citizens traveling in disturbed areas of the world are requested to keep in touch with the nearest American Diplomatic or Consular officers."

"Truth to tell, from the moment he had boarded the *Queen Mary* with his companion," Rabbi Levy later wrote, describing his younger self, "he had been conspicuously different from the other travelers, with his *payos*, long sidelocks which hung down his cheeks, and his Chabad-style prayers, prayers which grew lengthier and more enthusiastic."

On the ship were some prominent Jewish community and Zionist leaders, en route to a conference in Europe. They often engaged the two bright yeshivah students in conversation. One of the passengers was the editor of one of the largest daily Jewish newspapers in New York. He boasted to the young men that it was forty years since he had put on *tefillin*.

Emboldened by the unusual circumstances in which they found

themselves, the boys reproved the famous editor to his face. Standing nearby was an equally prominent leader of the religious Zionists, who berated the boys and asked them to speak courteously, or better yet, hold their peace.

To everyone's shock, the editor turned to the Zionist leader and said, "They are right! They are truly religious Jews. They should speak as they did to those who willfully disobey the commandments, rather than flatter us as you and your friends do."

Rabbi Levy later mused, "I wonder if that prominent religious Zionist leader remembers the unpleasant rebuke he received because of us. We surely never forgot it."

The trip took ten days, including a stopover in England. While the other passengers looked forward to exploring London, Berel considered it an annoying delay on his journey to his rebbe. "That great country aroused not a flicker of interest," he wrote in a 1978 article. "It was a minor stopover on the major road to Otwock."

When the two boys finally arrived in Poland, Berel immediately felt at home. "We hardly felt any strangeness in [our] new surroundings," he wrote. His family and friends in America seemed very remote to him compared to the scene in Otwock, "which seethed with hundreds of students from every part of Europe, and hundreds of chassidim arriving for *yechidus*, private audiences with the rebbe."

A few days after their arrival, there was a *farbrengen*, Chassidic gathering, where the Rebbe Rayatz delivered a Chassidic discourse. Most of the students were not permitted to attend these gatherings due to lack of space; however, the two new arrivals from America were permitted to go in.

Berel had not had a chance to eat a solid meal since his arrival, but he was not about to miss the opportunity to hear the rebbe speak. Standing on the side of the packed room, weak with hunger and still seasick

For Berel (center right) and Avraham (center left), the trip to Poland was a courageous step into the unknown. Rabbi Jacobson (third from left) encouraged them, however. In this photo, taken before they departed, Rabbi Avraham Paris (left), another Chabad chassid, appears with Herschel Schacter (right) and Mendel Baumgarten (second from right), two regulars at Rabbi Jacobson's Tanya class.
Courtesy of Lubavitch Archives

from the voyage, he looked over to where a table had been set with cakes and other refreshments, and fainted.

Influenza was spreading through Poland, and the two students, weak from their travels, caught the virus. For two weeks they were bedridden with fever. Unfazed, Berel pushed himself to recover as soon as possible, and began his regular study schedule. With the help of his friend Shlomo Zalman Hecht, he acclimated well.

Rigorous Study

Some doubts still remained about the Americans' ability to excel in Otwock, however. Reb Chatche Feigin wrote to Rabbi Jacobson to com-

Otwock was an idyllic vacation town. Students of the Lubavitch Yeshivah study among the trees (1930s). Courtesy of Rabbi Zev Katz/Lubavitch Archives

plain that the school administration had not been informed that the students were coming.

"You need to understand that American youth are not going to tolerate the amenities we currently have," the rebbe's aide wrote. "They also need additional attention and assistance in their studies," which would take the school time to arrange.

Berel, however, was perfectly content with the accommodations, writing to Rabbi Jacobson that he had all he needed. The rebbe told Berel to follow the regular study schedule of the yeshivah, the faculty paired the two Americans with the best students in the yeshivah for study partners, and Berel invested all his energies in learning.

"He changed our whole outlook about America," recalled Rabbi Yosef Wineberg, who was studying in Otwock at that time. "What we knew about America was that the stones are *treif* [unbefitting for a Jewish lifestyle]. Here you have an American with long payos."

The daily schedule was long and demanding, and the yeshivah expected students to make the most of every minute. Rabbi Levy recalled one example: Breakfast and supper were served in the yeshivah, and for lunch, students were given a voucher to purchase something to eat at a local store. If a student came late, he would not get the voucher. "Students quickly learned to be disciplined with their time," he said.

Berel especially liked the long, scholarly Chassidic discourses of the fifth Chabad Rebbe, Rabbi Shalom Dovber Schneersohn, from the years 1905 and 1906, known as *Samech-Hei* and *Samech-Vov*. After Chassidic gatherings, where students would spend hours telling stories, sharing ideas, singing *niggunim* (soul-stirring melodies) and saying toasts of *l'chaim* to each other, a tipsy Berel would recite long passages of these discourses from memory.

Years later, he would tell his son Rabbi Don Yoel Levy, "This is what you should be doing when you have a drink of *l'chaim*."

In a private audience, the seventh Chabad Rebbe, Rabbi Menachem Mendel Schneerson, told the younger Rabbi Levy, "Your father was an intellectual scholar. Follow in his ways and study scholarly Chassidic discourses."

Discrete Roommate

The American students were placed in the same room with Mendel Tenenbaum, one of the yeshivah's top students. Then just 21 years old, Mendel was already known to spend hours contemplating Chassidic philosophy each morning before dedicating many more hours to prayer.

Berel was deeply impressed with his new roommate. He had heard that one should study before praying from Rabbi Jacobson, but to see a refined young man putting the idea into practice was a powerful experience that he would frequently recall.

The two Americans, Berel (center) and Avraham (left), quickly grew comfortable in their new surroundings. Courtesy of Thelma Levy

"I would lie in bed, pretending to be asleep," he remembered. "Mendel would glance at us to see if we were sleeping. When he thought that we were in a deep sleep, he would spend hours reciting the *Krias shema al hamitah*," the prayer said before going to bed.

In his terse style, Rabbi Levy said, "There was what to hear and see!"

The Tough American

Berel had not lost any of his strong will and determination, and he soon made a name for himself as someone to be reckoned with. He recalled several incidents from his time in Otwock when he stood up for himself and others.

The yeshivah students were petrified of the local Polish citizens.

At times the Polish children would throw stones at the students sitting in the yeshivah courtyard. The students never retaliated, knowing that the authorities always took the side of the non-Jews. Once a boy threw a stone at Berel, expecting to get away with it as usual. Berel grabbed the boy by his pants and hung him from the branch of a tree. The boy dangled in the tree, terrified, until he finally managed to get down and run away.

The Polish boy went home and told his father what had happened. The next day, the father came with the police to the yeshivah study hall looking for the student who had "terrorized" his young son.

When the students realized whom they wanted, they told the police, "The student you are looking for is the new American student." They knew that the small-town police would not want to start up with an American. Sure enough, the officer immediately turned to the father of the boy and berated him for letting his son harass the students.

On another occasion, Berel was sitting on a bench in the study hall, and a young boy sat down next to him. The lad expected Berel to get up. The American did not understand what the issue was, and refused to move. The boy tried to push him off, and a brawl started. "We are in the yeshivah; let's go outside," Berel told him.

The two went outside, and the American bloodied the kid's nose. Berel found out later that the boy was Dovber Gurary (later known as Barry), the Rebbe Rayatz's grandson, who was a wild, obnoxious child.

Later that day, he got called to go to the Rayatz. "What happened?" the rebbe asked him. Berel said, "What do you want from me? I didn't start with him. He hit me, so I hit him back." The rebbe told him that he understood; "however, you should make up with him."

When Berel came to him, Barry accepted his apology. "You are an American," he said. "Teach me how to box."

One Shabbat, there was no hot water for coffee in the yeshivah.

Some of the students asked one of the younger students to go to a specific study hall in the town to bring some hot water. For whatever reason, some of the people there shoved the student under the table and started kicking him.

When he did not return immediately, the students asked Berel to go see what had happened. The American went to the study hall, grabbed one of the people there and told him, "Let the boy go, or else…"

They immediately released the boy.

English in Poland

Berel had brought a bunch of English books with him to Otwock, and would read them in his spare time. The school faculty was not happy that he was reading secular novels, and reported this to the Rayatz.

The rebbe called Berel in and asked him why he was reading secular books. "I read them because I don't want to forget my mother tongue," Berel said, "which I expect to resume speaking naturally when I return home, after my studies in Otwock."

"What sort of books are they?" the rebbe asked. "If they are scholarly books, it is a *shad der moach* [a waste of mental efforts]. If they are simply romantic stories, novels and such, then it's a *shad di hartz* [a waste of emotional efforts]. In any case, it cannot be of any great usefulness to you."

The Rayatz suggested that Berel's mother send the "News in Brief" section of the *New York Times* to him, so that he could "read the news reports in English from there."

Berel asked his mother to send him the sections, and she would include the "News in Brief" with her letters to him.

Walks with the Brisker

As a youngster, Berel had heard how the famed Rabbi Boruch Ber

Five months later, Avraham (standing, second from right) had a grown beard. He and Berel (standing, right) are seen here at the goodbye gathering for Rabbi Moshe Pinchus Katz (sitting, third from left), who married an American, Mindel Stockhammer. Also pictured is Rabbi Feigin (second from left), who organized the Americans' trip to Poland. Courtesy of Rabbi Zev Katz/Lubavitch Archives

Leibowitz, who headed the Kaminetz Yeshivah, was once visiting the United States to fundraise, and came to visit Rabbi Levine. Rabbi Leibowitz was one of the prized students of Rabbi Chaim Soloveitchik ("Reb Chaim Brisker"), who devised a classic method of studying the Talmud.

It was said that Rabbi Leibowitz spent the entire visit standing in silence before Rabbi Levine. When Rabbi Leibowitz left, he told his entourage, "Someone who *shushkit* [spoke in whispers] with my teacher, you must stand in front of him in awe!"

When he heard the story, Berel asked his uncle what his private chat with Rabbi Soloveitchik had been about. Rabbi Levine told Berel how, when he once met Rabbi Soloveitchik in Minsk, Belarus, the Talmudic scholar was struggling with some lines in Maimonides' *Moreh Nevuchim (Guide for the Perplexed)*. Rabbi Levine began explaining the lines to him. Some of the students wanted to listen in, and Rabbi Soloveit-

Berel enjoyed his walks with Rabbi Yitzchok Zev Soloveitchik (right) in Otwock.

chik motioned that they should discuss the text in hushed tones. When he finished explaining the difficult text, Rabbi Levine told him, "That was the simple explanation of the text. If you want, I could explain it to you according to Chabad teachings. Then you will have a totally new appreciation of it."

Rabbi Soloveitchik was an ardent Talmudist who respected Chabad leaders and their teachings, but preferred not to study them himself. He thanked Rabbi Levine and declined the offer.

When Berel was in Otwock, Rabbi Chaim's son Rabbi Yitzchok Zev, known as Reb Velvel Brisker, was there too. Berel introduced himself to the younger Rabbi Soloveitchik as the nephew of Rabbi Levine. Rabbi Soloveitchik greatly honored Berel for his family connection with one who was honored by his father, and invited him to come back often to visit him. While Rabbi Soloveitchik was in the town, Berel would regularly go on walks with him and discuss his Talmudic studies.

Rabbi Soloveitchik tried to convince Berel to join a non-Chassidic yeshiva, and suggested that he go learn at the Novardok Yeshiva in Baranovichy, then in Poland. The school was some 250 miles from Otwock, and Berel went there to visit. But, remembering his uncle's insistence on simple, non-modern dress, Berel was not impressed. "All the students were wearing white suits," he said. "I cannot learn in such a yeshivah."

Honoring Parents

Berel flourished in Otwock. In later years, he would treasure the "many wonderful memories... memories of the special atmosphere, the yeshivah schedule and the rebbe's manner." One thing, however, weighed on his mind. He was pained that he could not properly honor his parents.

"I knew I was doing the right thing when I left to study in Europe," he wrote. "But still, in my heart I could not forget that our sages taught that Jacob was punished for the 22 years that he was separated from his father and could not perform the mitzvah of honoring his parents. I was saddened by my distance from home."

He kept in touch with his parents by post. Although his father did not pay for Berel's voyage to Poland, he did send him 25 dollars a month, a fortune at the time, which he would use for his basic needs. Years later, he learned how much "pleasure and *nachas* I gave my father by my journey."

Then Berel received word that his father was dangerously ill. He rushed to inform the rebbe, and the Rayatz gave him a penny and wrote a letter: "In response to what you write about your father's failing health… May G-d send to him a cure, and give him an abundance of livelihood, materially and spiritually."

The Rebbe then added, "For you, may G-d help you to be a chassid, G-d-fearing person and a scholar." Berel sent the letter to his father in America. A few weeks later, he was delighted to hear that he had recovered.

Many years later, in the late 1950s, Rabbi Levy's father was becoming frail (Rabbi Levy's mother passed away in 1951), and family and friends advised him to stop driving. He refused to stop, however, and when Rabbi Levy asked him why, Eliezer Levy produced the penny and the letter from the Rayatz.

With deep faith and shining eyes, the father told his son: "Do you see? As long as I carry them with me, I have protection, and I need not fear anything!"

"I had practically forgotten the entire incident," Rabbi Levy wrote. "When I observed my father's boundless trust, I was proud and happy that I had sent the letter."

Rabbi Levy told his family not to worry about his father's driving. "Father knows what he is doing. No harm will come to him."

In July 1960, however, Rabbi Levy received a phone call at the close of Shabbat, informing him that his father had been hurt in an automobile accident.

Rabbi Levy rushed from his home in Elizabeth, New Jersey, to Bridgeport, to find his father in the hospital, badly hurt. As soon as Rabbi Levy entered the room, his father mustered up his strength to tell him, "It was Friday night. I wasn't carrying the penny."

His father had been walking home from synagogue and had been struck by a car. "He had nearly completed his crossing [the street] when he suddenly turned around or fell backwards into the path of a southbound car," the *Bridgeport Telegram* reported on July 20. Having become more observant later in life, he wasn't carrying the letter and penny, because Jewish law prohibits carrying objects in the public domain on the Sabbath.

Eliezer Levy never returned home. A few days later, on Tuesday, he died. At the funeral there was a huge line of cars, with many people coming to pay respects "to the sweet and kind coatmaker."

"The letter is now in my hands, an inheritance from my father," Rabbi Levy wrote. "When I look at it and the address from Otwock, the memories return to me in all their force. Memories of those precious

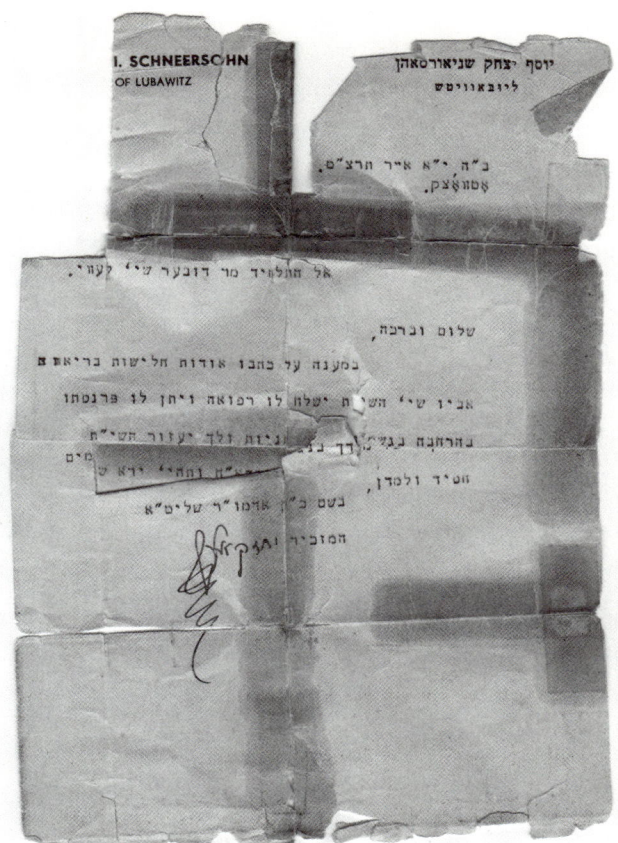

While Berel was in Poland, his father fell ill. Rabbi Schneersohn wrote this letter with a blessing for his recovery, and Eliezer Levy kept the letter in his pocket for over two decades. Courtesy of Thelma Levy

days, days when we were surrounded and protected by the holy spirit of the Rebbe."

More Americans

Seeing that Berel and Avraham had adjusted well to life in Otwock, the Rebbe Rayatz wrote to Rabbi Jacobson, suggesting that he send a larger group of Americans. "These students will be the nucleus," the rebbe wrote, "for a future yeshivah in your country."

Rabbi Jacobson turned to the class of Torah Vodaath students whom he had been mentoring over the past several years. "The most significant, and in some ways the most rewarding, of my projects was the class for yeshivah students that met every week in my home," he wrote in one of a series of autobiographical articles in *Di Yiddishe Heim* about those early years of Chabad activism in the United States. "They developed into truly Chassidic young men, who learned and understood Chassidism, who lived a Chassidic life."

Rabbi Jacobson discussed the rebbe's letter, and the students began to talk about the possibility of going to learn in Otwock. "It was their dream," he wrote.

The coming war had already cast a dark shadow over Europe, however, and the parents of the boys refused to consider the possibility of a trip to Poland. "Their parents were understandably adamant in their refusal to this ill-timed venture, and the idealistic teenagers were forced to agree," recalled Rabbi Hecht, who was one of the six students who planned to travel to Otwock.

The trip was canceled. Mordechai Fisher, another of the students, wrote to inform the rebbe, but the Rayatz responded immediately that "there is nothing to be afraid of," Rabbi Avraham Hecht wrote. "When I heard about this unexpected reply, my heart soared at the door of opportunity that had suddenly opened up for our small Europe-bound group."

The parents' objections were overruled. Rabbi Jacobson made arrangements for the trip, on which he planned to accompany the students, and on August 16, 1939, after a week's travel, the group arrived at the Lubavitch Yeshivah in Otwock.

The American students began to study, but it was difficult to concentrate. The situation in Europe was deteriorating rapidly. The Rebbe Rayatz delivered harrowing talks that were obviously a response to the political and social climate in Poland. One discourse, said specifically for the American students, focused on the famous line from the High

Holiday liturgy: "Repentance, prayer and charity avert the severity of the decree."

Despite his own obvious concern, the rebbe was adamant that people should remain calm. "Why are they making such a tumult over nothing?" he asked one of his aides, "It is a fallacy!"

In retrospect, Rabbi Wineberg said, it seems that the rebbe was trying to push off the war. "A righteous person, with a belief in something, helps to bring it into reality," he said in a 2004 interview. "The commentaries explain that the reason Noah did not want to enter the ark, even though G-d told him that there would be a flood, was because he wanted to push [it] off."

In the meantime, the American parents were worried, calling their sons and sending telegrams asking about their situation. "The thought of war was no longer a distant haze," Rabbi Hecht wrote, "for it had materialized in the form of a ferocious dragon right at our doorstep."

When Rabbi Jacobson asked whether it was perhaps too dangerous for the American students to remain, the rebbe told him not to worry. "They are American citizens, and if something happens, they could immediately go to Riga," he said.

On August 29, it became known that the Germans were planning an attack on Poland. The American consulate in Warsaw warned American citizens of the situation and directed them to leave.

Around this time, Rabbi Soloveitchik saw Berel walking in Otwock one morning. "What are you doing here?" he demanded. "Get out of here as soon as you can. Don't stay here!"

But Berel was determined to listen to his rebbe.

WAR

"The yeshivah was mobbed, full of *bachurim* [students] from all over," said Rabbi Avraham Barnetsky, describing the state of the Lubavitch school before the war. At times, the American students would study on the porch of their lodging to get away from the crowds and noise in the study hall. "Otwock had very good air," he said. "It was a pine tree resort area."

That was where they were on the morning of September 1, when fighter planes roared over their heads. A small debate erupted, because some of the student thought the planes were Polish. "They are too good to be Polish," Berel told them.

The students were not certain what was happening at first, though from the porch they could see the bombs falling. Venturing out, they saw craters in the ground and heard the sounds of people fleeing in confusion. The Jewish orphanage across the road was bombed. Berel stood frozen in horror at the sight of arms and legs lying scattered in the street.

He never forgot the scenes of that morning. "The planes were shooting indiscriminately," he later said, "just to instill panic. There was nothing strategic about bombing a resort town."

Instinctively, the American students made their way to the residence of the rebbe. "The room was crowded with many chassidim and their families," Rabbi Hecht recalled, "but no one was given permission

On September 1, 1939, the Germans bombed an orphanage across the street from where Berel was staying. Courtesy of Yad Vashem

to enter the rebbe's sanctuary at this difficult time."

At one point, the rebbe's aide emerged and approached Berel and Avraham with instructions that they should go to the home of the rebbe's mother, Rebbetzin Shterna Sarah, and assure her that there was nothing to fear. They immediately agreed.

Emerging from the rebbe's home, however, they were thrown into a world of chaos. The streets were full of the injured and the corpses of those killed by the bombing. "The streets absorbed mountains of pain and anguish without flinching, but our hearts were incapable of accepting the scene…" Rabbi Hecht wrote.

The short walk seemed to take an eternity. Finally, they arrived and delivered the rebbe's message, which noticeably calmed the rebbetzin.

On the way back to their lodging, the two tried to make sense of the situation and plan a course of action. Their first step was to call the U.S. consul in Warsaw to find out if war had been declared.

"I believe that this is only an attempt to intimidate the Polish people so that they will agree to Germany's demands," the official told them. "In the meanwhile, just listen to the radio. If necessary, I will have instructions broadcast in English for the American citizens."

Somewhat relieved, the students hurried back to the yeshivah to resume their studies as well as they could. But, a few hours later, another of the Americans called the consul and received a very different message. "Germany just issued an official declaration of war," the diplomat said. "I strongly advise you to travel immediately to Warsaw, and we will arrange your return to safety."

The students packed their suitcases and, hoping to get one last audience with the rebbe, made their way back to his house. A little over four hours after the first bombs fell, they found themselves in the rebbe's study.

The rebbe was dressed in his Shabbat clothing and looked calm. The students felt his serenity embrace and uplift them. "I think you should go to Warsaw for the time being," he told them. "You should be aware that every movement of a Jew is beloved in Heaven. Your coming here from America and your departure, you should know that it is beloved in Heaven… Know that every bomb has an address, and your address is not on a bomb."

From Warsaw, he advised them to travel to Riga. "Go without confusion or emotional excitement," he said. In Riga, Mr. Mottel Heifetz would be able to organize a study program for them. "I don't know when I will see you," the rebbe concluded. "I am wishing you to be inscribed for a good new year. May G-d help that we should meet again in good health."

Before they left, they asked the rebbe how they could observe Shabbat during their trip (it was Friday). The rebbe replied that the Hebrew date was Elul 18 – the birthday of the founder of Chassidism, the Baal Shem Tov, and of Chabad, Rabbi Schneur Zalman of Liadi – and that in the merit of these two, they would find it was not necessary to violate the Sabbath.

Outside, taxis already loaded with their luggage were waiting to ferry the ten Americans to Warsaw. They arrived at two o'clock that afternoon to find the consul irate. "Why didn't you leave when we told you?" he asked. "Didn't we warn you that war was going to break out and you all need to leave the country immediately?"

As the bombs were falling, Rabbi Schneersohn asked Berel and Avraham to assure his mother, Rebbetzin Shterna Sara (above), that there was nothing to fear. Courtesy of Lubavitch Archives

The students were shocked. Was this the same man they had spoken to earlier in the day, who kindly told them that he would take care of their travels to Riga? Then it dawned upon them that he had not known they were Jews. The realization "surprised and enraged the biased official, and twisted his features into a portrait of hate," Rabbi Hecht wrote.

At one point, the consul threatened to call the police. They realized they were on their own and would need to make arrangements for Shabbat before it was too late.

As the sun began to set, several of the students, Berel among them, decided to approach the famed Rabbi Menachem Ziemba, a great Talmudic genius who refused to take a rabbinical position and instead ran a store in the city. They went to his home and asked whether it would be permissible for them to desecrate the Sabbath in this time of need. The rabbi insisted that they first sit down to eat something before he would discuss any issues in Jewish law.

While they ate, Rabbi Ziemba went to the window and said that it was now safe to go out. "The Germans won't shoot at citizens walking around in the streets [in the evening]," he said. Later, after 11, it would be permissible to sign their names in order to check into a hotel, since to remain in the streets then would be dangerous. He showed them how to hold the pen and write in a way that would not constitute a biblical-level desecration of Shabbat.

Returning to the group, the students shared the rabbi's guidance. However, they all decided that since the rebbe had said they would not need to violate Shabbat, they would make every effort not to do so.

A Calming Voice

Berel and several of the other students found lodging that night, without having to sign, at the Imperial Hotel. They made the best meal they could with food that a widow back in Otwock had prepared for their trip.

The next day they went to pray at a small synagogue. The place was packed with refugees who had no place to eat. When the service was over, the owner of a catering hall announced that anyone who wanted to eat could come to the hall. There was supposed to be a wedding that night, he said, but surely due to the war it would be canceled.

Relief engulfed the students, and they went to the hall with the other refugees. As they ate, they discussed their situation and what the future might hold. Without the assistance of the consul, they were stranded, separated from anyone who might wield the slightest influence on their behalf.

Then, behind them, they heard a calming voice. "I am glad to see that you have managed to obtain sufficient amounts of nourishing food," the man said. "You will need all the strength you can muster to face the uncertain future."

The representative of the American Jewish Joint Distribution Committee echoed the rebbe's advice that they should make their way to Riga, which was still untouched by war. Visas, he told them, would need to be arranged. From the catering hall he took them to collect their luggage, and then to the Latvian embassy. But by the time they arrived, it was closed.

The man said he would find another way to get the visas, and disappeared, taking their passports with him. The students anxiously awaited his return, wondering if they had been foolish to trust him with their most precious possessions. To their great relief, he came back a short while later. He told them he had gone to the Latvian official's home and convinced him, after a few minutes of haggling, to give them visas.

Returning their passports, the Joint representative advised them to go to the train station immediately, but they waited until Shabbat ended before leaving. They found the station packed with refugees. The next train was scheduled to leave at five o'clock the next morning.

The trip was a harrowing one. As the train sped over mountains and across cliffs, the students witnessed gunfights between German and Polish planes. At one point a plane began shooting at the train. On a narrow pass with steep cliffs on either side, the train stopped, and the conductor commanded all of the passengers to make their way out of the cars and lie down on the tracks.

Looking out of the door, Berel realized that if he slipped as he climbed out, he would fall right off a cliff. "I will stay here," he told the conductor.

"If you do not go out, I will shoot you here," the conductor replied.

Berel obeyed, but the experience had a permanent effect on him. Although he was an exceptionally courageous individual, his son Rabbi Don Yoel said, "For the rest of life he was scared of heights."

Not Safe Yet

The students arrived in Riga on Monday, where they were greeted by Chabad chassidim. The locals immediately began to argue about who would have the merit of hosting the Americans. In the end, they held a lottery to decide the question.

The Americans immediately sent a telegram to Chabad in America, so that their families would know they were safe:

> Riga, September 4, 1939
>
> Agudas Chabad
>
> Arrived safely Riga out of danger, Rabbi [Schneersohn, the Rebbe is] well [in] Otwock. Three Hechts, Barnetsky, Levy, Kolodny, Gordon, Greenberg, Fisher, Altein.

Though it was not addressed to him specifically, the telegram was intended for their beloved teacher, Rabbi Jacobson. He had left Otwock shortly before war broke out, and they assumed he had already returned to America. In fact, he was stuck in Paris, waiting for a ship to take him to New York.

His immediate concern was for the American students in Otwock, but he could not help them while he was trapped in Europe. He recalled waiting in line at the United States Lines ocean liner company to obtain a ticket to America and being told there was a waiting list of nine hundred names. As he stood there with a heavy heart, a man approached and asked what was bothering him.

"I poured out my troubles," Rabbi Jacobson wrote, "that I had left my children [students] and others for whom I was responsible in Poland, and must get home to America to save them. And here I am stuck in France, and who knows when I will get home. Their lives are in terrible danger."

The man spoke to some officials at the company and miraculously obtained a coveted ticket for Rabbi Jacobson.

Meanwhile, the students had resumed their studies in the local Chabad synagogue in Riga, where, as the rebbe had promised, Mr. Heifetz arranged their schedule.

American students Avraham Barnetsky (right) and Yitzchok Kolodny traveled through Stockholm, Sweden, on the way to the United States. Courtesy of Agudas Chasidei Chabad Library

They remained in Riga for the High Holidays, when they had the opportunity to observe some of the great Chabad luminaries in prayer. "[Their] unparalleled devotion… seemed to form a straight path toward [the prayers'] destination on High," Rabbi Hecht wrote.

The Americans were so inspired by the chassidim in Riga that they were in no hurry to return home. "Since we, too, want very much to stay here as long as we can in order to fulfill our purpose for which we originally came [to Europe]," Mordechai Fisher wrote to Rabbi Shmuel Levitin, who was in New York, "we have decided to remain here at least until after the holiday of Sukkos."

The local chassidim, in turn, were impressed with the Americans. "With great wonder," Rabbi Elya Chaim Althaus, a Chabad activist in Riga, wrote to Rabbi Jacobson, "people were asking, 'Is it possible that America could truly produce such prosperous fruit?'" referring to the students. "I cannot describe to you their lack of will to leave Europe, the land where the rebbe and all those connected to him are found."

During Sukkot, however, it became clear that the war would soon reach Latvia, and the students realized they could not stay.

Immediately after the holiday they made their way via a small boat to Norway. There was a storm at sea, and what should have been a short journey became a long one. From Norway the group traveled to Stockholm, Sweden, where Rabbi Israel Zuber, a Chabad disciple, was the local rabbi. He arranged for them to stay at a hotel, and the students continued their studies in his synagogue, while Rabbi Jacobson, now back in New York, worked to secure them safe passage to America.

After several weeks in Sweden, the Americans boarded the *S.S. Mormaxport*, an American cargo ship, and embarked on the final, and most dangerous, leg of their journey. The German U-boats were known to sink vessels with no provocation, and the ship was stopped several times. The Germans repeatedly threatened to capsize the ship, "until they realized that they were dealing with American citizens," Rabbi Hecht wrote.

Stormy winter weather made the trip more difficult. There was little to eat on the boat, and the students survived on hard crackers. "It was like when the Jews were in Egypt," Rabbi Hecht later said. "They used to eat [something like] this cracker. It was made just from flour and water."

On November 4, a Shabbat, the students arrived in Hoboken, New Jersey. Their families and friends, who had not heard from them since

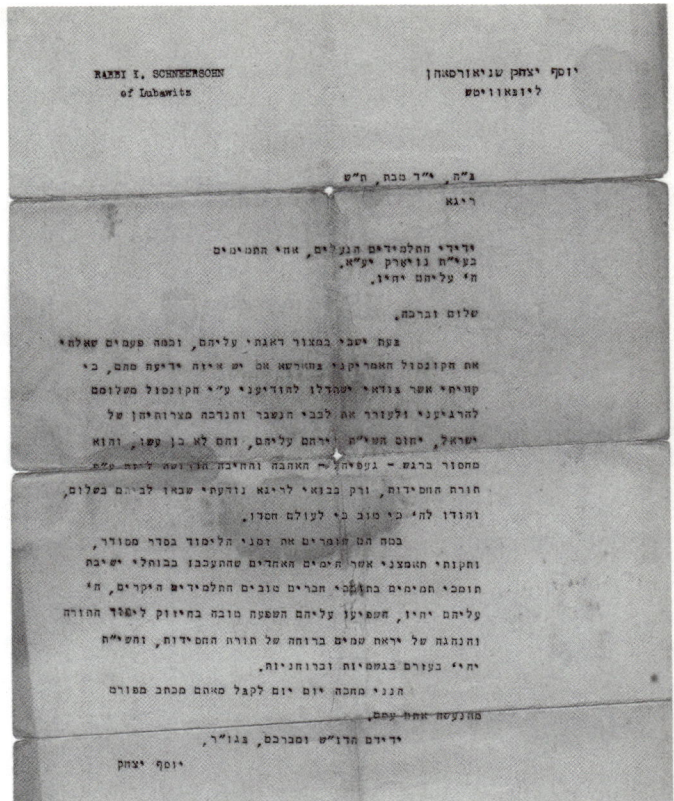

Rabbi Schneersohn wrote, expressing his surprise that the students had not kept him informed about the progress of their journey to the United States. *Courtesy of Thelma Levy*

the telegram from Riga, were surprised and overjoyed to see them.

The Levys had already given up hope that their son would survive the war. "They thought I was dead," Rabbi Levy recalled. When he arrived at their doorstep, his mother fainted in shock. Three times they woke her, and she passed out again and again.

"I Worried About You"

Despite her joy at his return, Berel's mother maintained her opposition to his religious observance, refusing to support him as long as he

While his son went on his own path, Eliezer Levy (center) came to appreciate his son's choices in life. Courtesy of Thelma Levy.

continued studying in yeshivah. Undeterred, he returned to his studies at Torah Vodaath.

During the trip he had gotten lice in his hair, and shaved it all off, including his long sidelocks, which he never regrew. He also gave up the dress code he had adopted as one of the Malachim, and began to wear a suit. It was a different Berel Levy who now applied to be admitted to the school he had left under his uncle's influence.

The dean, Rabbi Shlomo Heiman, tested him as an incoming student. When he heard that Berel had been studying at the Lubavitch Yeshiva in Otwock, where the dean was Rabbi Yehudah Eber, Rabbi Heineman said, "Ah, Rabbi Yehudah Eber. He is a great Torah scholar. If he would have been a dean in the Lithuanian Torah world, they would have considered him to be like Reb Chaim Ozer," referring to Rabbi Grodzinski, a great Talmudic scholar and the head of the rabbinical court in Vilnius, Lithuania.

The American students continued to follow the situation of the rebbe, who had traveled from Otwock to Warsaw, where he remained under German bombardment for some time. On December 17, 1939, he and his entourage arrived in Riga. It was there that he first learned that the

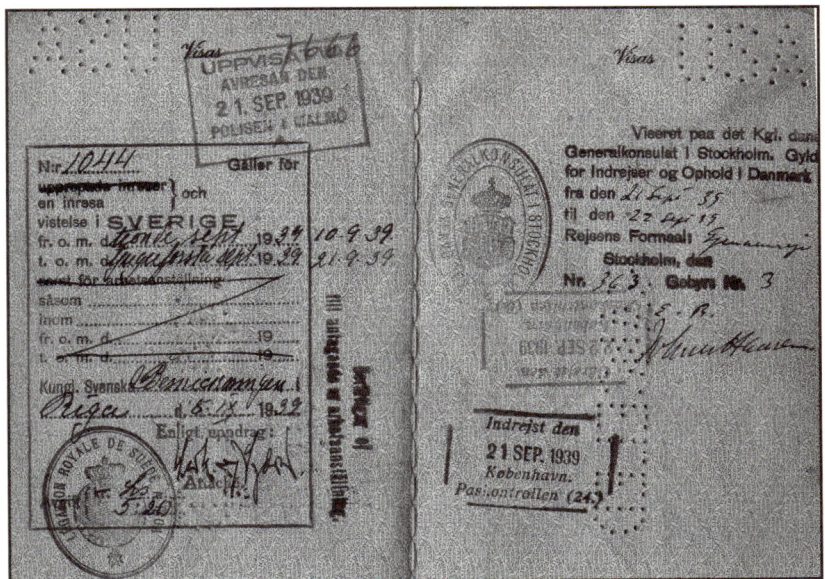

Berel's passport, with stamps from Riga (Latvia) and Stockholm (Sweden), dated September 1939. Courtesy of Thelma Levy

students were safe in the United States.

"While I was enduring the siege, I worried about you," the rebbe wrote to them ten days after his arrival in Riga, noting that he had asked the American consul what their situation was. "I expected that you would surely try to let us know of your welfare through the consul in order to calm me and to give encouragement to my heart that is broken and shattered from the misfortunes of the Jewish people – may G-d have mercy and pity upon them."

Though he himself had been in mortal danger, he was thinking of them. He reminded the students of the "love and affection that is expected according to the teachings of Chassidism" and described how, upon hearing the news that they were safe, he had echoed the Psalmist, "Give thanks to G-d who is good, for His kindness is eternal" (107:1).

LAYING THE FOUNDATION

In March 1940, the Rebbe Rayatz, having miraculously escaped the inferno in Europe, arrived in New York and proclaimed, "America is no different." Just as Torah scholarship and observance had flourished in Europe, so it would flourish in the *goldene medina*. He and his followers would do all they could to save European Jews from destruction, but education in America was an equally urgent matter. He would not go to sleep, he said, before a school was established.

Berel was one of the original ten students who joined that first school in the basement of the small Oneg Shabbos Synagogue in Brooklyn's East Flatbush neighborhood. The yeshivah would later move to Crown Heights, where the rebbe established his court, at 770 Eastern Parkway.

"The group of Americans that came to Otwock had great self-sacrifice," said Rabbi Wineberg, "and it was through them that the yeshivah [was] able to be replanted in the United States. Rabbi Levy was one of those who laid the foundation for what Chabad is today in America."

With little money and no support from his parents, Berel persevered in his studies under very difficult conditions. He would spend his days at the Lubavitch Yeshivah, but at night, in the bitter cold winter, he slept in a small rented room without much heating. Twice he ended up in the hospital with pneumonia, a life-threatening illness at the time.

The treatment for pneumonia was sulfa drugs, which had severe

When Rabbi Schneersohn arrived in the United States in 1940 and opened a new Lubavitch Yeshivah, Berel (left) immediately joined. Courtesy of Agudas Chasidei Chabad Library

side effects, impeding his ability to walk. Berel knew he could not stop taking the drugs, but he also refused to lighten his study regimen. With what little strength he had, he managed to cope with the side effects and fight off the infection while keeping to his rigorous schedule.

"When I was in school," Rabbi Levy told a reporter in March 1982, "I studied Jewish law from seven a.m. to midnight daily, with Friday afternoons off to prepare for the Sabbath. Sometimes I slept on a bench in school. I never went home; I'd get up in the morning and start studying again."

The local draft board in Brooklyn had decided that yeshivah students did not qualify for student exemptions, and many of the Chabad students were summoned to appear for examinations.

Thelma's parents, Yitzchak and Sarah Horowitz, were immigrants like Berel's; however, they remained faithful to their Jewish roots. Pictured are their three daughters (left to right), Julia, Thelma and Regina. Courtesy of Thelma Levy

"Berel was very religious," Shmuel Popack, a fellow student, recalled. "When he was examined, he refused to remove his tzitzis." At the time, the four-cornered garments, with fringes attached, were made with a slit in the front, and the students of the Chabad yeshiva would sew a button onto the top.

A chest x-ray was required as part of the exam, and on Berel's x-ray, the doctors mistook the button on his tzitzit for a lung lesion from tuberculosis. He was granted a medical deferment.

A Fellow Greenhorn

Around this time, Buddy Chenovsky, Berel's neighbor in Crown Heights, told him about a nice girl named Thelma Horowitz, whom he had met at an event in The Bronx. The event was a mixer, organized by Hapoel Hamizrachi, in an effort to facilitate the matchmaking process for religious girls and boys. "Every once in a while, we used to have some kind of an affair," recalled Mrs. Levy, who was 18 at the time. "The Bronx was not the place for the dating scene.... Therefore, someone would arrange for the Brooklyn people to come to The Bronx."

Berel called her and asked her for a date. Thelma's parents, Yitzchak and Sarah, were immigrants like Berel's; however, they remained faithful to their Jewish roots. Her grandparents were esteemed rabbinical figures in their respective cities in Galicia, a small kingdom in Eastern Europe that no longer exists. Yitzchak and Sarah arrived shortly before World War I as teenagers, wed at a young age and had three girls: Regina, Thelma and Julia.

Born in The Bronx in 1924, Thelma grew up speaking Yiddish. Thus, even though she was born in America, people would refer to her as a *griner*, a greenhorn. Until today, Thelma wears the title with pride. Her father supported the family, working long hours for a meager wage as a waiter in a local restaurant.

Now 92, Thelma vividly recalls the sacrifices her mother made so that her children could get a Jewish education. At first, they studied *alef-beit* after school at a synagogue across the street from their home, where she and her older sister were the only girls in the class. When they got older, her mother enrolled all the girls in Congregation Kehilath Israel's Talmud Torah afternoon Hebrew school.

Mrs. Levy remembered the synagogue, which was across the street from Crotona Park. "From a staircase in the back of the synagogue, we had to climb five flights of stairs to our classrooms," she said.

Yitzchak and Sarah Horowitz (above) were pleasantly surprised when Thelma decided to marry a yeshivah student. Courtesy of Thelma Levy

Kehilath Israel was in a more well-to-do neighborhood of The Bronx, a 15-minute walk from the Horowitzes' home. Thus, her mother spent every afternoon walking her children back and forth to the school. "We were three girls of three ages," Mrs. Levy said, "so of course we had to go to three different classes."

Julia, the youngest sister, went first, at four o'clock. By the time Mrs. Horowitz returned, she would have only a few minutes to rest before she had to take Thelma and pick up Julia. Leaving Julia at home, she would walk the oldest daughter to her class, which began at six; pick up Thelma and deposit her at home; and return one final time to pick up Regina, arriving home around 7:15 in the evening.

"Mrs. Horowitz, you have no boys," a neighbor once said to her. "Why do you run back and forth, back and forth, three times a day to bring your girls?" Girls' education was not a priority for most parents at the time.

"I am not asking by you," Thelma's mother replied.

Shabbat was a special day in the Horowitz home. Mrs. Horowitz would spend Thursday night baking challah bread, coffee cake and rugelach. "If we were good children," Mrs. Levy said, "we got cookies, which was something round dipped in cinnamon and sugar. And if we were very good, we got an onion bun."

She recalls her father singing the traditional *zemirot* during the Shabbat meal ("He would love that time") and then retiring for some well-deserved rest.

"There was no such thing as going places, doing things," she said of her childhood. But the Horowitz children did not feel deprived. "There were no cars. Playing was out in the street. We played tag, ball. We had a broomstick for a bat."

She was 16 years old when World War II broke out. For the first time, the family purchased a radio. "I remember my mother standing and listening to what was going on," Mrs. Levy said. "They were worried about their family left back in Europe."

By the time she met Rabbi Levy, she was working as a bookkeeper. After their first date, she could see that they shared a deep commitment to Judaism. He recounted his adventures in Poland, and she told him

Thelma received a Jewish education thanks to her mother's self-sacrifice. She graduated as valedictorian in May 1937. Courtesy of Thelma Levy

Rabbi Schneersohn in his office. Courtesy of Agudas Chasidei Chabad Library

about her work.

Late in 1944 they decided to get married. "My parents were shocked that I was going to marry a yeshivah student," Mrs. Levy said.

Several times before the wedding Berel came to the Horowitz home for Shabbat. One Friday he arrived without a change of clothing for the next day. "Did you lose it?" Thelma asked.

No, he told her. He had a cousin, living on the East Side, who was emotionally disturbed. "I met him, and he didn't have what to wear," he said. "I gave him my clothes. Let him enjoy them for Shabbos."

There was one area of her fiancée's life about which Thelma would have much to learn. "I never heard the word Lubavitch before I met Berel," she said. Only when they were already engaged, and Berel took her to meet the Rebbe Rayatz in Crown Heights, did she get a taste of what life as a Chabad chassid would be.

After completing his studies at the Chabad yeshivah and receiving rabbinic ordination, Rabbi Levy taught at the Lubavitch grade school on Bedford and Dean in Brooklyn, where his gift for education was first discovered.

He also received a BA in education from City College of New York, and was a member of the Hebrew Teachers Federation of America.

PART TWO

DAY SCHOOL MOVEMENT

When the Rayatz miraculously escaped war-torn Europe and arrived in New York, Jewish observance in America was on the decline. The primary reason for this, he felt, was the dire lack of authentic Jewish education. Making Jewish education affordable and accessible was the only way to revive Torah Judaism and ensure Jewish continuity, the rebbe reasoned.

"The Jew in the European ghetto had G-d constantly before his mind," wrote Hyman Grinstein in his monumental book on that period, *The Rise of the Jewish Community of New York*. "The Jew of New York was aware of G-d only on certain occasions and in certain times and seasons. As religious practice declined, there was no longer a feeling of nearness to G-d in the intimate acts of daily life."

While many Jewish children did attend the classic after-school Talmud Torah Hebrew schools, the results were less than a basic Jewish education. There were a few Jewish day schools, but the Rayatz felt that their educational priorities were skewed toward secular studies. Even New York, which boasted several small schools, seemed to him a wasteland of true Torah education.

In a short period the rebbe established boys' and girls' day schools, and dozens of after-school programs, across the New York metropolitan area. He also created an organization that gave free Jewish classes to children in public schools.

The rebbe then turned his attention to the rest of the country, where Jewish education was almost nil. State by state and city by city, the Rayatz's son-in-law Rabbi Shmaryahu Gurary led a miniature army of young adults, many of them Torah Vodaath graduates—now full-fledged Chabad followers—in building a network of Jewish day schools.

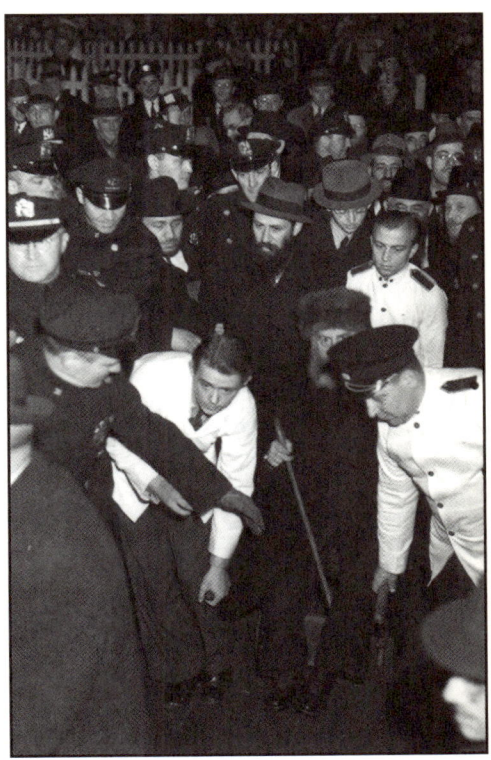

Rabbi Schneersohn arrives in New York in 1940. The rebbe beseeched American Jewry to do all they could to save Jews in Europe, while promising that "America is no different" than the homeland in terms of the need for Jewish education and observance. Courtesy of Lubavitch Archives

These young men and women became principals, teachers and community activists. The Rayatz demanded much from them, sending them to places where religious Jews were not welcome. But, emboldened by the rebbe's confidence in them, they convinced thousands of parents to send their children to the new Torah schools.

Rabbi Avraham Hecht, Rabbi Levy's fellow student from Torah Vodaath, who later became the leading rabbi of the Syrian Jewish community in the United States, told how the Rayatz transformed the young

Americans into community leaders. "The rebbe said we should speak to parents about sending their kids to yeshivahs," he said. "I never spoke [publicly]. I was very shy. But the Rebbe said, 'You have to go talk.'"

Rabbi Hecht, then 18, was scheduled to speak at one of Brooklyn's large synagogues. "I came. I was scared," he said. "You don't know how scared I was. I never opened up my mouth in public." As he made his way to the podium, though, he kept thinking about how the rebbe was depending on him to speak about Jewish education. The speech went over very well, and from then on he had no issues with public speaking.

"The Rebbe could take a *shteken* [stick] and make it into a speaker," he said. "It was tremendous. After that, I spoke in the biggest synagogues. Nothing bothered me."

The Rayatz laid the ground rules for the schools: Their purpose was Jewish education. General studies should be of the highest quality, but should not come at the expense of Jewish education. Scheduling secular studies first thing in the morning was out of the question. The prime time of the day must be devoted to Torah.

The rebbe encouraged his young emissaries to see the schools as the centers of larger communities, to reach out to their students' parents with the aim of bringing the families closer to their Jewish roots. He advised them to establish synagogues that would welcome the families and their children, and to make gatherings outside of school hours.

At first, much of the funding for the schools came from the central office of Lubavitch schools. This made it clear that the philosophy of the schools and their general structure would be dictated by headquarters, and not be influenced by locals who might have wanted laxer standards in Jewish law.

The fundraising effort was led by Rabbi Gurary, a tireless advocate for Jewish education. He would arrive at offices unannounced and plead with apathetic businessmen to support his fight against the assimilated

Rabbi Schneersohn (at microphone) inspired young men and women to open Jewish day schools. Here, at a dinner to support the schools, he is seen with Rabbi Gurary (left), who led the day school effort. Also pictured is the rebbe's son-in-law, Rabbi Menachem Mendel Schneerson (third from right), the future leader of the Chabad movement. Courtesy of Agudas Chasidei Chabad Library

lifestyle many of them had embraced. As the school network grew, however, centralized funding was no longer viable, and by 1946 most of the schools were on their own.

Following in the Rayatz's footsteps (and to a certain extent in response to his work), Rabbi Shraga Feivel Mendlowitz and Rabbi Aharon Kotler established Torah Umesorah, the National Society for Hebrew Day Schools, in 1944. The organization took a different road toward the goal the Rayatz had identified. Torah Umesorah chose to inspire local communities to build their own schools. The efforts were not led by rabbinical figures, but rather by American-looking educators, many with prestigious titles and degrees.

Dr. Joe Kaminetsky, director of Torah Umesorah, was charged with convincing Jewish communities across the United States to open Jewish day schools. Here he is seen (standing, center) with the staff at Torah Umesorah (1950s). Courtesy of Torah Umesorah

"There were one or two organizations at work in the field at the time," wrote Dr. Joseph Kaminetsky, the national director of Torah Umesorah, in a 1963 promotional pamphlet. "The Lubavitcher movement… had brought to this country its fiery zeal to set up institutions of Torah. Reb Feivel Mendlowitz felt that an institution more indigenous to America had to be founded."

Torah Umesorah staff worked at convincing communities to build schools—schools that would be their own, to fund and care for. If you need assistance with the curriculum and teachers, they told locals, we are always here to help.

Often it was a difficult proposition to sell. Rabbis were too busy with their synagogue duties; some feared they would not be able to find teachers; and some claimed that there would never be enough funds.

When the schools succeeded, it was usually because of laypeople who contributed their time, energy and money to make them a reality. Dr. Kaminetsky would tell stories of triumph: the woman who baked bread to raise money for school furniture, and parents who gave all of their savings to purchase school buildings.

In contrast to Chabad's approach, Torah Umesorah took a laid-back attitude to the schools they helped establish. Of course they hoped that administrators would follow basic guidelines of curriculum and adherence to Jewish law, but the standards were rarely enforced.

"Dr. Kaminetsky understood well that one must deal very sensitively with people who are far removed from traditional Yiddishkeit," wrote Rabbi Joshua Fishman, the organization's executive vice president for close to three decades, "and that imposing very stringent conditions could mean the complete collapse of a day school initiative."

Despite their differing approaches, the two organizations coexisted and flourished. Torah Umesorah has built hundreds of Jewish day schools in North America, and Chabad has sent out thousands of directors, principals and teachers to build Jewish day schools and communities across the globe.

A Mission

In 1944 the Rayatz sent Rabbi Mordechai Altein to begin the process of opening a Lubavitch school in New Haven, Connecticut. The consensus at the time was that a Jewish school was not viable in New Haven, a previous attempt at starting one having been unsuccessful. But the Rayatz felt that abandoning the community was not an option, and that if the school had the right leadership, it would be a success.

In a private audience, during the future Mrs. Levy's first visit to Chabad headquarters, the Rayatz spoke to Rabbi Levy about the plans and asked him to lead the school. The rebbe discussed what he saw the school accomplishing and how it should be done. He had a clear vision, and Rabbi Levy was to follow the guidelines.

Then, the rebbe, who did not speak clearly because of an illness, turned to Thelma and said that surely she would also teach at the new girls' school. Her face turned white.

"I felt like someone shot me," Mrs. Levy recalled. "I was trained to be a bookkeeper. I didn't know how to go into the classroom and say good morning to the children."

Seeing her reaction, Rabbi Levy motioned for her to calm down and not to respond.

Her mind racing, Thelma heard nothing else during the audience. Outside of the rebbe's office, all she could say was "I don't know what I am going to do."

"Don't worry," her fiancée told her, "I will guide you in your teaching."

The young bride quickly realized that joining her husband in Chabad would mean developing the mindset of a soldier. After that, she said, "I was ready to accept and never complained."

Rabbi Mordechai Altein did the preliminaries and made contacts for them in the community, and after their marriage the couple moved straight to New Haven. Rabbi Levy was to lead the school, and Mrs. Levy was to be a teacher. Rabbi Velvl Schildkraut came to assist. It was summertime, and they began the school immediately with four children in the dining room of a private home.

By the fall, the school had already purchased a new building and enrolled tens of students. To attract more students, current students marched through the Jewish neighborhoods singing and chanting Jewish slogans. The children also came to synagogue with new kippahs emblazoned with the school's name.

After they wed, the Levys moved to New Haven, Connecticut, where they founded a Chabad day school (1947). Courtesy of Thelma Levy

"Entering into their new comfortable location, the New Haven day school grew in quantity and quality and is acclimating very well," reported the periodical *Kovetz Lubavitch* in the fall of 1944. "The school is headed by an alumnus of the Central Lubavitch Yeshivah in Brooklyn, the talented Rabbi Berel Levy."

At the time there were roughly 25,000 Jewish families in New Haven. They were mostly first- or second-generation European immigrants who arrived shortly before the Great Depression in the 1930s, when many lost their jobs and families went hungry.

These families just wanted to be left alone to build their financial stability. "They focused their outlook sharply on assimilation," wrote Zalman Schachter, who taught at the school in the 1940s, in his autobiography. "Trying to establish a Hasidic day school [in New Haven] proved

Rabbi Levy (second from left) poses with the New Haven school staff in May 1946. Also pictured are Velvl Schildkraut (left) and Zalman Schachter (second from right). Courtesy of Thlema Levy

to be among the most daunting tasks I have ever faced."

In those early years, Rabbi Levy fought valiantly to keep the school running. Every morning he would ferry the children from their homes in a makeshift "school bus." He would then run the school with an inadequate staff. After he dropped the children at their homes, he went to work recruiting more students and fundraising to cover the school's deficit.

The school grew, and soon there was an active girls' school as well, where Mrs. Levy taught. "Every single day he used to tell me what to do," said Mrs. Levy, who taught for several decades and was honored by Torah Umesorah as one of the top teachers in the Jewish Day School movement, "and that is what I did and was successful."

New Haven resident Micky Epstein recalled the Levys' arrival in the community. "They were very good people," she said. Before they came, there was no one in the city she felt she could look up to and learn from as a Jewish role model, "but they were really wonderful," the 87-year-old said. "It was so nice having them in New Haven. I still think about the Levys and the impression they made on me."

Rabbi Levy also established a branch of the school in West Haven. "Rabbi B. Levy, principal of the Yeshivah Achei Tmimim Lubavitch of New Haven, announces that a branch afternoon school has been opened," a local newspaper reported. "Jewish residents of West Haven who have wanted to give their children a Jewish education will now be able to do so."

In 1946 a new administrator was hired for the school, who took control of the budget and ruled with an iron fist.

For Rabbi Levy, who was still covering the school's budget, things became really difficult when a prized donor gave him an ultimatum: if the school did not become coed, he would cease to support it. Feeling that this was an existential crisis, Rabbi Levy travelled to New York to consult the Rayatz. The trip was not simple in those days, and he seldom went.

Rabbi Levy described his dilemma in a private audience with the rebbe. "If you make it mixed," the Rayatz responded, "for what do I need the entire school?" The idea was dropped, and the donor withdrew his support.

In 1946, Rabbi Levy left the school and became the executive director of the Hartford Yeshivah day school. Shortly after his arrival, he headed a building campaign to raise $150,000.

"The Yeshiva is our assurance that Judaism will live," Rabbi Levy wrote in the *Connecticut Jewish Ledger* on August 23, 1946, "that the torch of Jewish life and learning shall be held aloft to give spiritual light and guidance to a sorely tried people.... Yeshiva needs a new modern building for a student body of close to 250 boys and girls. Right now there is no space for many applicants who are waiting for admission."

In 1947 he entered the business world, though he continued teaching Hebrew school at the Emanuel Synagogue in Hartford and in a synagogue in New Britain, Connecticut.

Paying Debt

Rabbi Levy first tried his hand at selling venetian blinds. But the business was a failure. For many years the family lived very simply, from hand to mouth.

When Rabbi Levy's daughter Fruma was engaged in 1965 to Rabbi Zvi Gartenhaus, the news in the family was that "the debt was finally paid off."

The young Don Yoel asked his mother what this meant, and she explained that when Rabbi Levy was in the blinds business, he went into debt. Instead of declaring Chapter 11, he paid it off over time. "It took him years, but he paid back every penny," she told her son.

In 1970, before the marriage of his second child, he finished paying off another debt he had incurred as a guarantor on someone else's loan.

Lakewood

In 1951, Rabbi Levy decided to return to the field of education, and turned to Torah Umesorah for assistance. Dr. Kaminetsky contacted Rabbi Hillel Henkin at the Hartford Day School as a reference.

"I know him [Rabbi Levy] to be a very fine fellow, easy to get along with, has a nice personality," he wrote. "[He] is a hard worker." He added that Rabbi Levy not only diligently fulfilled his salaried duties, but also organized adult education classes and created a children's club, "all gratis." The Hartford rabbi concluded that he "has shown sincerity and

Rabbi Levy's fundraising capabilities and problem-solving skills eventually gained him national recognition and a job at Torah Umesorah. He appears here at a New Jersey hotel with donation receipts in hand (1953). Courtesy of Thelma Levy

devotion, listens to reason and at all times is zealous in propagating religious Jewish living."

With this recommendation, Torah Umesorah strongly encouraged the Lakewood (N.J.) Hebrew Day School to hire Rabbi Levy. The school at the time was coed, which made Rabbi Levy hesitant to accept the position. However, he decided that while he would not establish a coed school himself, he could take a job in one.

As executive director, he was both the school's principal and its primary fundraiser. He was successful in the role, working to erect a new building. According to the *Asbury Park*

Rabbi Levy brought his skills from New Haven to Lakewood, New Jersey, where he became a principal and fundraiser. A newspaper clipping from that period describes his efforts.

Press, from the time Rabbi Levy arrived at the school, the enrollment doubled from 70 children to 140. "An increased enrollment made the addition necessary."

The newspaper praised the new construction, which used "fluorescent lighting and rubber tiled floors." The paper reported that "all the classrooms and the gymnasium were financed by interested citizens, according to Rabbi Bernard Levy, executive director and principal of the school."

The building is still in use today by the Cheder Bnei Torah.

It was in Lakewood that Rabbi Levy met Rabbi Aharon Kotler, with whom he developed a close relationship. Although Rabbi Levy was a proud Lubavitcher, and Rabbi Kotler was a known antagonist of the

Lubavitch movement, the two found a common language that surpassed their differences.

In May 1952, Rabbi Levy made his first appearance on the national stage at Torah Umesorah's fourth annual convention for their National Association of PTAs, with a speech entitled "The PTA and the School's Overall Financial Program."

He also started a radio program, *Jewish Variety*, where he would interview prominent Jewish figures and present Jewish ideas and music. The weekly 55-minute program, the *Asbury Park Press* reported on November 22, 1952, would also include a "question box" segment, during which Rabbi Levy would answer listeners' questions about Judaism on air. "Rabbi Levy says he will try to make the program a means of increasing better understanding of the Jewish customs…"

The program was well received. "I was happy to learn that the 'Jewish Variety' program started on WJLK on Sunday morning will be a weekly attraction," wrote Gilbert Cantor in a local Jewish newspaper. "The hour was very enjoyable to me… a word of praise is due to Rabbi Levy."

Elizabeth

In 1954 the Levy family moved to Elizabeth, New Jersey, where Rabbi Levy became the executive director of the city's Jewish Educational Center. "Appointment of Rabbi Bernard Levy of Lakewood," the *New York Times* reported on September 11, 1954, "as executive director of the Jewish Educational Center was announced today by Samuel Cohen, president. Rabbi Levy will coordinate activities of the center's affiliate organizations and direct a building fund campaign for a new branch in North Elizabeth."

Rabbi Pinchas M. Teitz had built a large following and a Jewish school, and Rabbi Levy was brought in to build a network of local donors to support it. A master fundraiser, over seven years he created a solid network of support and formed many personal relationships in the

In Elizabeth, Rabbi Levy became a dynamic force in the community, where he headed the building of a new synagogue and the growth of the day school. Here Rabbi Levy shakes the hand of a graduating student. Courtesy of Thelma Levy

town.

"He was a good fundraiser," recalled Sholom Lifchetz, who spent time with the Levy family when he came home to Elizabeth from his Talmudic studies at the Telshe Yeshiva in Cleveland, Ohio. Rabbi Levy always answered requests for money generously, he said. "He was a very good person. He liked to do a *chesed* [kind deed]. He was always easy to approach by someone who was in need."

Rabbi Levy also raised funds and opened a new synagogue, Congregation Adath Israel, known locally as the North Avenue Synagogue. He became the unofficial rabbi there, leading prayer services and giving regular Torah classes.

The Levy home was always open to visitors. "My father was a lively people person. The locals would feel good being around him, stopping by our home to talk to him," Fruma Gartenhaus said. Community members still recall the strong influence Rabbi Levy had on their lives, and several said they had increased their level of Jewish observance at his urging.

However, Elizabeth was not the kind of community the Levys envisioned raising their children in. "We always need to look at our future," Rabbi Levy would tell his wife, "which is moving back to the Jewish community in New York."

"The environment in Elizabeth was not very religious," said Rabbi Don Yoel. "Most of my classmates were not observant Jews, yet my father instilled in us an extremely strong religious foundation. Later, when my sister and I went to fully religious schools, we blended in naturally due to the strength of the foundation."

He recalled how there was once a dance at the school, and some of the students had a great idea: "You are the rabbi's son. Why don't you ask the other rabbi's daughter to the dance?"

"Thank you very much," Don Yoel told them, "but I don't go to dances. I don't dance with girls."

"I was always used to being different," he said. "I grew up that way. I knew I could not eat everything that my friends were eating. My father didn't have to stress it with me. This is something that I grew up with."

Rabbi Don Yoel's most vivid memories from that time are of his father focused on his studies of Talmud and Jewish law. "My father could sit down with a *sefer* [Jewish religious text]," he recalled. "If you would bang him on the head, he wouldn't hear you."

Rabbi Levy also continued to study Chabad Chassidism in Elizabeth, and had a weekly class with Rabbi Shalom Ber Gordon, a well-known Chabad rabbi in Newark, New Jersey.

Rabbi Levy was successful in his work in Elizabeth, but he and his wife felt that it was not the right place to educate their children. Pictured are Fruma (left) and Don Yoel. Courtesy of Thelma Levy

Burgeoning Interest

Even then, kosher was a subject of significant interest in the Levy home. "When we were kids, most people would look at the ingredients of a candy, and if it did not say lard or tallow, they would eat it," Rabbi Don Yoel said.

He remembers his father telling him it wasn't so simple. In his spare time Rabbi Levy would visit factories to see how foods were made. He would come back and tell his family, "You could eat this, but that you can't eat."

At the time, vegetable shortening was considered a kosher ingredient. But the family stopped using it when Rabbi Levy discovered that it was often processed on the same equipment as meat fat.

Rabbi Levy warned his family that companies could not be trusted to label their products accurately. Even when ingredients were listed, people were not familiar with the additives and byproducts being used. "Then he started doing research on what these ingredients were," Rabbi Don Yoel said. "We found out that whey was in fact derived from milk. No one knew this."

Gatherings in New York

After the passing of the Rebbe Rayatz in 1950, Rabbi Levy had begun to build a relationship with his successor, Rabbi Menachem Mendel Schneerson, the seventh Lubavitcher Rebbe.

Even in those early years, Rabbi Levy realized that the Rebbe's ideas were visionary. He began to travel to New York for the large Chassidic gatherings, *farbrengens*, where the Rebbe would speak.

He also invited members of the Elizabeth community to accompany him on his trips. A prominent individual in the community learned about these excursions and insisted that they stop, but Rabbi Levy ignored the request.

Entrusted by Rabbi Pinchus Teitz (left), Rabbi Levy grew the local Jewish day school's financial support. Courtesy of Thelma Levy

Rabbi Menachem Hacohen recalled his first visit to the United States in the late 1950s as rabbi of the Histadrut, Israeli's organization of trade unions, a very powerful institution at the time. His brother, Rabbi Levy's friend from Connecticut, asked if Rabbi Hacohen could stay with the Levys.

"He waited for me at the airport," the nonagenarian recalled. "Instead of heading to New Jersey, he took me straight to the Rebbe in Brooklyn."

After the passing of Rabbi Schneersohn, Rabbi Levy became a follower of his successor, Rabbi Menachem Mendel Schneerson, known simply as the Rebbe. Rabbi Levy would regularly bring members of the Elizabeth Jewish community to farbrengens, Chassidic gatherings presided over by the Rebbe. Courtesy of Ezzie Schaffran/Lubavitch Archives

Rabbi Levy had arranged from him to meet the Rebbe. The audience lasted several hours, and Rabbi Hacohen returned to the Levy home early in the morning for his "supper." Rabbi Levy combined religious fervor with an appreciation for the diversity of the Jewish people, he said. "I would say that is what Chabad is today, accepting of others for who they are."

Rabbi Levy was devoted chassid, he concluded, who never acted without seeking the Rebbe's guidance, "and a *chacham*, a very intelligent man."

Rabbi Levy received a Grundig portable tape recorder as a gift, and began bringing it with him to New York and recording the Rebbe's talks. Recording and photographing the Rebbe was discouraged in the Chabad community, and in the middle of one farbrengen, someone approached Rabbi Levy and asked him what he thought he was doing.

The man was large and overbearing, but Rabbi Levy, with his usual determination, refused to back down. Just then someone else walked over, took the tape recorder, placed it in his own bag and nonchalantly asked for the keys to Rabbi Levy's car.

When the large man asked him for the recorder to get rid of the reels, Rabbi Levy told them that it was gone.

A short while later, in a private audience, Rabbi Levy told the Rebbe what happened. "If the Rebbe doesn't want me to have them," he said, "I will give the Rebbe the recordings."

The Rebbe asked what the talk had been about, apparently wanting to see if Rabbi Levy wanted the recording as a collector's item, or if he was actually listening in order to learn.

He repeated over the general ideas of the talk and, satisfied, the Rebbe said, "You can keep it."

The Gold Watch

Over the years, part of the school faculty became jealous of Rabbi Levy's success, and the situation in Elizabeth grew difficult for him.

Things boiled over after a dinner that he organized for the school. The event was successful, and to show their appreciation, the dinner committee presented him with a gold watch. Rabbi Levy had never expected such a gift, and thanked them graciously.

Some did not appreciate the gesture, however, and one member of the board berated him for agreeing to accept such an extravagance.

NATIONAL EDUCATION

It was not long before Rabbi Levy's talents as a fundraiser and school administrator became known outside of Elizabeth. By 1959, he was being called on regularly to help schools across the country. During his vacation, he would travel around to the schools. "To him it was very important not to do the wrong thing," Mrs. Levy said, "to work for someone while he was being paid by someone else."

Eventually, Rabbi Levy was offered the position of director of development for Torah Umesorah, which, in addition to fundraising and other duties, included being a problem-solver for schools in their network.

Rabbi Levy immediately consulted the Rebbe, who advised him not to take the job. Accepting this advice, he rejected Torah Umesorah's offer and continued his work in Elizabeth under the same difficult circumstances.

"The Rebbe did not say why," recalled Mrs. Levy. "But, if the Rebbe said no, that was no." Meanwhile, the situation in Elizabeth deteriorated, and certain individuals became openly hostile to Rabbi Levy.

A year later, Torah Umesorah called again and told him they desperately needed his services. Rabbi Levy went back to the Rebbe and described in detail how painful his current situation had become. To his surprise, the Rebbe said he should now accept the position.

"Why did you say no last year, and now you are saying yes?" he asked.

"The organization then was going through a hard time with someone from Yeshiva University," the Rebbe said. "I didn't want you to get involved in the situation and perhaps be made to leave. Now that everything was solved, you can go."

Rabbi Levy accepted the offer and threw himself into his new job. By the time Rabbi Levy arrived at Torah Umesorah in 1960, the growth of Jewish day schools had reached a plateau (between 1958 and 1968, a total of four new elementary schools were added).

When Rabbi Levy arrived at Torah Umesorah, the organization's financial situation was precarious, and it was cutting its programs. Courtesy of Thelma Levy

Schools were opened, but schools also closed. The organization's focus had become to support the existing schools rather than to open new ones. They provided curricula and teaching materials, and when needed, they would step in to help schools with financial issues or in managing their relationships with parent boards.

Their two most significant programs were the yearly PTA conferences and their flagship children's magazine, *Olomeinu – Our World*. When Dr. Kaminetsky reached out to Rabbi Levy, the organization's financial situation was dire – they were on the brink of collapse. Programs were being closed, and the focus was to minimize costs.

In the November 1960 issue of the Torah Umesorah *Monthly Report*, under the heading "New Director of Development," Dr. Kaminetsky wrote, "His newly created position will entail working out the plans for the expansion of Torah Umesorah's public relations and fundraising services to all Hebrew Day Schools throughout the country. He will also begin plans for the eventual setting up of a National Torah Fund for Day Schools in the country and will direct the Dinner Campaign of Torah Umesorah."

Two months later, the national director described Rabbi Levy's first months at the organization in a memorandum to the board: "This year, we at long last have our own fundraiser, Rabbi Bernard Levy, who has thrown himself into the work with great zeal. This wonderful addition will enable the rest of the Staff to concentrate on the actual work of Torah Umesorah."

Soon it became known that there was an inseparable trio at the Torah Umesorah office: Dr. Joseph "Joe" Kaminetsky, national director; Mr. Amos Bunim, CEO of Eden Textiles, a philanthropist and tireless activist for Jewish education, who at the time was the associate chairman of the organization's board; and Rabbi Levy, the new director of development, who dedicated his life to Torah Umesorah.

Fundraising Master

Fixing the financial situation at Torah Umesorah required enormous patience and nerves of steel. "He would travel around the country, meeting with individuals and befriending people," explained Mr. Bunim in a 1990 interview. "His role was basically in fundraising. He was very good at it; he really put Torah Umesorah on a very solid financial footing."

To many, Rabbi Levy was the public face of the organization in the field. "When he represented Torah Umesorah, it was really respected by the people he went to visit," recalled the businessman. "I went with him on many occasions, and it was beautiful, the reverence people had [for] him."

As a lay leader with an active involvement in the daily fight for the organization's existence, Mr. Bunim was afforded a firsthand look at the whirlwind called Berel Levy. "Going out with him, seeing his tremendous dedication and devotion and care and concern, was something very special. He was truly interested to see that the organization should be able to go on."

Frequently, Dr. Kaminetsky and Rabbi Levy would come to Mr. Bunim's office to discuss how they could make the organization grow while fulfilling their other duties. "The following report spells out all details of the 'big events' and projects which should occupy our minds – and at which we should work hard – during the coming year, please G-d," began the report from one such meeting.

Dr. Kaminetsky considered Rabbi Levy his right-hand man. When a school had an urgent problem and the national director was on vacation, the principal spoke to Rabbi Levy. He was privy to all the details and would discuss the issue with the principal at length.

When another school turned to the organization with a complicated problem, Dr. Kaminetsky immediately delegated it to Rabbi Levy. "I gave Berel Levy all the correspondence, all the records, etc….," he wrote to the school official.

Grand Affairs

In the 1950s, Torah Umesorah's annual dinner would draw one hundred attendees at the most, Mr. Bunim said. The event brought in a third of the budget. One of Rabbi Levy's first tasks was to make the dinners into grand affairs in which donors would be honored to participate.

During his first years with the organization, planning for the dinners took up most of the time at board meetings, with Rabbi Levy leading the conversation.

His efforts proved successful. The second dinner he organized, in 1962, according to a report, "was the greatest success we ever had financially, thank G-d," raising half of that year's budget.

"When he first arrived, those dinners were rather small and didn't bring in very much. But after he put his tremendous effort into it, the annual Torah Umesorah dinner became a major, major event, which it still is today," said Mr. Bunim. "We together built it up to eight hundred or a thousand people."

In a first for the organization, Rabbi Levy began to follow up after the dinner with potential donors. He also organized that people who donated to the schools in the Torah Umesorah network should support headquarters as well.

Teachers' Institute

Even before he started Torah Umesorah, Rabbi Mendlowitz saw the need for a place where he could educate Jewish educators. In 1941 he founded Aish Dos, which he called a place to educate "Torah paratroopers." The institute taught young men pedagogy coupled with Jewish activism. It did not last long, however.

More unsuccessful attempts were made in 1945, 1948 and 1956. At one point Dr. Kaminetsky arranged for teachers from the Torah Umesorah network to take education classes at the United Lubavitcher Yeshivoth during the summer months. The classes had been implemented there in the 1940s.

The need for a teacher's institute was great, but financial support was lacking, and Torah Umesorah gave up on the idea for the time being.

One of the aspects of his job that Rabbi Levy cherished most was the opportunity he had to interact with, seek advice from and fulfill the wishes of the greatest Torah giants of that time, such as Rabbi Moshe Feinstein, the great *halachic* decisor of the 20th century, and Rabbi Aharon Kotler, founder of Beth Medrash Govoha in Lakewood, New Jer-

Rabbi Levy relayed the Rebbe's directives to the board of Torah Umesorah, which led to the establishment of a teachers' institute. Here Rabbi Aharon Kotler (left) attends a Torah Umesorah event with Rabbi Levy. Also pictured are Rabbi Eliezer Silver (standing) and Rabbi Avraham Kalmanowitz. Courtesy of Torah Umesorah

sey.

While Rabbi Levy knew Rabbi Kotler from his time in Lakewood, their relationship grew much deeper at Torah Umesorah, where Rabbi Kotler was the head of the Rabbinical Administrative Board. Rabbi Levy spent hours on the road traveling to Lakewood to discuss issues with him. Mr. Bunim, an ardent follower of Rabbi Kotler's, was often present.

Rabbi Levy used to say that the person closest in approach and style to his rebbe, the Lubavitcher Rebbe, was Rabbi Kotler. Both had an eye on the future and, looking beyond their immediate communities, focused much of their energy on supporting and strengthening the Jewish nation as a whole.

That was how, after being called for a private audience with the

Rebbe in the early 1960s, Rabbi Levy found himself once again on the road to Lakewood. The Rebbe had said that there was a great need for a school to educate teachers. "The yeshivah student leaves the yeshivah," he said, "he doesn't know teaching methodology or classroom pedagogy. If they had this training, many of them would be recruited by Jewish day schools. We have to educate them how to teach."

Rabbi Levy felt passionate about the idea and planned to make it happen. He presented the idea to Rabbi Kotler, without telling him where it originated, and Rabbi Kotler, too, got very excited.

Rabbi Kotler had his differences with the sixth Chabad Rebbe, the Rayatz, but that did not stop him from working closely with his ardent follower, Rabbi Levy. Rabbi Levy would always say that he never heard a negative word from the Rebbe or from Rabbi Kotler about each other or the groups they respectively led.

In the lively discussion that ensued, Rabbi Kotler explained how he would like to see the student-teachers educated. It was then that he alluded, for the first and last time, to Rabbi Levy's connection to Chabad. "There are *tzaddikim*, *beinonim* and *resha'im*," he said, referring to the righteous, the average people and the wicked, concepts explained at length in the *Tanya*, the foundational text of Chabad Chassidism written by the first Chabad Rebbe, Rabbi Schneur Zalman of Liadi. Turning to Rabbi Levy, Rabbi Kotler said, "*Nu*, Reb Ber, you know what we mean here; you studied *Tanya*!"

Rabbi Kotler was then already old and weak. Yet, as always, he did not leave it up to others to present his ideas. He called for a meeting of Torah Umesorah's Rabbinical Board, where he lamented the lack of a teaching institute. "Reb Aharon Kotler, Chairman, opened the meeting with a discussion on the need for a Teacher Training Institute. [He said that] this is a most vital matter," read the report from the May 1962 meeting.

With the board's permission, Rabbi Levy and Mr. Bunim initiated a campaign to raise awareness about the need for the institute and to raise funds. That year the institute opened its first branch in Ner Israel Rabbinical College in Baltimore, Maryland. Another branch opened the next year in New York in the Torah Vodaath building. The school was named after the longtime treasurer of Torah Umesorah, who died suddenly in January 1963.

"The Joseph Shapiro Teachers' Institute, a professional school for the specialized training of Hebrew day school teachers, was formally opened here today under the auspices of Torah Umesorah," reported the *Jewish Telegraphic Agency*. "Admission to the school is open to senior students in major rabbinical seminaries, who will be trained to fill vacant positions in Hebrew day schools throughout the country where a shortage of teachers currently exists."

The program would take two years, and at the end the educators would receive accreditation by the organization. Around twenty people signed up the first year. Only two-thirds of them, however, ever showed up to the classes. In June 1963, Dr. Kaminetsky and Rabbi Levy went to interview the students. Only nine of them expressed interest in continuing the program, and all of them said that they would soon have no time to continue. Most were not genuinely interested in becoming teachers. They were in fact working as salesmen. According to Mr. Bunim, in a November memorandum by Dr. Kaminetsky, the project was called "a failure."

When Rabbi Kotler passed away in November of that year, the project lost its most high-profile supporter. Mr. Bunim and Rabbi Levy, however, would not give up. They pressed the Torah Umesorah board to work on ways to make the program a success.

Rabbi Levy felt there was a need to create a fellowship program, where graduates from yeshivah high schools could receive a stipend for their attendance during specific hours of the day. "If we would have had something in the way of a fellowship for these students," Rabbi Levy told the board, "we would have gotten more of them to be interested in continuing."

In addition, he said, the institute needed a building of its own, away from the yeshivah. "In order to give the training status, it must have its own building, adequate facilities for the students to study, to do research, a pedagogic library," he told the board. "Only in a central institute could we create the necessary serious environment for this type of program, and only through a central institute could we hope to encourage others to enter the field."

At the next meeting, the board voted to implement these ideas and create a budget. A December 1963 report by Dr. Kaminetsky stated that the new building would include classrooms, a library on pedagogy, a reference library, a publications department, a conference room and a research institute. During the summer, the institute would offer classes in education for working teachers.

Finding a building was left to Rabbi Levy and Mr. Bunim.

In a letter to members of the board from December 1963, Dr. Kaminetsky wrote about the importance of getting the institute opened as soon as possible. "The Conservatives have announced a plan for 30 new Solomon Schechter schools, and they constitute a real menace," he wrote. "And thus it is very important for us to set up a system of training teachers."

The Shapiro family, for whose patriarch the institute was named, had agreed to pay for the new building, but Rabbi Levy and Mr. Bunim still had to contend with Moe Feuerstein, the executive committee chairman of Torah Umesorah, who vehemently opposed the idea of a new building because he felt the rabbinical board would not agree.

"The members of the Rabbinical Administrative Board will have to understand this in view of the menace of the Conservatives," Dr. Kaminetsky wrote. Rabbi Levy felt that if Rabbi Yaakov Kamenetsky, the

Part of Rabbi Levy's job as director of development was to travel around the country helping schools solve their financial problems. Here he meets with a Jewish community (circa 1963). Courtesy of Thelma Levy

head of Mesivta Torah Vodaath, who had replaced Rabbi Kotler on the rabbinical board, could be convinced, he would overrule the objections of the other members. He volunteered to present the case for the new building to Rabbi Kamenetsky.

When Rabbi Levy and Mrs. Shapiro found a building on New York City's Madison Avenue, the board said it was too expensive and there was no need for such a large building. In the end, they could not find a building that satisfied everyone. The fellowships, though, proved to be a success, and several more locations for the institute were added.

Over the more than five decades since Rabbi Levy first pushed to create the programs, thousands of educators have received their initial and continued training at the institute, named today for its original predecessor in the early 1940s, Aish Dos. More recently, the organization finally got its own building in Brooklyn, where the teacher training is conducted.

Federation Support

When Mr. Irving Stone, a philanthropist from Cleveland, Ohio, was organizing federations to support Jewish day schools in the 1960s, some objected to schools in the Torah Umesorah network taking the money. They argued that the federations would meddle in school policy. Rabbi Levy consulted Rabbi Kotler about what the policy should be, and he said that schools should be permitted to accept the money.

"Many day schools are dependent upon the support of a federation, and we cannot tell them to refrain from taking such much-needed support," Rabbi Kotler said.

Rabbi Levy's passion for education became well known. On one trip to visit Florida day schools, he was invited to meet the Satmar Rebbe, Rabbi Yoel Teitelbaum. The two discussed education through the night. Despite their differences in philosophy—Satmar's approach is to shun nonobservant Jews, while Chabad reaches out to them—they were able to have a productive conversation.

The Firefighter

Many of Rabbi Levy's trips around the country were taken together with Dr. Kaminetsky. The two would make whirlwind visits to cities to check on the schools there. Of their visit to Chicago in December 1962, Dr. Kaminetsky wrote, "We had a rather exciting time in that windy city."

When there was a crisis, however, Rabbi Levy was usually dispatched to deal with it alone.

"Whenever a yeshivah had a problem, he went down and worked it out," said Mrs. Levy. "It was a 24-hour job. The phone never stopped ringing, and there were many, many meetings."

Before Rabbi Levy left to deal with a problem, he and Dr. Kaminetsky would identify the best people to work with in the community. Choosing the right people was essential, because they would be the ones to implement the changes Rabbi Levy recommended.

"Rabbi Bernard Levy of our office is coming to Detroit for a day or so on Monday, please G-d," Dr. Kaminetsky wrote to Mr. and Mrs. Arthur Selmar in 1963. "We have not been in Detroit for a long time, and we want to get an objective picture of what is happening with yeshivah education in your town. I told Rabbi Levy that you two folks would be in a position to give him an unbiased, clear, objective picture of the whole situation."

When Rabbi Levy returned from these trips, the director would write to thank those who helped him during his visits: "Rabbi Levy just returned from his trip, and he has reported to us how helpful you were to him in every phase of his work when he was in Detroit. We are very grateful to you."

In January 1965, the Torah Umesorah day school in Augusta, Georgia, was facing difficulties. In a letter to Dr. Kaminetsky, Charlotte Denny, a local supporter of the school, wrote, "I have waited until now to write to you hoping that the school would get better, but as of now nothing could be worse.... Our school is going to close."

Dr. Kaminetsky heard more rumors that the school had closed down, and wrote to the school's director, "They told me that the school closed down.... I would appreciate hearing from you as to how things are getting along and whether there is some ground to this rumor."

As usual, Rabbi Levy was sent to iron things out and see if the school could be reopened. "I am sorry that things are developing the way they are," Dr. Kaminetsky wrote to Mrs. Denny. "I will try to get Rabbi Levy out there as soon as possible."

In a subsequent letter in May, he wrote to Harold Denny, "[Rabbi

Levy] brought back wonderful regards from you. He told me how devoted you are to the day school, and I am very proud to get the report."

As a direct result of Rabbi Levy's trip, Mr. Shapiro offered that his Adas Yeshurun Synagogue would subsidize the Hebrew department of Augusta's day school. "This is a wonderful gesture, and I want to convey our thanks to everyone in the synagogue," Dr. Kaminetsky wrote.

He ended his letter, "I am glad that you folks have a little bit of peace of mind now, and I wish you well."

If Rabbi Levy could not find a donor to support a school in need, he used other means to secure funding. "Reb Berel was terrific in San Diego," reported Rabbi Simcha Wasserman, famed dean of Ohr Elchonon in Los Angeles. "He most probably has given you a report already."

In 1963, Rabbi Wasserman's yeshivah owed the IRS tens of thousands of dollars. The school had planned a fundraising dinner a few months down the line, but the debt had to be paid immediately.

"While this situation threatens to be choking [us]," he wrote to Dr. Kaminetsky, "as I mentioned to you, there are some good outlooks for placing the yeshivah on a much higher standard for the coming year, if we should survive with the help of the Almighty."

In an urgent telegram, Rabbi Wasserman wrote that the IRS had given him a final date. "[I] am wiring Rabbi Levy," he wrote. "Please assist."

Dr. Kaminetsky and Rabbi Levy secured large loans for the school. Shortly thereafter, Rabbi Wasserman wrote, "The situation with the IRS worked out in time. Please deliver in my name thanks, from the depths of my heart, to our friend Rabbi Levy."

Over time, Rabbi Levy became an expert in trimming and revamping school budgets. "As soon as possible, I should like to get an audited report of your expenses and income for the past two years – with the projected budget for next year," Dr. Kaminetsky wrote to the principal of the day school in Atlantic City. "I will submit these to Rabbi Levy of our

One of Rabbi Levy's greatest accomplishments at Torah Umesorah was the organization of successful fundraising dinners. Here, he (extreme right) appears at a Torah Umesorah dinner. Courtesy of Torah Umesorah

office for intensive study. Rabbi Levy will be in touch with expert advisers and will visit your school as soon as possible to recommend further economics and the like. We will do all we can to trim the budget down to the barest minimum, I assure you."

The schools appreciated Rabbi Levy's efforts immensely. When the director of an Ohio school heard that Rabbi Levy's visit had been delayed so that he could prepare for an upcoming conference, he replied, "I would much rather see Rabbi Levy's talents applied where they are most needed; although selfishly speaking, I certainly would like to see him come here."

Common Ground

Over the years, Chabad and Torah Umesorah had their fair share of conflicts. "Our school-building initiatives out of town sometimes met with resistance among local Lubavitch representatives," Dr. Kaminetsky wrote in his autobiography. "They had preceded us as pioneers in some places and must have looked upon us as carpet-baggers, strangers meddling in local affairs."

(In one unusually aggressive move, after the passing of the Rayatz, several Torah Umesorah activists made efforts to quash the Chabad schools in their areas, hoping that the movement would crumble. Those efforts were quickly put to a stop by Dr. Kaminetsky, and peace reigned.)

The central staff at Torah Umesorah clearly had no axe to grind. Between Rabbi Gurary and Dr. Kaminetsky there was a cool, though cordial, relationship. Several times Dr. Kaminetsky noted that he could not find common ground with Rabbi Gurary, though he had made every effort to.

When Rabbi Levy joined Torah Umesorah, he made a concerted effort to improve relations between the two organizations. He encouraged Dr. Kaminetsky to discuss the challenges facing Torah Umesorah with the Lubavitcher Rebbe and his chief aide, Rabbi Chaim Hodakov.

Dr. Kaminetsky took advantage of this new channel of communications to resolve issues when they arose. "I would write the Rebbe or take up the matter with Rabbi Chodakov [sic], and after some difficulty, we would manage to work out a *modus vivendi*," he wrote.

After Dr. Kaminetsky's first private audience in 1962, he wrote to update the Rebbe on what they had discussed, and proposed that Torah Umesorah and Chabad should join forces in organizing the national Parent Teacher Association. The Rebbe reviewed all the material that he sent with the letter and replied, "I was glad to read the good and tangible results in connection with our conversation, and surely there will be even more improvements in all of your holy work in education, and surely you will not withhold the good news and inform me."

During another audience, the Rebbe asked Dr. Kaminetsky what the day schools in his network did about textbooks that contained problematic information from a Torah perspective. "We tear out the pages," the director answered. The Rebbe told him that it was not a good idea: "It just makes the kids more curious to seek out what it says there." He suggested that Torah Umesorah should produce its own accredited curriculum.

Over the years the relationship grew stronger. During a controversy over whether a particular school in the Midwest should be supported by Torah Umesorah, a local philanthropist suggested that the Rebbe decide if the school had merit. Dr. Kaminetsky had a long conversation on the matter with Rabbi Hodakov, which he then relayed to the philanthropist.

"In general, the Rebbe does not give *hechsharim* [stamps of approval]," the head of Torah Umesorah wrote in 1963, "neither for foods nor for schools. But if somebody would come to him and say, for instance, that a school uses a *'Kitzur Chumash'* [an abridged version of the Torah, which the Rebbe decried at the time], then, naturally, he cannot accept this as part of the Torah program."

In another letter, Dr. Kaminetsky quoted the Rebbe's advice on fighting negative reports in a newspaper: "It is worthwhile to work with the people who have mimeographs in their basements."

Dr. Kaminetsky and other members of the Torah Umesorah faculty visited the Rebbe during the 1968 teachers' strike in New York City. The strike lasted for more than a month, and left thousands of public school students, including many Jewish children, without schools.

"There are so many Jewish children walking around the streets," the Rebbe said. "Why hasn't the aggressive stance been taken that we will offer children a 50 percent discount on day school tuition? We need to enroll them into Jewish schools. Once you have them in the schools and the public schools reopen, some will leave, but many will not."

The Rebbe also made comments on the various Torah Umesorah

publications. Dr. Kaminetsky recalled that the Rebbe "would send pointers for how to make the [*Jewish Parent*] magazine more effective." He advised them to make the magazine livelier, "so that the Jewish mother would want to read it before she went to sleep."

The Rabbinic Board

As a part of his duties, Rabbi Levy attended the meetings of Torah Umesorah's rabbinic board, in which Rabbis Aharon Kotler, Mordechai Gifter and Yaakov Kamenetsky, among others, participated. Rabbi Levy would report back to the Rebbe about the meetings, and occasionally he would convey the Rebbe's position on an issue to the board. Once he asked the Rebbe why he didn't attend the meetings himself. "Surely if the Rebbe would go," he said, "it would have much more influence on them…"

In response, the Rebbe said that the fifth Chabad Rebbe, Rabbi Shalom Dovber Schneersohn, had a large following in Russia, and his views were widely respected and accepted. When his son, the Rebbe Rayatz, left the Soviet Union and came to Poland, he left many of his followers behind, and his influence diminished accordingly. If he wanted to address a certain issue, he would express his views through others, great rabbinical leaders such as Rabbi Chaim Ozer Grodzinski.

"I do like the *shver* [father-in-law] does," the Rebbe said, stating a principle that guided much of his conduct.

The rabbinic board knew that Rabbi Levy was speaking to the Rebbe about the meetings. Rabbi Gifter, the dean of the Telshe Yeshivah in Cleveland and one of the leading figures of Orthodox Jewry in the United States, once said to him during a meeting, "Ask by the Lubavitcher Rebbe. He will know what to do. Don't ask him in my name, but he would know."

Rabbi Levy's presence did not prevent the rabbis from making critical remarks about Chabad on occasion. When Rabbi Levy repeated

The rabbinic board was an integral part of Torah Umesorah. Here the organization's founder, Rabbi Aharon Kotler (right), is seen at a Torah Umesorah fundraiser. Also pictured (from right to left): Samuel Feuerstein, president of Torah Umesorah; Rabbi Leo Jung, rabbi of the Jewish Center of New York; and Rabbi Dr. Samson R. Weiss, national director of Young Israel. *Courtesy of Torah Umesorah*

these, the Rebbe never said anything, simply ignoring the negative talk.

One issue on which the Rebbe sought to influence the board was summer vacation. "I don't understand why they closed the schools during the summer," the Rebbe told Rabbi Levy, "but now that they closed the yeshivahs, we have to make sure that the children should go to camp and not roam the streets." (As a direct result of that conversation, the OK maintains a camp fund until this day.)

At the request of Dr. Kaminetsky, Rabbi Hodakov wrote a letter outlining the Rebbe's approach to summer vacation. It was published in the winter 1964 issue of *Hamenahel*, a publication geared to Torah Umesorah school principals, with this introduction: "The following letter from Rabbi M. A. Hodakov, secretary to the Lubavitcher Rebbe and director of Merkos L'Inyonei Chinuch, Inc., will undoubtedly be of great interest to our principals."

The three-page letter included eight suggestions for educators on making the most of the vacation period. It included, "It is necessary that the teachers, in good time, before the summer recess begins, convey to their students… what the purpose of the summer recess is, so that they should… derive the utmost benefit from it, in accordance with the purpose.… The summer is also an investment for success in the coming school year."

Not Your Father!

In the mid-1960s, Rabbi Levy's son Don Yoel was studying at the Talmudical Yeshiva of Philadelphia. In honor of his birthday, he traveled to New York for a private audience with the Rebbe. "Don't ask the Rebbe permission for your father to also go in," Rabbi Leibel Groner, one of the Rebbe's aides, warned him. Rabbi Groner knew that if Rabbi Levy went in, all those scheduled for an audience would be kept waiting for hours as the Rebbe discussed Torah Umesorah with him.

"Your father is here?" the Rebbe asked as soon as the young man entered his office.

Don Yoel did not know how to respond. The Rebbe saw his hesitation and asked, "What is the matter?"

He told the Rebbe that he had just been told that there was no permission for his father to enter the Rebbe's office. "I am scared of him [Rabbi Groner]," he told the Rebbe.

The Rebbe smiled and said, "It's okay, tell your father to come in." Don Yoel walked out of the office and told the aide that he was going to get his father, who was waiting in one of the rooms. When Rabbi Groner gave him a sharp look, Don Yoel said, "I didn't do anything. The Rebbe asked me to call my father in."

Rabbi Groner's prediction proved accurate. After speaking to the young man, the Rebbe spent hours talking to Rabbi Levy.

Possible Merger

In one New England town, the staff of the Torah Umesorah school felt that the Chabad school there should close and join forces with them. "We had a day school, and there was also a Lubavitcher day school," Dr. Norman Lamm later recalled. "My concern was that there was competition for very few students."

Dr. Lamm discussed the issue in a private audience with the Rebbe in the late 1950s. The Rebbe had long held a definite opinion on such questions. He felt that it was not a good idea, because when it came to Torah, competition was a good thing. "He took a *halachic* [Jewish legal] stance that there is no *hasagas gevul* [encroachment]," recalled Dr. Lamm, "no encroachment when it comes to disseminating the Torah."

In the early 1960s, after Dr. Lamm left, the Torah Umesorah school in question was once again on the verge of closing, with insurmountable debt. "The situation in ... has us all down here [worried]," Dr. Kaminetsky wrote. "It is one of the toughest problems we have come across, and we are working hard to help solve it."

After a board member visited the school, the organization gave the school a staggering loan, equal today to $115,000. "Were it not for the emergency loan which was extended to us by your bank, there is no doubt that our school would have, G-d forbid, closed," the director wrote in September 1963.

The administration of the school and the local clergy felt that the situation of two schools competing for funds and children was unbearable. They were unaccommodating to the Chabad school, and made every effort to torpedo the purchase of a local synagogue for its use. "There is simple [sic] no justification for maintaining an institution which produces nothing but a pinpoint on a map," the Torah Umesorah school's principal wrote.

In a letter to the Lubavitcher Rebbe, Dr. Kaminetsky described the situation. "The present day school is in a precarious position. It needs all the help it can get. The merger with Lubavitch – however few their forces – in my humble opinion will give real Torah a chance to thrive."

He requested that the Rebbe tell the local Chabad representative that he should merge with the Torah Umesorah school. But the Rebbe seldom involved himself in the network of Chabad schools that was established before the sixth Chabad Rebbe passed away, leaving the schools under the directorship of Rabbi Gurary.

"Rabbi Chodakov [sic] called me on Thursday to tell me that the whole matter is really out of the hands of the Rebbe, himself," he wrote to the principal. "It belongs to Rabbi Gurary of the Tomchei Tmimim Yeshivos, which is part of the network."

Rabbi Levy was in the Midwest when the issue flared up again in September. He reached out the Chabad representative in question to help mediate the conflict. The Lubavitchers believed that the goal of the "merger" was simply to swallow their school. Rabbi Levy conveyed the message to headquarters: there would be no merger. "Even if there will be only five children in the Lubavitch school, they will not give up an institution," Rabbi Levy said. "This is a matter of principle with them."

After receiving another derogatory letter from the school's principal about the Chabad representatives, Dr. Kaminetsky replied, "It is not for me to question the procedures of the Lubavitchers. They are chassidim, and they have different ways of looking at matters. I would not be concerned with them. If I were you, I would devote all of my energy to building up a bigger and better school."

Both schools continued to struggle for many years. In the end the day school cut ties with Torah Umesorah, and the Chabad school maintains a small but steady enrollment.

Not Just Kids

During his time at Torah Umesorah, perhaps more than anyone else, Rabbi Levy came to see what the Jewish day school movement was achieving. "[It has] to its credit some awe-inspiring achievements," Rabbi Levy later wrote. "It is now giving a basic Torah education to more than

50,000 children."

The schools were bringing thousands of their graduates into Jewish high schools, thus assuring the future of Jewish life on American soil. Having had to fight to get a proper Jewish education in America himself, he keenly appreciated this phenomenon. "It is presently beginning to have a revolutionary impact in almost two hundred communities such as would have been unimaginable a few brief years ago," he wrote.

Yet, he felt, the movement had not achieved its full potential. It was reaching thousands of children, but its impact was still individual rather than collective. Day schools had not transformed American Jewry into a Torah community.

He believed the solution was in "the twin pillars of home and school." It was not enough for children to be enrolled in Jewish schools; the Jewish values and instruction they were receiving had to penetrate the home as well. The answer, he told his colleagues at Torah Umesorah on numerous occasions, was adult education programs.

On a local level, Rabbi Levy had made parent programming part of his work in the various cities where he had headed schools. Newspaper clippings from that period describing how he had detailed the Yom Kippur laws or told the story of Chanukah for parents attest to his longstanding interest in adult education.

The Parent Teacher Associations (PTAs) that Torah Umesorah been instrumental in organizing around the country would be the perfect vehicles for this initiative, Rabbi Levy argued. "The many thousands of parents who are drawn to PTA participation may be initially motivated only by the desire to enhance the educational welfare of their children through the conventional gamut of PTA functions," he said. "But they can at the same time be exposed, and ultimately attracted to, the beauty and truth of the life of Torah."

PTA fundraising activities – bazaars, raffles, journals and similar projects – were important. However, the Jewi[sh day school movement] needed to place central emphasis on adult ed[ucation. The movement] must expend every effort to attract [adults to Torah study,] he said. "It must offer organized classes in every [community for adult] learning, in as sustained, efficient and attractive a [manner as possible."]

The project did not come to fruition during [his tenure at] Torah Umesorah. But a few years later, in 1974, the [OK estab]lished Project Seed, a major component of which w[as Torah] study for community members.

When, under Rabbi Levy's direction, the OK began producing a glossy magazine, the *Jewish Homemaker*, he made it a priority to publish extensive articles on Judaism and Jewish practice in addition to those about kosher supervision.

The Cholent Dilemma

Personal relationships are paramount to a director of development, and over the years Rabbi Levy built friendships in communities across the globe. One was with Rabbi Baruch Poupko, a pioneer of Jewish education in the United States who moved to Pittsburgh in 1941. There he was the senior rabbi of Shaare Torah congregation, the president of the Rabbinical Council of Pittsburgh and one of the original founders of the Hillel Academy of Pittsburgh, established in 1947 and affiliated with Torah Umesorah.

The two rabbis shared an ongoing joke about the need to persevere and to stand in the front line by having *mesirat nefesh*, personal self-sacrifice, for Jewish education. "Now that I know that Rabbi Levy will be here for Shabbos," Rabbi Poupko once wrote to Dr. Kaminetsky, "please ask him in our name to be our guest Shabbos morning – tell him that our cholent is an expression of the finest tradition of Jewish martyrdom."

Dr. Kaminetsky replied that Rabbi Levy had already committed himself to eat with another family. His suggestion was to invite Rabbi Levy for the *melava malka* meal after Shabbat. "If Berel feels brave enough, he will eat your cholent then, although it may in truth be 'an expression of the finest tradition of Jewish martyrdom' at your home."

Save the Money

In 1964 the Hillel Academy in Denver, Colorado, was contemplating hiring an executive director. Such important hires fell under Rabbi Levy's jurisdiction, and he was asked to help determine if it was a good idea.

Rabbi Levy told the administration in Denver that only 10 percent of schools have an executive director, and the need for one depends on the leadership. Some schools, he said, are "so well organized they can function efficiently without one. On the other hand, there are schools with only one hundred students that find the need for an executive director."

Worried that the expense would be too much for the school, he advised them to examine their financial capabilities and see if the same objectives could be accomplished without paying a director's salary.

In a meeting at Torah Umesorah headquarters, a board member pointed out the possible problems with asking the school to evaluate its own financial status. Rabbi Levy, always an advocate for transparency and objectivity in financial considerations, noted that the organization's accountant had stopped participating in the meetings. "Our accountant came to our meetings to present a financial report, but he was never called on," he said.

Having expended so much of his time in fundraising, Rabbi Levy was adamant that the organization should spend its money wisely. A proposal was once floated in a board meeting that the yearly principals' conference should take place in Israel. The suggestion was that the organization would bring them to Israel in order to learn from the educational practices there and compare them to those used in America.

Rabbi Levy felt that this was a total waste of precious charity funds.

Despite their differences, the Rebbe and Dr. Joseph Kaminetsky (above) found common ground to work together on behalf of Jewish education. *Courtesy of Torah Umesorah*

"It's very nice, but I don't think that Torah Umesorah should be doing that. The education issues in Israel are not the same problems we have here. We don't need to spend the money on a trip to take all the principals there. We need the funds for other important projects," he said. His opposition to the idea created tension in the meeting, and those who had proposed the trip accused him of being anti-Zionist.

Helping Others

Even with his busy schedule, Rabbi Levy always had time to help people. In 1962, Rabbi Leibel Posner and his wife, Thirza, wanted to move back to New York from the Midwest, but the young rabbi was having a difficult time finding employment. He had applied for a teaching position in New Jersey that was well paid, and had high hopes that he would be hired.

Rabbi Levy had been helping him find a job, and when Rabbi Posner told him about the position, he said he knew the principal of the school well and would call him to recommend Rabbi Posner. Rabbi Levy immediately picked up the phone. After a few moments of conversation, however, he became crestfallen. The principal had said that Rabbi Posner's Hebrew was not up to par.

"What struck me most was his attitude," said Rabbi Posner. "He seemed all broken up because he couldn't help me. In fact, I started to console him."

In the meantime, Rabbi Dov Liebenstein, who ran the placement office at Torah Umesorah, walked into the office. "Dov, this young man needs a job. What do you have for him?" Rabbi Levy asked.

Rabbi Liebenstein answered that there was a position open in Yeshiva Rabbi Samson Raphael Hirsch in the Washington Heights section of Manhattan. Rabbi Posner was interviewed that day, and the next day he was hired for even better pay than the New Jersey position had offered.

A week or so later, Rabbi Posner called Rabbi Levy about an afternoon job. Rabbi Levy told him to call the Board of Jewish Education and speak to Rabbi Samson Isseroff, who had an opening. Rabbi Posner received that job as well.

Saving Olomeinu

Around the time when Rabbi Levy joined Torah Umesorah, *Olomeinu – Our World*, the organization's student magazine, was faltering. The magazine had been started in 1945, shortly after the organization was founded, and included stories, holiday supplements, Hebrew pages, cartoon strips, puzzle pages and short biographies of Jewish greats.

"We have discontinued publishing *Olomeinu*, our children's magazine," Dr. Kaminetsky wrote in February 1960. "I have talked to our people about going into the publishing business again, by they are very reluctant. We have lost a great deal of money on our publications and have had to curtail matters drastically."

He continued to push for the magazine, with little success. "We have to see that the magazine continues to appear. It is not an easy job!" he wrote in November 1960.

Rabbi Levy also believed the magazine was important, and made every effort to convince the board to reestablish it, which it finally did the next year. "*Olomeinu* was in deep trouble," Mr. Bunim recalled. "Rabbi Levy put all his strength behind it to raise the funds to keep it alive."

The publication continued to flounder, however, pulling the entire publications department down with it.

"A study of the publications department's financial status was made," Rabbi Levy wrote in a January 1961 report on the organization's financial health, noting that the situation there was not good.

Rabbi Levy wanted a new chairman for the department. "This department is very vital because there is a great need for many more publications. It is also of utmost importance that this department is run with maximum efficiency," he wrote.

The report suggested further study on the budget and a closer look at the department's accounting books. Rabbi Levy also wanted *Olomeinu* to have its own chairman. "There is much work needed in order to secure its existence," he wrote.

The efforts turned out to be in vain, and the magazine once again found itself on the brink of closure, recalled Mr. Bunim. The lay board of Torah Umesorah "had no financiers to go on with it [the magazine] and threatened to close it," he said.

It was then that Rabbi Levy decided to bring Mr. Bunim to the Lubavitcher Rebbe to discuss what to do with the magazine.

Chabad had its own set of publications, among them several magazines for children—the beloved and long-running *Talks and Tales* appeared monthly. They also published, years before Torah Umesorah, history books and books on Jewish holidays in English. Torah Umesorah schools, not on policy, rarely utilized these publications.

Chabad officials noticed, and complained about it. "I wonder how many principals and teachers are thoroughly familiar with the publications of [Chabad]," wrote Dr. Nissan Mindel, chief editor of Chabad's children's books, in a chapter published in Torah Umesorah's *Hebrew Day School Education: An Overview*, "and to what extent they are availing themselves of such publications as our monthly *Talks and Tales*, our Festival series, our textbooks on Jewish history and other literature?"

From the tens of hours that Rabbi Levy spent with the Rebbe discussing Jewish education and Torah Umesorah, he knew that to the Rebbe, all that was beside the point. To reach and inspire more Jewish children was the Rebbe's passion, which Rabbi Levy wanted to utilize.

"[The Rebbe] was an advocate for what was going on [in Torah Umesorah]," Mr. Bunim said in a 2002 interview, "even though he was not involved in Torah Umesorah. He might have been… in the 'other camp,' but he still had the integrity to understand how important it was."

The Rebbe told them that under no circumstances should *Olomeinu* be allowed to die. "The magazine must go on; this is very important for the children," Mr. Bunim paraphrased the Rebbe.

"He gave a very strong *brachah* [blessing] for its future success, and then handed Rabbi Levy a substantial amount of money, adding that from this sum should grow the financial support needed to restore the magazine to its proper vitality."

Two days later, Rabbi Levy and Mr. Bunim went to see a good friend of the Bunim family, Mr. Arthur I. LeVine, a very successful businessman who owned a large, well-known printing company, Ad Press Ltd. Rabbi Levy impressed the importance of the magazine on Mr. LeVine, who agreed to print quite a number of issues of *Olomeinu* gratis.

This gave Rabbi Levy the time in which to raise the money to put the magazine back on its feet. "If it wasn't for what he [Rabbi Levy] did, I don't know if *Olomeinu* would be in existence today," Mr. Bunim said.

Dr. Kaminetsky acknowledged the Rebbe's generosity: "Such a sum was significant. This was an especially generous gesture, considering that the Lubavitch movement had its own children's publication."

Torah Umesorah's parents' magazine, the *Jewish Parent*, could not be saved, however, and succumbed to financial struggles. "I could not challenge the Torah Umesorah board, and we suspended the publication," Dr. Kaminetsky wrote. "It was a great loss to Torah Umesorah."

Reflecting on the Rebbe's role in saving *Olomeinu*, he wrote, "Had there been more such instances of goodwill and understanding between Lubavitch and Torah Umesorah, the Hebrew day school movement would have been the real winner."

Telephone Study Partner

Rabbi Levy had not been at Torah Umesorah long when his professional relationship with Mr. Bunim blossomed into friendship. "I liked his integrity; I liked his feeling for other people; I liked his feeling for learning Torah, of course, which was paramount in both of our lives," Mr. Bunim recalled. "He was really a true loyal friend."

Naturally, said Mr. Bunim, they began studying Talmud together. Mr. Bunim's office was ten blocks away from the Torah Umesorah's offices in Manhattan. Each morning, before work hours, Rabbi Levy would come over to Mr. Bunim's office to study. "We learned whatever Gemara we wanted to," the businessman recalled. "It was a very beautiful *chavruta* [study partnership]."

Though they approached Talmud study with differing methodologies—Mr. Bunim in the Brisk tradition and Rabbi Levy in the Chassidic—they were able, "in a very fine way," to reach an understanding of the difficult texts.

The *chavrutah* continued for many years. When Rabbi Levy was not in Manhattan, they learned on the telephone at seven o'clock every morning. Mr. Bunim liked to say that theirs was the first-ever tele-

In the Torah Umesorah offices, Rabbi Levy met Amos Bunim, a legendary figure in the Jewish world, who became a lifelong personal friend. Here, Mr. Bunim (sitting) at the 1963 Torah Umesorah dinner. Also in the photo is Dr. Kaminetsky. Courtesy of Torah Umesorah

phone study partnership. He recalled that many times Rabbi Levy used to soothe his youngest son, Eliezer Yitzchak, with one hand and hold the phone with the other.

The daily Torah study enhanced Mr. Bunim's life immeasurably. "He was a *chavruta* that really related to you in every which way," he said. "We were totally engrossed in the Gemara. There was nothing else."

Such long phone calls were very costly in the 1970s. Once, when Rabbi Levy was on the road for close to a month, the phone company noticed a drastic drop in his bill and called to inquire if everything was okay.

"To me, that was the most cherished thing, the learning of Torah," said Mr. Bunim, summarizing the relationship. "Everything else was really secondary."

Mr. Bunim and the Rebbe

Rabbi Levy often discussed his friendship with Mr. Bunim and the businessman's activities on behalf of Jewish education with the Rebbe. "The Rebbe kept tabs on me through him," Mr. Bunim said.

Like the rest of the Torah Umesorah staff, Mr. Bunim appreciated the keen advice and suggestions that Rabbi Levy relayed to them from the Rebbe.

In 1963, Mr. Bunim became involved in a heated debate about whether federal funding to Jewish day schools violated the separation of church and state. At the time a few Jewish organizations had joined with other religious groups to argue that if funding were not used directly for religious education, there was no reason why religious schools should not receive government funding for their basic needs. The Rebbe joined the effort and became active in promoting the cause.

Around this time Rabbi Levy brought Mr. Bunim to a private audience with the Rebbe that lasted many hours. When Mr. Bunim entered the Rebbe's room, the Rebbe invited him to sit down, but he refused out of respect. The Rebbe insisted, however, taking pains to make the businessman feel at ease. "It was as if two friends were speaking to each other," Mr. Bunim recalled.

The Rebbe then began to inquire about Mr. Bunim's efforts in Washington, D.C. There was tremendous resistance to the idea of funding religious schools from many government bodies. Mr. Bunim had met with many legislators to explain in detail how Jewish day schools operated and assure them that there would be no breach of church and state. The Rebbe questioned him in detail about every meeting, which officials had been receptive to his message and which had been antagonistic.

As the audience stretched well beyond the time allotted to it, the Rebbe's aides began ringing the buzzer to signal that the audience should end. The Rebbe ignored them: "Forget about the buzzer," he said.

"He was very interested to understand how this whole thing worked," Mr. Bunim recalled. "His understanding was tremendously deep as to what he was searching for. [The meeting was] really a fascinating experience, I must say."

The conversations with Mr. Bunim assisted the Rebbe in his own efforts to promote federal aid for Jewish schools.

Over the next decade, Mr. Bunim would continue to meet with the Rebbe periodically to discuss his work in education. He estimated that he spent over fifteen hours in the Rebbe's office in all.

The struggle to get funding for day schools continued, but Mr. Bunim did have success in another area: Pointing out that the federal government was already giving money to Catholic colleges, Mr. Bunim successfully lobbied for Jewish institutions of higher education to receive aid as well.

During one of their meetings, the Rebbe asked Mr. Bunim to meet with the administration of United Lubavitcher Yeshivoth and see if he could help them receive funding for their higher education department. Mr. Bunim did so, and afterwards the Rebbe's aide called to thank him. The Rebbe was on the other line, "whispering [to the aide], telling him exactly what to say," Mr. Bunim said.

Overload

Rabbi Levy became so integral to the functioning of Torah Umesorah that at times he was tasked with more than he could possibly do. Occasionally he was unable to address pressing issues due to his overwhelming workload.

Once Rabbi Levy and Dr. Kaminetsky were visiting a donor in Los Angeles, when a comment Dr. Kaminetsky made in jest was taken the wrong way. The donor was offended and threatened to withdraw his support.

"I am just sorry that we got ourselves into some of these problems, and certainly we will sit down and evaluate these things," Dr. Kaminetsky wrote in January 1964. "I am sorry that Berel is so tied up in his other work at present that I do not have the time to sit down and evaluate matters from our angle."

Much of Rabbi Levy's time at home became consumed with work as well. "He was always out in the field or on the phone," Mrs. Levy said. "Sometimes he was gone for a day, sometimes a week."

End of an Era

As the years passed, Rabbi Levy clashed with several of Torah Umesorah's board members. Their disagreements usually centered on Rabbi Levy's unwillingness to compromise Jewish law. Rabbi Levy turned to Mr. Bunim, who had also noticed the friction, and asked if he should consider looking for another job as a backup. The businessman agreed that his friend needed to find solid ground outside of the organization.

With Mr. Bunim's encouragement and financial backing, Rabbi Levy acquired Rabbi Kohn's supervision, and during the times that he was not working for Torah Umesorah he visited factories to review their operations.

Some of the Torah Umesorah board members were heavily involved in the Orthodox Union's kosher supervision and viewed Rabbi Levy's work as a conflict of interest, Mr. Bunim recalled. "That compounded the problem tremendously, and that brought forth the real problem [the board members had with Rabbi Levy], and they wanted him out."

The situation festered for a while, and finally came to a head before Passover 1965. One of the companies Rabbi Levy took over from Rabbi Kohn was Barricini Candies, which for years had been competing with Bartons Candy for the Jewish market. The competition was especially fierce around Passover time, when a Bartons chocolate box was a staple at the Seder table.

"Rabbi Named Kashruth Overseer," reported Jewish newspapers across America in February 1965. "Rabbi Bernard Levy, prominent member of the Union of Orthodox Rabbis of the United States and Canada and the Rabbinical Alliance of America, is now supervisor of Kashruth for Barricini Candy for the whole year and for Passover."

The president of Bartons, Stephen Klein, was also the vice president of the board of Torah Umesorah. He was extremely angry, feeling that Rabbi Levy had deliberately entered into the bitter war he had with Barricini. Mr. Klein and Mr. Feuerstein impressed on the other board members that their employee should not have another job as a kosher supervisor. It was one or the other.

Rabbi and Mrs. Levy at their daughter's wedding, 1965. Courtesy of Thelma Levy

Rabbi Levy was given an ultimatum by Dr. Kaminetsky: If he did not give up his work in kosher supervision, he would face the consequences.

The situation pained Rabbi Levy deeply. He was willing to leave the world of kosher to keep his position and continue to bolster the organization that was so dear to him. As he always did when faced with a momentous decision, he made his way to the Lubavitcher Rebbe. The Rebbe told him that the field of kosher was very important and he should not stop his work.

When he came back to Torah Umesorah with his decision, they asked him to resign. He went back to the Rebbe, who told him: "No! Go every day to work, sit at your desk as you always did, and do what you have to. Do not resign."

For several weeks Rabbi Levy continued to go to work every day. He sat at his desk and found himself doing nothing. He was a man of action, and they were some of the most difficult weeks of his life. But he knew that this was what his rebbe wanted him to do, and he would follow through until the end.

At Torah Umesorah, not everyone was happy. "The organization was in such desperate straits that it would be a very big mistake for him to leave," Mr. Bunim said later. "I felt that this was very important for the continuity of Torah Umesorah financially. We got into a big battle, and I did not win that battle."

Torah Umesorah relieved Rabbi Levy of his duties. "I was very badly hurt by it on a personal level," Mr. Bunim said, noting that he resigned from the organization when he learned that they had fired Rabbi Levy. "I felt that the very dynamic force in the organization was taken away. I felt that it was a very big loss."

When Rabbi Levy told the Rebbe he had been fired, the Rebbe asked if they were paying him severance. They were not. The Rebbe told him that he should see to it that they paid him his due severance pay. The organization refused, and things went to a court of Jewish law, a *din Torah*.

From the beginning, Mr. Klein did his best to influence the outcome of the trial. Rabbi Moshe Feinstein heard the case, however, and his integrity and impartiality prevented Mr. Klein from exerting any undue influence.

The din Torah proved very difficult for Mr. Bunim, who backed Rabbi Levy. "I testified in that *din Torah*," he recalled. "I testified against Torah Umesorah. That was very hard for me." He eventually returned to Torah Umesorah to work on the federal aid programs.

In the end Rabi Levy won the case and was paid a severance package, a painful ending to an era of extraordinary productivity in his life.

"He loved his work there," Mrs. Levy said. "He always said those were the best years of his life."

To the credit of Torah Umesorah, Rabbi Levy's departure did not damage the good relationship that had developed between the organization and Chabad. Years later, when Rabbi Nochem Kaplan took a position as principal in a Torah Umesorah school in Norfolk, Virginia, Dr. Kaminetsky told him, "You know that we had Lubavitchers here? You know that Rabbi Levy was here? You could work with me. I am telling you, the Rebbe is my friend."

When Rabbi Levy was let go from Torah Umesorah, there was a dispute about whether he should receive severance pay, and certain parties sought to influence the decision. Rabbi Moshe Feinstein (above) made sure the terms of the agreement were in full compliance with Jewish law. Courtesy of Torah Umesorah

PART THREE

THE INVESTIGATOR

According to folklore, the original formula for Dr. Pepper was cut in half and held in the vaults of two banks in Dallas, Texas. During his 1976 visit to the Dallas syrup plant, however, there was no hiding the ingredients of the sugary soft drink from Rabbi Levy.

"Kosher supervision today is rather complicated," Rabbi Levy told the *New York Times*. "We must know the highly secret formulas of synthetic flavorings, as well as who is selling and who is buying from whom."

In a profile written at the time, *Dial-Clock Magazine* dubbed Rabbi Levy "the Sherlock Holmes of the food industry." The "smiling, black-hatted, bearded rabbi is at home between large beverage-production equipment," the reporter wrote. "He pokes his fingers into pipes, smells the compounds and tastes other raw ingredients. Rabbi Levy's knowledge of food technology is current to the latest information on natural and synthetic flavorings and compounds, and he has considerable knowledge of beverage chemistry."

Dr. Pepper is the oldest of the major soft drink brands in the United States. It was originally developed and sold out of a Texas pharmacy, until the demand for it exceeded the pharmacy's production capacity. The

When Rabbi Levy entered the kosher world, he envisioned a certification that would trace every ingredient to its source. Here he visits a manufacturer of pasta in China (circa 1985). Courtesy of OK Kosher

drink gained international recognition at the 1904 World's Fair Exposition, the same expo that featured the hamburger bun and the ice cream cone.

The soda company first sought kosher supervision in 1970. At the time, Rabbi Levy was waging a campaign to educate kosher consumers about the need to know where a product's ingredients came from and how it was made before pronouncing it kosher.

Dial-Clock testified that Rabbi Levy made sure that anything the product came into contact with during production was kosher. "His inquiry is probably as comprehensive as one devised by any battery of inspectors."

He told the magazine that there were no ingredients that would make Dr. Pepper non-kosher, but the concern was that the raw ingredients might be made in the same place where non-kosher animal derivatives or meat and dairy products were manufactured. In such a case, the reporter wrote, the "preparation vessels and mixing tanks are purged with boiling water, [a process] witnessed by Rabbi Levy."

In a 1975 profile, the *New York Times* reported on the OK's supervision of the General Foods Corporation, maker of Post cereals. "You have to have a thorough knowledge of food technology and food chemistry," Rabbi Levy told the paper. "If you are not up to date on these aspects, you can be most knowledgeable on Jewish law, but not qualified to do this work."

Rabbi Levy lived in both worlds: in books of Jewish law and in consultation with the great rabbinical leaders of his generation, and in the world of food chemistry and manufacturing. "Those who are in the field," he wrote in 1985, "must be extremely knowledgeable in modern food technology. Changes in formulas are made every day."

Educating Consumers

When Rabbi Levy entered the elite world of kosher supervision agencies, he realized that he needed to educate the Jewish community about why processed food items required supervision. In the inaugural issue of the *Jewish Homemaker*, published in January 1969, he expressed his hope that learning about the complexity of food production would make consumers more conscious about what they eat.

"The fact is that most foods brought into the average American household today go through some sort of processing and packaging," he wrote. "Every major company in the industry has a laboratory and a research department. These companies are constantly looking for ways to improve their products and to lengthen their shelf life."

Around that time, the Fair Packaging and Labeling Act (FPLA) was signed into law. The regulations required that all food be labeled with an accurate list of ingredients.

"Many homemakers," Rabbi Levy wrote, "are in the habit of reading these labels and relying on their limited knowledge of ingredients, accepting the products as Kosher. Everyone knows that there are laws requiring these listings and that there are penalties for fraud. But what is not common knowledge is that these laws are limited in their requirements."

These limitations had become clear to Rabbi Levy during the five years he worked in kosher supervision before acquiring the OK. The purpose of the OK's new publication, he wrote, would be to clarify and answer modern-day questions about kosher, "in order to make it easier and more pleasurable for you, the Jewish Homemaker, to keep a kosher home."

Running a kosher supervision agency was a serious undertaking, which became only more challenging as advanced machinery was introduced and the demand for kosher food grew, Rabbi Levy wrote in 1985. He gave the example of the processing of chicken and meat, which by then was done on a mass scale. A *shochet* [slaughterer] slaughtered an average of 1,200 chickens or 50 to 90 cattle an hour. In order to accomplish this, he wrote, "besides being a most sincere, G-d-fearing individual, he must be an expert and have years of experience." The agency that assumed responsibility for the process "must carry a tremendous moral obligation."

This obligation, which the kosher consumer placed in the hands of the agencies, applied to all of the products under supervision. Over the years he described instances where his investigation of seemingly innocuous products led to unexpected discoveries.

A food manufacturer under OK supervision once wanted to purchase vegetable shortening produced in Europe. On a trip to Europe, Rabbi Levy visited the shortening plant, and while all the ingredients there seemed to be kosher, something didn't seem right. Looking around, he realized that there was no equipment to produce shortening in the factory. He inquired where the shortening was from, and it turned out that this plant purchased their shortening from other plants and then resold it. This critical piece of information necessitated a visit to another plant before approval could be given to the U.S. manufacturer, which never would have guessed that it was buying resold shortening if Rabbi Levy hadn't known what to look for.

"There is never a dull moment," he wrote in 1983. "Day in and day out we are confronted with new twists and new problems. One might think that after being thoroughly involved in the field for more than twenty years, there would be few surprises. Far from it, as I have discovered numerous times in recent weeks."

The Kosher Demand

"Kosher is the fastest-growing segment of the domestic food industry," Sue Fishkoff wrote in the *New York Times* in 2010, "with bigger sales than organic. One-third to one-half of the food in American supermarkets is kosher-certified, representing more than $200 billion of the country's estimated $500 billion in annual food sales, up from $32 billion in 1993."

These statistics lead to a startling conclusion: "Given that Jews make up less than 2 percent of the population, and most of them don't keep kosher, it's clear that the people buying this food are mostly non-Jews."

Sociologists can debate why food with kosher certification is attractive to non-Jews. One hypothesis is that consumers understand that kosher supervision is more thorough and comprehensive than government oversight. "Kosher certification agencies are more proactive and prospective than government agencies," wrote Timothy D. Lytton in *Kosher: Private Regulation in the Age of Industrial Food*. "Whereas most state regulators are merely reactive to complaints, kosher certifiers actively seek out problems before they affect consumers and set new policies to avoid trouble later."

In a 1977 letter to a spice company, Rabbi Levy compared the kosher agency to an accountant doing an audit: "Supervision for Kashruth certification no more means the manufacturer is untrustworthy than an audit by a CPA does. The function of the rabbi and his staff in Kashruth supervision is much the same as the auditing CPA and his staff vis-a-vis financial statements. The Kashruth supervisor must see that the Kashruth regulations are adhered to, and that inadvertent or other errors by company personnel do not occur."

Rabbi Levy reserved the right to make unannounced visits to the factories he certified, which he would regularly do. One company that produced both kosher and non-kosher soup bases had agreed to make the kosher products and affix the labels only when an OK supervisor was present. But on a surprise visit, it was discovered that they were producing the product and affixing the kosher labels themselves. "Naturally, we canceled," Rabbi Levy wrote of the company's kosher certification.

Another reason for consumers to prefer kosher food is that supervision is not limited to the United States. Many of the ingredients used in processed food come from foreign countries where food safety standards may be low or nonexistent. Rabbi Levy traveled the world, visiting the sites where raw ingredients were produced. In a December 1981 article about coconut oil, he wrote, "The coconut companies have very sophisticated equipment and they are very strict about the cleanliness of the plant. They are as modern as the most modern plant in the USA. The only ingredient used is a chemical which keeps it white."

Policy Driven

Rabbi Levy was a master of detail. From his small home office in the Borough Park neighborhood of Brooklyn, where with his wife, Thelma, he ran the financial division of the business, he created policies that applied to any company the OK certified, and he made every effort to ensure that they were followed. When they were not, kosher certification was immediately revoked.

This Hunt-Wesson memo from the 1970s gives a sense of the transparency and information the OK demanded of companies:

> Rabbi Bernard Levy, through regular inspection of our plants and detailed knowledge of our formulas, certifies most of our products as kosher…
>
> In these inspections, he may review or ask questions about the processes, ingredients, and labels involved in any or all of the products produced at that location.
>
> When a new product is still in the concept stages, a Marketing decision is made as to whether it should be a kosher product. If so, the product development personnel prepare ingredient specifications calling for kosher ingredients and a process is developed which is also kosher. Before labels for the product are approved, in which the OK would be incorporated, the rabbi is contacted and given full particulars as to the formula, the source and nature of the ingredients, and the location and nature of the processing equipment.

"He had no patience for anything but the optimum standards on compliance and efficiency," recalled Ira Axelrod, a long-time kosher supervisor who accompanied Rabbi Levy on visits to factories and today works for the Star-K. "I am sure he was well aware of the fact that he would not win popularity contests in many a place, but that was not his role; ensuring kosher was."

His refusal to bend under pressure and his knowledge of the food industry earned Rabbi Levy the respect of the companies he worked with. But he also did his best to accommodate their needs whenever possible. "He didn't just come down like a ton of bricks," recalled his son Rabbi Don Yoel. "He would try to help them. He understood that you need to

Rabbi Levy visits the Erewhon warehouse in Japan (1980). He would regularly walk into food-production areas unannounced and scan the floors, looking for ingredients that had not been approved. Courtesy of OK Kosher

be tough, but you still need to remember that they are people." If an ingredient turned out not to be kosher, the OK would work with the company to find an alternate supplier.

The OK's first policy was not to solicit business. "Solicited companies do not feel that they must comply with all the requirements for true supervision," Rabbi Levy wrote in January 1977. "They feel that they can set the time and standards of *hashgacha*." In addition, chasing customers would cheapen their image. "It is not dignified," he explained, for a kosher agency that sets high standards to behave like any other money-making enterprise.

By the same token, the OK never took a percentage of product sales, on the grounds that it would lead to compromises for the sake of profits.

"You want them to have more business," Rabbi Levy said, "so you start cutting corners. We are not anyone's partner in the sales."

In factories that produced both kosher and non-kosher food, Rabbi Levy required daily supervision by a local rabbi to ensure that products would not be mistakenly – or maliciously – mixed.

Adding a new company is not a short process, and adjustments would need to be made, either in ingredients or on the production line. When a company that produced butter cookies requested certification, it was determined that since the factory also produced non-kosher products, constant supervision was required.

When this policy was not implemented by other agencies, this saddened Rabbi Levy. "There are, unfortunately, butter cookies that are being imported today," he wrote in February 1978, "which are produced in factories where Kosher and non-Kosher varieties are produced, and the word of the company is taken that no animal fat is being used in the Kosher cookies. There is no constant supervision. I hope that we will be able to change this situation."

Taught by many years of experience, he required that every meat restaurant and catering establishment under OK supervision have a constant full-time mashgiach. "This was true even in cases where the owners were known to be observant Jews," Rabbi Don Yoel said.

Every Ingredient

Rabbi Levy insisted on tracing every ingredient to its source, which was often a complicated endeavor. Processed food items sold in American stores may contain dozens, even hundreds, of ingredients. Many of these components are manufactured outside the United States, in dedicated factories that produce just one chemical or additive. Rabbi Levy became the first kosher supervisor to travel to all corners of the world on a kosher quest. "His seemingly endless energy, exhaustive investigations and phenomenal memory made him a walking encyclopedia of kosher information," said Rabbi Don Yoel.

In 1979, Rabbi Levy told the *New York Times* that he had already logged millions of miles. The reporter described him as having "the sinews of a young man and the gray beard of a patriarch," evidence of the fact that he spent three-quarters of the year away from home.

"He had just returned from West Germany," the article continued, "where he looked into the production of kosher cysteine hydrochloride made from human hair provided by cooperative barbers.... Rabbi Levy stopped in Denmark to check on candy, and in the Netherlands to inspect cookies.... He thinks back also to his efforts in Japan (rennet), Taiwan (mushrooms), Spain (olive oil), England (sweets), Portugal (sardines) and Belgium (chocolates)."

By the 1980s, Rabbi Levy's perseverance in investigating even basic ingredients had made him the face of kosher in America. "He was much more than the OU was; he was much stronger," said Rabbi Yosef Wikler, publisher of *Kashrus Magazine*. He attributed Rabbi Levy's dominance to his willingness to travel, as opposed to other agencies, "where a lot of people were sitting at home and making telephone calls."

One of the ingredients Rabbi Levy investigated was oil. Natural oils were universally accepted as kosher by other agencies. "What could go wrong with coconut oil?" many in the industry said. But on visits to oil plants and other factories around the world, Rabbi Levy discovered that a lot could, and did, go wrong with oil.

Chief among Rabbi Levy's concerns were the ships and ISO tankers that transported the oils. The tankers also carried lard, tallow, non-kosher refined glycerin and fatty acids. If kosher oil was placed in the tankers after such a shipment, it would be rendered non-kosher. To resolve this, Rabbi Levy introduced a system for monitoring the tankers, much of which is still used today.

Another concern was that factories often fried multiple foods in the same oil. Banana chips, for example, might seem perfectly innocuous, if one didn't know that they were fried in the same oil as cheese rings, pork rinds and other non-kosher foods, Rabbi Levy wrote in 1981.

In fact, manufacturers were not even required to list the oil a product was fried in as an ingredient. One company told him that "as long as no vegetable shortening was used in the product, and the product was only cooked in vegetable shortening – or any other shortening – the law did not require the listing of the shortening as an ingredient on the package." Shocked, Rabbi Levy wrote, "The company could be frying the product in lard and there need be no mention of it on the package, and they would not be breaking the law!"

In April 1974, Rabbi Levy recounted how one company had asked for certification, asserting that they used only vegetable fats in their baked goods. All the labels on their products made the same claim, and during Rabbi Levy's visit, a company executive repeated it.

As they stepped into the factory, however, there in front of them was a row of newly stacked cartons of blended animal and vegetable fats. "What's this?" Rabbi Levy asked. "It must be a mistake," the executive stammered. "I really don't know."

"This is serious," Rabbi Levy told him. "Your label states that you use only vegetable oil." The executive responded, "We never said our products are kosher."

For the company, it was simple economics: the prices of vegetable and animal fats at the time were fluctuating and competing with one another. At one point, the cost of animal fat was substantially below that of vegetable oil. "It was much more economical for the company to use animal fat blended with vegetable fat," Rabbi Levy wrote.

While consumers relied on companies to disclose their ingredients, he explained, one could not always trust a label. Labels were expensive to print, and if a temporary change were made to the ingredients, the company would not destroy all their valuable labels.

He illustrated this point with a story: On a visit to a marshmallow factory, he had engaged the owner in a long conversation about how the product was made. Not realizing that Rabbi Levy had an extensive knowledge of food production, the owner tried to conceal the fact that the marshmallows contained gelatin, a problematic ingredient for kosher products.

After a while, he was forced to admit that they did contain non-kosher gelatin, although, as Rabbi Levy pointed out, it was not listed as an ingredient on the packaging. "The manufacturer promised to correct this oversight and to list gelatin on the label," he wrote.

Rabbi Levy would frequently remind his supervisors of the need to be alert when they visited factories. Sometimes small details could point to a larger problem. During a visit to a pretzel factory in 1970, he asked if the plant produced anything else besides these pretzels. The response was "no." Something didn't seem right, however, and as he walked around the factory, he noticed cheddar cheese powder in drums.

When he asked what the cheese was for, the manager explained that once a week they run a small order of cheese pretzels. "We don't really count this as anything," he said. But to Rabbi Levy, it counted a lot. He explained that the stove and conveyors would have to be koshered after the cheese pretzels were made for the regular product to be certified kosher.

That same year Rabbi Levy visited a candy factory where everything seemed to be in order, until he noticed a pan full of grease. The workers referred to the grease as a release agent. "Without this, the candy sticks to the machine," he was told. Upon further investigation, it turned out that the grease was an animal product. When he asked why he had not been told about that ingredient, he was told, "This is not considered as an ingredient. It is not important."

Not a "Posek"

Given the complexity of food production techniques, Rabbi Levy was often faced with questions that only a true expert in Jewish law could answer. He told the *Times* reporter about a product he was considering certifying that contained an enzyme derived from the tongue of an animal. "I'm a nervous guy," he said. "I don't trust anybody. There are questions you don't have answers to, so you're stringent."

With such questions, he would go to Rabbi Moshe Feinstein, "the Lower East Side's most celebrated expert on difficult questions of religious law. Rabbi Feinstein ponders precedents, pierces mysteries and writes opinions known as Responsa."

Rabbi Levy told the newspaper that if Rabbi Feinstein ruled that the enzyme was not kosher, he would drop the company immediately, though it would mean a loss of revenue. "Some people make a nice living from certifications I turn down," he said. Noting that rabbis are also human beings with weaknesses, he said, "It's an unfortunate situation. There's nothing that I can do about it except cry."

As it turned out, Rabbi Feinstein said that the enzyme was kosher, and gave specifications on the process for extracting the enzyme from the tongue (see *Igrot Moshe*, vol. 6, pp. 228–9).

"He never felt that he was a *posek*," said Rabbi Avraham Feigelstock, who leads a kosher agency in Vancouver, Canada. "He would tell me, 'I will call Rabbi Feinstein.'"

Most of Rabbi Levy's contact with Rabbi Feinstein took place over the phone or in person, but some of it was in writing. In the early years of his work in kosher, he asked whether soap derived from non-kosher ingredients could be used to clean dishes. Rabbi Feinstein, in a well-sourced response (ibid. vol. 5, p. 39), explained that if a product is not fit for a dog to eat, it is okay for it to contain non-kosher ingredients.

Because they were in contact so often, Rabbi Levy became close

Rabbi Levy responds to questions after a lecture at Bais Chana Women's Institute in St. Paul, Minnesota (1977). Courtesy of OK Kosher

with the Feinstein family over the years. Before Pesach, he would bring matzah to Rabbi Feinstein from the Lubavitcher Rebbe. Once they were both in a car with someone who began speaking ill of the Rebbe. Rabbi Feinstein spoke up: "While you are talking ill of great Jewish scholars, please let me off at the curb and I will find my own way home."

Mrs. Levy recalled that they once paid a visit to Rabbi Feinstein in his home in the country with their young son Eliezer Yitzchak. At one point, Rabbi Feinstein said, "I will go outside and play with the young child," which he promptly did.

Outspoken Critic

Rabbi Levy was an outspoken critic of the practices of other kosher agencies. Following the example of his predecessor, Mr. George Goldstein, he used the OK's publication, which he renamed the *Jewish Home-*

maker, to highlight issues in the kosher world.

In contrast to the food-centered *Kosher Food Guide* produced by the previous owner of the OK, the neatly designed magazine carried interesting articles with a focus on Jewish observance and pride. At the time one of only a few Jewish magazines, the stories and profiles it published softened the sharper tone of Rabbi Levy's editorials, which were printed under the heading "Keeping Kosher," usually the last article in the magazine.

"Though he was careful to avoid making frontal attacks on the other kosher agencies… it was clear from his attitude that Rabbi Levy had his own standards for doing things," said Mr. Axelrod. "He made no secret of his feelings – his way was far superior."

"At the time in the kosher world," Rabbi Wikler said, "if you were not vocal, if you did not openly speak about the issues, no one would have ever corrected them. This is why I believe Rabbi Levy did what he did."

While his criticism was not always well received, it certainly had an effect. "His critique of the OU helped the OU improve," said Rabbi Zushe Blech, author of *Kosher Food Production*. "Having the opposition certainly wasn't a bad thing."

From its inception, the *Jewish Homemaker* fearlessly addressed some of the most controversial issues in the world of kosher supervision. In 1971, Rabbi Levy learned that Baskin-Robbins was telling its stores to inform customers that their ice cream was kosher. Many turned to the OK to confirm the claim. Rabbi Levy always answered them in the negative, but when someone showed him the store manual, he could not keep quiet and wrote to the company.

"You say that the ice cream is kosher," he wrote. "I believe that you are doing this because you do not have a thorough knowledge of exactly what is involved." He suggested that they set up a meeting so he could explain.

At the meeting, however, the executives only reiterated their claim that their ice creams were kosher.

In the pages of the *Homemaker*, Rabbi Levy lambasted Baskin-Robbins. The ice cream was made by several companies, and several locations, "that I have visited," he wrote, used non-kosher ingredients on the same equipment. What bothered him the most, however, was the company's statement that a rabbi would not be able to visit the many plants and factories. "If a rabbi is unable to properly supervise the product, how can it be kosher because of, or through, a mere statement of prejudiced owners?" he demanded.

In November 1977, Rabbi Levy weighed in on one of the great kosher controversies of the 20th century: the ground-fish problem. The question was whether factories that supplied filleted and ground fish for kosher products like canned tuna and gefilte fish needed to have constant supervision to ensure that every fish was kosher and that kosher fish were not soaked with non-kosher fish.

In the previous issue of the *Homemaker* Rabbi Levy had written that he was unwilling to address the issue, since he had no first-hand knowledge of the process. "I am planning to go to the West Coast," he wrote, "and will attempt to make my own investigation so that I may find out for myself what the situation really is."

At the time the OK was not certifying the fish, nor were they asked to. Yet, wrote Mr. Axelrod in a 1988 obituary, "He had thoroughly investigated the field, mainly in order to develop his own first-hand knowledge about a topic then a raging controversy, and one which still has not completely subsided. With nothing to gain financially, he arranged to go aboard a West Coast tuna boat, to observe the methodology in the catching and processing of tuna. He also personally visited some processing plants."

After his investigation, Rabbi Levy questioned the permissibility of tuna, or any ground or filleted fish, including the Shabbat staple gefilte fish, as they were then prepared, processed and distributed.

At a tuna factory he was told that their supervising rabbi came only twice to check that the oil they were using was kosher. He did not inspect the fish itself, relying on the workers to make sure the species were kosher. Some agencies, he wrote, certified all the tuna a company produced without ever visiting their plants in other countries.

During these visits he made another discovery. Many of the plants also produced pet foods that contained chicken and meat, and the cans of tuna and pet food were heated together. "I saw them place regular tuna fish and pet food in the same retort and cook them together," he wrote.

Although the cans were sealed, he explained that the hot water used in the process rendered the tuna non-kosher. The experience confirmed his conviction that factories producing kosher and non-kosher products required constant supervision. "Can these plants be trusted when non-kosher products are at hand and there are only occasional inspections by a mashgiach?" he asked.

Filleted fish presented another set of possible problems. "A mashgiach from a fishery in Canada told me his plant was so large – and open 24 hours a day – it was impossible for one person or several persons to inspect all the fish that was handled," he wrote. "He said he walks through the plant every once in a while merely to let the workers know he is around. He does not inspect every fish. And this fish is filleted for gefilte fish!"

Rabbi Levy opined that every piece of fish should be kept with the skin attached until it could be reviewed to make sure it was kosher.

He described how in one plant he had visited, several species of fish were being filleted, including catfish, which is not kosher. After the fileting, the workers determined what species of fish they were dealing with by texture. "I tried it," he wrote. "I picked up a piece of filleted catfish and a piece of an allegedly kosher species, and I couldn't tell the difference."

He turned to the manager and asked, "Isn't it easy for the women to make a mistake?"

The manager replied, "No one dies from catfish."

Rabbi Levy's articles in the *Homemaker* were intended to keep consumers informed, but he sometimes asked for their help as well. In the 1980s the price of sugar skyrocketed in America, and corn syrup became the sweetener of choice for most food companies. This was an issue for kosher agencies, because many Jews do not consume corn on Passover. "On Pesach, all these companies must go back to using cane sugar," wrote Rabbi Levy in April 1983. "This is very costly to them."

Soft drink companies in particular struggled with this issue, with many threatening to discontinue their kosher-for-Passover products or find rabbis who would allow the use of corn sweeteners. Rabbi Levy lamented that there were agencies ready to give in to the companies' demand so as not to lose their business. "I bring this to the attention of readers, hoping that they will maintain their strong stand in this matter," he wrote.

Another issue the *Homemaker* took on was the price of kosher food. In a May 1982 article Rabbi Levy described a Russian immigrant who came to pray regularly at a certain synagogue, but was discovered not to be keeping a kosher home. Amazed, several congregants confronted him and asked why. "I can't afford to keep a kosher home," he told them with considerable shame. "Kosher chicken costs $1.49 a pound, non-kosher chicken costs 49 cents a pound!"

Rabbi Levy acknowledged that kosher chicken should cost more because extra expenses were involved. But he felt there was no reason for such a large difference in price. "In the past, when a *shochet* used to slaughter 75 chickens an hour in a retail market, a kosher fowl cost a few cents more per pound," he wrote. "Today, a shochet slaughters between 1000 and 1200 chickens an hour, and the price of kosher chicken is three times the price of chickens that are not kosher.

"What is the excuse for the tripling of the price?" he asked. "I have not found a single shochet who has become a millionaire slaughtering chickens. Yet the producer was able to realize a fine profit, even though he was selling the chickens for substantially less than any of the other producers!"

Rabbi Levy also protested the price hikes for Pesach food. One company was relabeling cottonseed oil for Passover and advertising that it had supervision from the time of pressing. "In the U.S.A. there is no such thing!" Rabbi Levy wrote in February 1973. "Wesson Oil… has exactly the same kind of supervision as any cottonseed oil." He was bringing this to readers' attention, he wrote, "because of the unnecessary raising of prices before Pesach."

In one of his last articles, in September 1985, Rabbi Levy lamented that Jewish publications had taken to publishing a disclaimer such as "We do not assume responsibility for the Kashrus of any product or service advertised in these pages." He pointed out that the letters were very small, and that even if they had been larger, the disclaimer did not do enough to deter readers from believing that the product or store advertised was kosher.

Especially laughable, he wrote, was when one publication printed the disclaimer in some unnoticed corner, and then, in large and prominently placed letters, implored its readers, "Please patronize our advertisers!" Rabbi Levy suggested two solutions: either the publications in question should stop advertising food, or they should advertise only foods that carry a reliable kosher certification. At the very least, he wrote, they should print the disclaimer in larger letters.

KOSHER COMPLICATIONS

Rabbi Levy liked to say that the question one should ask is not whether a food is *treif* (not kosher), but rather, "Is it kosher?" In the past, he would say, people would come to a rabbi to ask whether foods they cooked at home might have become treif by accident. But processed foods, he said, should be considered treif until proven kosher.

He often told the story of a travel agent he knew who was once on a flight to Detroit, when someone asked him whether a certain bagel was kosher. He responded that it was not, but the man pressed him again, "Are you sure that the bagels are treif?" The agent responded, "Let me ask you: if it was a question of poison, and I were to tell you that the bagels may be poisoned, would you then ask 'Are you sure they are using poison?' Foods must be definitely kosher before you eat, not definitely treif!"

Ensuring the kashrut of mass-produced, processed food was a complicated endeavor, to be attempted only by an expert. Over the years, Rabbi Levy said, he discovered that many people in the business of kosher supervision had either "some knowledge of the *halacha* [Jewish law] and no knowledge of food technology," or "some knowledge of food technology and no knowledge of halacha." Rabbi Levy felt strongly that one needed both, and the various problems and controversies he encountered during his tenure at the OK proved time and again that he was right.

Rabbi Levy devoted himself to the OK work completely, just as he had done with his work in education. When Sholom Lifchetz, who was involved in kosher supervision, moved to New York from Florida, Rabbi Levy offered him a position. He admired what Rabbi Levy had accomplished, and recalled that there were companies whose kosher status had been "pretty bad off, and he brought them into line. Everyone knew that the companies [he supervised] were in good hands."

He knew Rabbi Levy from Elizabeth, however, and was familiar with his work ethic. "Rabbi Levy worked 24/7," he said. "He could call at 2 a.m. with an issue and a solution for a particular company." He said that although Rabbi Levy offered to double his salary, he declined the position.

Ira Axelrod described his first visit to a factory with Rabbi Levy as the experience of a lifetime. Touring the floor, Rabbi Levy would question why items were there that should not be. "He didn't need to ask what the items were," Mr. Axelrod said. "He immediately knew that the items just should not be there. The ingredients were like old friends of his. It [kosher] was a part of him; it was a part of his skin."

Pulling the Seal

Revoking the kosher certification of a company or restaurant when it did not comply with OK policy was business as usual for Rabbi Levy. But for consumers it could be confusing. There was usually some speculation that the seal of approval, known as the *hechsher*, had been removed for reasons that had nothing to do with kosher. During the early 1980s this became known as the politics of the kosher world.

"Often it hurts when the word is used, for it impugns our sincerity," Rabbi Levy wrote in a June 1985 article. "I honestly do not know what people mean by this. I am not running for office, and removing a hechsher does not make me popular in the eyes of the public."

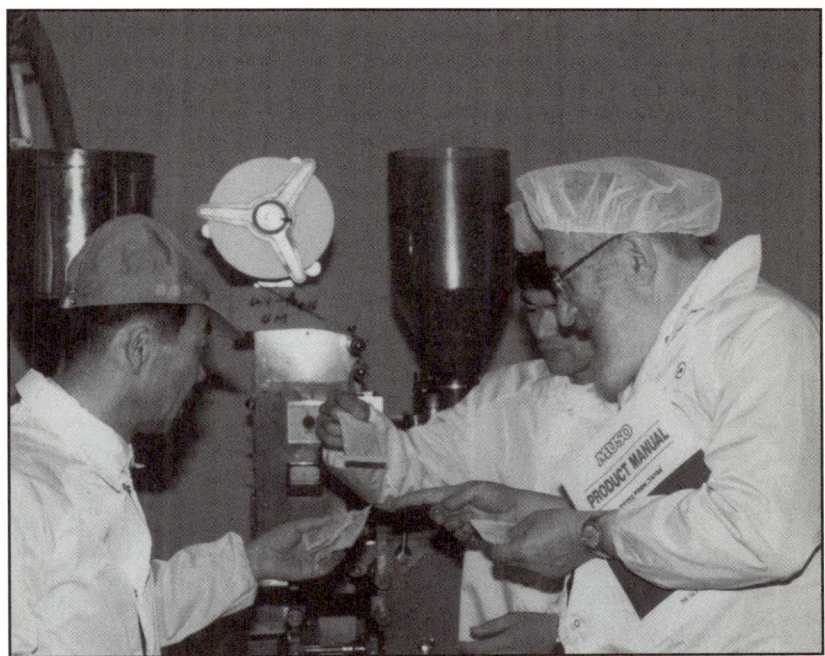

Rabbi Levy drills workers at the Hino Yakuhin tea company (1984). Removing the OK certification was not done lightly, but Rabbi Levy did not hesitate to act when companies refused to open their production lines and warehouses for surprise inspections. Courtesy of OK Kosher

There were many reasons a kosher certification might be revoked, and usually they had nothing to do with money. "I don't remember when I removed a hechsher because of money," he wrote. He did note, however, that finances could rightfully play a role at other agencies. "Sending *mashgichim* [supervisors] to inspect the plants costs money, [and] if the company doesn't pay we cannot afford to send mashgichim." He concluded that if people trusted the agency to ensure that their food was kosher, certainly they should trust them to say when it is not.

As an OK mashgiach at the Stevensville Hotel in the Catskills Mountains, Rabbi Yair Hoffman said he saw firsthand that Rabbi Levy was not in the business for the money. Rabbi Hoffman once discovered that someone in the kitchen was openly desecrating the Shabbat, which would affect the kosher status of the food. He approached the hotel administration, but they refused to remedy the situation.

As a last resort he went to Rabbi Levy, who immediately told the caterer, "If you don't put a stop to this right now, I am removing my *hechsher* [kosher approval] immediately and announcing it in the main dining room."

Rabbi Hoffman, who today is a popular author on contemporary issues and Jewish law, said that Rabbi Levy had "the strength of character to do the right thing. There was no 'I am making money from this company,' there was no personal agenda involved. The fact that he would lose the supervision had no impact on his decision."

In another article, Rabbi Levy wrote that removal of certification may be due to the "high standards of Kashruth with which we expect our companies to comply; or to the fact that a company no longer wants our supervision and finds it easier and more advantageous to work with other agencies. In some cases, we can say truthfully, the reason is known only to the company itself."

At the time, Rabbi Levy could recall only one time when a company had done outright fraud. The manufacturer in question had forged the signature of the supervisor on a product that needed to have continuous supervision. "In effect, they were producing their product without any mashgiach at all," he wrote.

At times he would use his column in the *Jewish Homemaker* to explain why certification had been removed from a particular item. "The Ice Cream Mix produced by Horstman Mix & Cream," he wrote in April 1976, "is *no longer* under our supervision and we no longer endorse the product. The reason for this is that we cannot accept the emulsifier they use as kosher."

When the McCormick spice company wrote to Rabbi Levy in 1977 that they needed to rethink the way the OK inspected their facilities,

Rabbi Levy balked. "It is understood that we will not accept any visit or inspection by you unless you have given us a prior call and we have advised you that our people would be able to take you around," wrote Jack Sassard, the West Coast CEO. To Rabbi Levy, that was unacceptable. Surprise visits were one of his most important tools to ensure that companies followed the kosher guidelines. The company's certification was removed.

Chocolate Debacle

Rabbi Levy's supervision of the Barricini candy company was what had originally led him to become involved in kosher supervision full time. Barricini and Bartons had been fiercely competing for years, and Rabbi Levy was fired from Torah Umesorah because he was giving approval to Barricini when Mr. Stephen Klein, the owner of Bartons, was heavily involved in the organization.

But even before he acquired the OK, Rabbi Levy found that he was hitting a wall with Barricini, who did not want to comply with all of his standards. The problem was gelatin, which is usually derived from animal products. At one time the company was making their own kosher gelatin, but when they decided to begin buying it, they could not find a product that was kosher according to Rabbi Levy's standards. At the time they were his largest company, and dropping them would mean losing most of his livelihood. Nevertheless, he told them he could no longer certify them.

A short while later, he went into a private audience with the Lubavitcher Rebbe and told him what had happened. "What is with the customers who are buying?" the Rebbe asked. Rabbi Levy did not know what to respond.

"You have to notify everybody who is buying [the candy] that there is no hechsher," the Rebbe said. "You have the responsibility." The Rebbe told him that he should get a list of customers from the company.

"It is a strange thing to do," Rabbi Levy later told his son Rabbi Don Yoel. "You go to the company and ask them to give a list? But the Rebbe asked me to do it. I will do it." Rabbi Levy called Barricini and told them that he was removing their kosher certification because of the gelatin, and asked for a list of customers so that he could inform them about the change.

Shortly thereafter, the company called Rabbi Levy to say that they had decided not to use the non-kosher gelatin after all.

Though it was unusual at the time, today informing customers is an accepted practice in many kosher agencies. "The Rebbe's primary interest," said Rabbi Don Yoel, "was making sure Jews had the information needed to buy properly certified food."

Ice Cream Crisis

When Rabbi Levy acquired the OK from the Goldsteins, they were already certifying large companies like Kraft Foods and Pillsbury. Perhaps the most daunting and risky certification, however, was Carvel ice cream, a contract that included hundreds of franchised stores across the United States.

"My predecessor gave them a certification," Rabbi Levy wrote in April 1973, "on the basis of checking out all of the products that are supplied to the Carvel stores.... He relied upon the franchise contracts, which do not permit the stores to purchase any products that are not supplied by Carvel Corporation. The Carvel company has inspectors who visit the stores and investigate to make sure that every store complies with the franchise agreement."

According to many rabbinical authorities, he wrote, this was sufficient to certify that the stores were kosher, but "I was not satisfied, and insisted that we have our own mashgichim inspect the stores regularly."

This was an expensive endeavor for the company and a very large undertaking for Rabbi Levy. He approached several rabbinical figures

Never losing his focus, Rabbi Levy would always question about companies about what was on their floor and the discrepancies that there might be. Here Rabbi Levy questions workers at a chemical company. Courtesy of OK Kosher

and asked if perhaps it would be better to just give up the contract. "They advised us not to, because so many Jews eat Carvel's," he wrote. "If we could be instrumental in keeping it kosher, it would be worthwhile."

The company agreed to cover the expenses of eight mashgichim, who began inspecting all the stores. When a store was caught with a product that was not kosher, it received a letter from Carvel:

> We have been advised by Rabbi Levy of the Organized Kashruth Laboratories that on a recent inspection of your store there was found an unauthorized product. This is a direct violation of your Dealer's License Agreement, and it jeopardizes the Kosher approval for the entire Carvel chain.
>
> This letter is being sent to you pursuant to Paragraph 17 of your Dealer's License Agreement, giving you 48 hours' notice to cor-

rect this violation and give us your written assurance that it will not reoccur in the future. We urge you to protect your investment and comply with this request within the prescribed time.

In most cases this letter helped. When was necessary, Rabbi Levy wrote, "A few franchises have also been taken away."

Carvel's demand that franchise stores purchase only Carvel products led to controversy, however. The New York attorney general charged the company with conspiracy to control franchise-holders through "a network of illegal tying and exclusive dealing arrangements," the *New York Times* reported on August 17, 1979. "These, the suit charged, required franchise-holders to purchase not only all ice cream ingredients and other exclusive formula products from the company – common and legal practice in the franchise field – but also all other supplies and equipment that the dealers might have obtained more cheaply elsewhere."

Over the next six years the company and Attorney General Robert Abrams fought a battle in court and public opinion. "The case was dropped in 1985," reported the *Antitrust Law Journal* on April 1, 1987. "Indeed, the attorney general was roundly criticized by the New York Supreme Court for having made these 'haranguing' statements, without alleging facts sufficient to support them."

The settlement that ended the case did secure changes in how the company dealt with their franchise stores, however, allowing them to purchase certain items from other suppliers. "None [of the changes] benefited a single consumer, but they were enough to end the nationwide kosher status of Carvel ice cream – to the detriment of a few hundred thousand American consumers," the *Journal* concluded.

The removal of Carvel's certification caused a furor, and many contacted the OK to ask why it had been done. "Our concern is Kashruth," Rabbi Levy wrote in June 1985. "Kashruth is our sole concern! We are not running for city, state or federal office!"

Fats Dilemma

When certifying companies that produced both animal and vegetable fats, Rabbi Levy would take extra precautions. "These companies supposedly keep completely isolated equipment for vegetable fats," he wrote in September 1983. But the temptation to use the vegetable lines for animal fat was strong. Therefore the company would have to submit to daily unscheduled inspections.

The company had several good reasons to want to mix the lines, Rabbi Levy explained. One was that mechanical problems were not uncommon, making it expedient to use the vegetable line while the animal one was being repaired. Another was that they often had large orders which could not be filled quickly using only one line. In addition, animal fats are usually blended with vegetable fats. Therefore, without supervision, the company might fill an order for vegetable fats from animal lines. The supervisor would need to monitor the pipes to make sure that vegetable fat could go to the animal line, but not vice versa.

"These companies have very complicated systems," he wrote, "and only experts can really know if the lines are truly separated. We have come across many cases where the companies thought their lines were really isolated, and our expert has found them not to be so."

This issue persisted in at least one case, when a shortening company was caught by the government selling animal fats labeled as vegetable. The government penalized them by making them bury the rest of the product. "Some of these companies have kosher supervision and are very popular with the consumer," he wrote.

Another issue, mentioned before, was the transport of oils and fats. When one New Jersey company wanted its fats to have approval, Rabbi Levy checked out their tanker and found it to be layered with fat. "If you want your oil certified as OK," he informed them, "you must thoroughly clean the tank and remove all residue of non-kosher fat." The company responded that it was impossible to do so. "In that case," Rabbi Levy told them, "I cannot give you supervision."

Hotel Issues

Hotels are difficult to keep kosher, because the food comes from many locations in the hotel. Certifying hotels as kosher for Pesach is an even greater challenge. "I do not say it is an easy job," Rabbi Levy wrote in April 1976. "I mention above how difficult it is to supervise one's own kitchen for Pesach for a small group – how much more so for thousands of Jews."

That year the OK had certified seven hotels for Passover. But in February 1981, Rabbi Levy told his readers that the OK had pulled back on its supervision of hotels. "We have limited the number of hotels which are offering OK supervision for Pesach," he wrote. "We have done so intentionally: Because it is extremely difficult to provide hotels with the quality of supervision which we feel all hotels require in this season, in accordance with the highest standards that OK Laboratories adheres to."

Rabbi Levy demanded that hotels only accept food from trusted distributors, dedicate a week before the holiday to make the kitchen kosher and have full-time supervisors as long as the kitchen was open. "Unquestionably, we could provide supervision for many more hotels on the North American scene," he wrote. "But we are not ready to compromise our principles. OK Laboratories has built a reputation of being scrupulous in its hashgacha: it does not give its certification easily or take its responsibilities lightly."

In a defiant tone, Rabbi Levy described how one owner of several hotels had yielded to the OK's demands begrudgingly. At every turn he complained that he should not have to follow the directions. Eventually, he and the agency parted ways. That year, Rabbi Levy said, the same owner had proposed that the OK provide supervision for only one hotel in the group. However, Rabbi Levy informed his readers that his conscience led him to certify only hotels whose owners he could trust.

When evaluating whether to certify a hotel, one of Rabbi Levy's main concerns was the location of the kosher kitchen. He demanded that there be no other kitchen in the section of the hotel where the food was being served, so that waiters should not mistakenly mix up the trays. One hotel in Acapulco, Mexico, turned to Rabbi Levy to give supervision, but when he heard that the kitchen was on the ground floor and the dining area on the twelfth, he nixed the idea. "We rejected the Acapulco proposal out of hand," he wrote. Every tray of food would need to be watched until it reached the plates. How, he asked, would it be possible to do that in such a situation?

That year Rabbi Levy approved only three hotels, and in the *Homemaker* he warned readers that many hotels did not have proper supervision:

> A word or two of caution: before you go to your Glatt Kosher hotel in Miami, be sure to find out how many mashgichim they have and where the mashgiach spends his time. Is he in the kitchen, where he belongs?
>
> We admonish our friends and readers – everyone who is sincere in his desire to observe Kashruth – to be exceedingly careful about choosing a hotel. This is particularly true for Pesach, when the minutest particle of *chametz* is prohibited.

Chewing Gum Confusion

In September 1973, Rabbi Levy stepped right into the messy issue of chewing gum. Gum has several ingredients that can be problematic from a kosher perspective: magnesium stearate, glycerin and glycerol resin. At that time most agencies did not approve any gum, besides for one rabbi who was approving Wrigley's. When he looked into the matter, Rabbi Levy was told that Wrigley's purchased their glycerol resin from the Hercules Chemical Company.

He called Hercules and asked how they transitioned from non-kosher product to kosher. They responded that they purged the equipment with the kosher product and then discarded the initial run. This was a red flag in Rabbi Levy's eyes, because it meant they were not cleaning the equipment. "They do not wait 24 hours from one production to the second," he wrote. "They do not use water for purging."

He was also told that no one from any agency was supervising the purging process. "This means that one must take the word of the company that they are using kosher glycerin, while the non-kosher product is available in the factory."

On his own initiative, Rabbi Levy visited the Wrigley's factory in London the next time he was in Europe. In an article for the *Homemaker* he described how the resin was cooked with glycerin and then released and deposited on gravel ground. The resin and glycerin harden for a day and then are removed with jackhammers, the kind used to break pavement.

He concluded: "One can imagine how difficult it is to completely remove the resin and clean away all the deposits [before the kosher product was run]. The company claims it would take at least a day. [Yet] it is possible that the final product may be kosher because of the amount of glycerol resin used, and other extenuating circumstances."

Though he left the final decision to the reader, it was clear from the tone of the article that Rabbi Levy had concluded that kosher consumers should not feel comfortable with chewing gum as it was then produced. This infuriated many gum chewers, who wrote to the OK to complain.

Rabbi Levy responded in the next issue, reiterating that he was not saying the gum was not kosher, but merely presenting the results of his investigation. "According to the kashruth certifying agencies you mention in your letter, the chewing gum is kosher.... I do not argue this point. They, however, will not disagree with me on the statement of the company that the glycerol resin is produced the way I describe it in my last article. I state emphatically in my article the reason why I wrote it."

He noted that many people would not buy the gum because they did not wish to rely on leniencies, which was their prerogative.

In July 1980, Rabbi Levy informed his readers that the Paskesz Candy Company had succeeded in producing a high-quality kosher chewing gum under the OK's supervision. He wrote that he had himself made two trips to Europe to review the process and ingredients. The factory producing the gum had agreed to have their equipment purged with water, though it was a costly process. A mashgiach from Belgium oversaw production, and Rabbi Levy was in constant contact with him.

SYMBOL TROUBLE

Though Rabbi Levy was not afraid to point out problems in the world of kosher supervision, his greatest joy lay in resolving them. And though his criticism of other agencies was sometimes withering, he never named them explicitly. "We are only human," he wrote February 1978, "and pray to the Almighty that these accidents be at a minimum."

In a private home there are sometimes accidents when food may be rendered non-kosher, he would say, and when someone asks a rabbi whether such an accident has occurred, it in no way impugns the kashrut of the kitchen or the integrity of the person. On the contrary, he wrote, this shows only that the person is "conscientious in doing the job right."

The same principle applied to mass-produced food, though on a larger scale. "Each company is a hundred times larger than the individual kitchen," he wrote in November 1979. Occasionally something is bound to go wrong. Real problems arose only when the errors were not corrected.

"There are always people or organizations that want to lead us to believe that their system of kosher endorsement is beyond reproach," he wrote, but it was simply not possible. Equally willing to admit his own failings, in April 1973 he wrote, "I am not infallible. If, *chas v'sholom* [G-d forbid], I make a mistake, I will be the first to rectify it."

When rumors began to circulate that the supervision of the OK's largest competitor, the OU, was not adequate, he stood up for them in the November 1971 issue of the *Jewish Homemaker*: "Let me say earnestly for all to see and hear: the rabbi who administrates the kashruth supervision of the OU is one of the most sincere and revered rabbis in the field of kashruth, and has more *mesiras nefesh* (self-sacrifice) for the dissemination and observance of genuine kashruth than any one person I know."

Rabbi Levy's passport photo (circa 1977). Courtesy of Thelma Levy

This attitude of respect and understanding allowed Rabbi Levy to maintain good relationships with the other agencies during his early years at the OK. In those years his greatest challenges came from outside the kosher world.

Forgery

During the 1970s, Rabbi Levy had to contend with two issues related to the OK symbol. One was companies who were lax about putting the symbol on their packages, even though they had been certified. The second, more difficult problem was the unapproved use of the symbol, usually out of ignorance, but occasionally with willful intent to deceive.

In September 1974, in response to a question about why Lazzara breads did not have an OK on their packaging, Rabbi Levy wrote, "Unfortunately, many companies are slow in complying with the requirement that their labels carry the OK. It is a matter of printing. You, the readers, can be helpful by writing to the companies and requesting them to hurry."

The *Homemaker* published a list of the companies with OK supervision to aid consumers, who began to find that the symbol, when it did appear, could not always be relied on.

The fraudulent use of the symbol was generally the result of the company's ignorance. Especially in the early days, before the OK had gained widespread recognition, many could not tell the difference between it and the simple K, which is used by companies who want to cunningly enter the kosher market without any supervision. Sometimes the symbol appeared by an error of the printers, who made labels for many products.

"Until recently, we had no idea that anyone owned the OK symbol, or that any problem existed with our use of the OK symbol," wrote the American Popcorn Company, in a letter that Rabbi Levy requested they send to all their distributors. "The OK symbol was placed on our JOLLY TIME Microwave Popcorn in the good faith belief that the contents were kosher and that anyone could use the OK symbol."

When notified of their error, most companies corrected it immediately. The OK tried to avoid taking these disputes to court. "We, of course, notify the manufacturers that they must cease and desist from using the OK," Rabbi Levy wrote in February 1978. "We try very hard to avoid litigation. We resort to this only if a company refuses to cooperate."

Unfortunately, it often took time for the products with the unapproved kosher symbols to be removed from the shelves. If Rabbi Levy knew that the product contained non-kosher ingredients, he would place ads to notify the public about the problem.

"We recently had this problem with Sweetzel's cookies baked by a bakery in Pennsylvania," he wrote in April 1981. "When it was brought to the attention of the OK… they were immediately notified and ads were placed in Jewish newspapers." However, after a few months the OK was still receiving complaints. "We had the district attorney's office contact them. The bakery assured the district attorney's office that the labels were destroyed, that these were old packages that would be removed immediately."

In 1983 the Hudson Pharmaceutical Corporation used the symbol on its vitamins without permission. When Rabbi Levy called them to ask that they cease, the reply was that as soon as they used up the labels bearing the OK, they would stop. That was unacceptable, Rabbi Levy told them; they must stop using it immediately. They refused, however, and lawyers had to get involved.

The company offered to pay the OK "if you would permit us to go on using your symbol, until none [of the labels] are left." Naturally, Rabbi Levy said that they would have to investigate the plant and determine whether all the products were indeed kosher. They scheduled a time, but then he received a call from a Hudson employee assuring him that all the products were under the supervision of another rabbi and that all the ingredients were kosher.

When Rabbi Levy arrived at the factory, he discovered that they were using non-kosher ingredients. "I demanded that they destroy all of their labels with our OK approval," he wrote. "Confronted with the facts, they complied right away."

Perhaps the most high-profile case of OK forgery was Glace, a non-dairy ice cream launched by Gloria Vanderbilt under the Dolly Madison label in 1985. The dessert was made with tofu, which was gaining popularity as a health food in the 1980s.

Glace's marketing team knew that the product would be a hit with kosher consumers, who were eager for a non-dairy dessert to enjoy after a meat meal. A kosher symbol would also appeal to people allergic to milk, who knew that kosher agencies had higher standards than the FDA for determining whether a food was truly dairy-free. Unfortunately, they neglected to seek supervision for the product before adding the symbol to the label.

Several readers of the *Homemaker* wrote in to inform Rabbi Levy about the Glace issue, and he immediately called the company. Realizing their mistake, they agreed to remove the ice cream from the shelves and to destroy all the finished product in the warehouse, which they did.

In a meeting with two representatives, Rabbi Levy was asked to assume the kosher supervision of all the new products they would eventually manufacture. "I told them this would be impossible," Rabbi Levy wrote in June 1985, "until all of the old product was removed from the stores, otherwise the consumer would not know which product was supervised and which wasn't."

Despite the company's efforts to resolve the issue, it hit the news. Gloria Vanderbilt, who made her riches from a clothing line and eventually became a celebrity, made the story newsworthy. "A Tale of Tofu: Gloria Vanderbilt Runs Up Against the Rabbis," ran the *New York Magazine* headline. "The way Gloria Vanderbilt's new tofu frozen dessert, Glace, has been marketed isn't quite kosher."

To Rabbi Levy's dismay, the article stated that another kosher agency had agreed to certify the ice cream that had already been produced. According to his assessment, there was no way to retroactively review how the production was done and what the ingredients were.

"How many notices have you seen of late about products whose supervision has been removed?" Rabbi Levy wrote in September of that year. "And how many, on the very next day or week, that another agency is giving this company its endorsement? I have been told by companies that the OK is too difficult to deal with, 'therefore we must change our supervising agency.' Our readers surely understand what this means. If a

When Rabbi Levy discovered a problem in a factory, he didn't just demand that it be fixed; he worked with the company to find a solution. Here he visits the 2 Alarm Chili Company in Texas (circa 1986). Courtesy of OK Kosher

company is not cooperating with the supervising agent and knows there is another Kosher certifier waiting in the wings to grab the certification, you can imagine what can happen to Kashruth!"

In *The Vanderbilt Women*, Clarice Stasz wrote that Glace was a failure in the end, in part because it "ran into trouble when a rabbi complained that his endorsement of its being kosher was not valid."

Unfortunately, symbol forgeries were not always so easily resolved. The OK expended a great deal of money and effort in court cases over copyright infringement. Rabbi Levy lamented that law enforcement did not take more of an active role in preventing these problems, leaving the courts to deal with them after the fact. "It is criminal that the laws do not sufficiently protect us in this matter," he wrote in April 1983. "The Department of Agriculture or the District Attorney will not help us."

Imitation

Over the years, Rabbi Levy expressed his unease at other agencies using the letter K in their kosher symbols. "The K within a circle," he wrote in February 1978, "has been used for more than 30 years. In recent years many newcomers in the field of Kashruth have been imitating the OK and confusing the public with symbols similar to the OK."

He quickly realized that he could not trademark the letter K, which was used by many companies without any supervision, and by some "who do not want to use another trademark on their packages, or are under the supervision of rabbis who do not have a trademark of their own."

What bothered him the most was when other kosher agencies incorporated the letter into their own symbols. In November 1979 he wrote that these agencies were trying to imitate the OK. "Many people think that these products are under our certification. I therefore again wish to caution our readers. I should be flattered by this, but, unfortunately, they do not live up to the high standards of the OK Laboratories."

Many of these new symbols were "extremely similar to ours," he wrote. "We tell our inquirers to inspect the seal a little more closely so they will see that it is not our seal. Legal steps are being taken to rectify this." In March 1981 the *Homemaker* published a list of symbols that could be mistaken for the OK. "The public is confused," Rabbi Levy wrote, "and many are being led astray."

Cutthroat Competition

A regular complaint voiced in the pages of the *Homemaker* was about the practice by some agencies of poaching companies from their competitors. "We feel that this practice is unethical," Rabbi Levy wrote in June 1978, "and unprofessional, and we were hopeful that such solicitation would come to an end."

Rabbi Chaim Goldzweig, known as the "super mashgiach" and in-

Rabbi Levy asks questions at the Nishin Shokai sesame oil manufacturer (circa 1984). Recognizing that his certification symbol had become synonymous with his high standards, he bristled when others sought to imitate it. Courtesy of OK Kosher

gredient maven at the OU, was very close with Rabbi Levy. "Berel spoke to me a lot; I spoke to him a lot," he recalled. "If I had a problem, or he had a problem, we spoke to each other about it. We helped each other as much as possible."

He said that Rabbi Levy would assist him with finding mashgichim in far-flung locations, and "we tried to make sure that we did not step on each other's toes."

Such peaceful coexistence between agencies was rare, however. Rabbi Levy described several episodes where competition became fierce. In Dallas, Texas, the contracted supervisor had shown him a letter he had received from a New York–based supervising agency, asking him to solicit a company that had been under the OK supervision for five years.

In Minnesota, a rabbi who supervised sausage plants in Chicago solicited a slaughterhouse which was under the supervision of a local rabbi. He promised the owners of the Minnesota slaughterhouse that if they took the supervision away from the local rabbi and gave it to him, he would permit his sausage plants to purchase meat from them.

This wheeling and dealing sometimes happened in the middle of the certification process. One cheese company had initially agreed to Rabbi Levy's requirement that a supervisor be intimately involved in making hard cheese. "The usual procedure is that the supervisor pours the rennet into the tank," he wrote in 1978.

The company never followed through with the certification, however, and Rabbi Levy learned later that "they found another rabbi who was willing to give them supervision with only an occasional visit to the plant."

Family Business

The OK was growing, and Rabbi Levy recognized that his son Rabbi Don Yoel would be an asset to the organization. In fact, he had already begun making plans to recruit his son when the younger Rabbi Levy got married in Israel to Malka Deutsch in 1970. He was forced to defer them, however, because the Lubavitcher Rebbe guided Rabbi Don Yoel to focus on his studies at the Chabad *kollel* in Kiryat Malachi, Israel, providing him with a rigorous study regimen, which he followed for seven years.

During that time, whenever Rabbi Levy brought up the topic of his son's returning to the United States, the Rebbe would always say, "If he is learning, why take him away from his studies?" Rabbi Levy once suggested that Rabbi Don Yoel could spend half the day studying and the other half working at the OK, but the Rebbe simply replied, "If he is able to learn the entire day, why take him away from his learning?"

Eventually, Rabbi Levy was at his wits' end. He asked the Rebbe if he could bring a partner into the OK to assist him. The Rebbe immediately

Rabbi Don Yoel Levy did not want to continue in his father's footsteps, preferring to become a Chabad representative in some remote location. At the Rebbe's behest, however, he joined his father in 1977. Here Rabbi Don Yoel (right) dances with his father on his wedding day (1970). Courtesy of Malka Levy

said that he should bring Rabbi Don Yoel into the business.

However, Rabbi Don Yoel was not happy. The gold standard for a Lubavitcher chassid, he felt, was to go on *shlichut*, to become a Chabad representative in a remote community. "I prefer to go and ask myself," he told his father.

In a private audience, the Rebbe told Rabbi Don Yoel that "kosher is included in spreading Judaism." The Rebbe described what he perceived as the biggest problem with kosher supervision at the time. "It is disturbing that many supervisors see nothing wrong with certifying products which they themselves would not eat," he said. "If the rabbi does not trust his own supervision, how much integrity could he possibly have?"

The question hit home for Rabbi Don Yoel. The OK's policy was to

Rabbi Don Yoel tours an Asian food manufacturing plant (circa 1982). Courtesy of OK Kosher

certify foods that were not *chalav yisrael* or *pas yisrael*, even though the Chabad community had accepted the stringency of not eating such foods. Some objected to this, but the elder Rabbi Levy maintained that his agency served not only the Chabad community but also the general Jewish community, which included many who did not adhere to the standards he set for himself.

The younger Rabbi Levy had always been bothered that his father certified products that he would not bring into their home. "My father's hechsherim are on non–*chalav yisrael* and non–*pas yisrael* products, which I do not eat. Under these guidelines set by the Rebbe…"

The Rebbe replied that since these products were not forbidden according to the strict letter of the law, there was nothing wrong with supervising their production. "The reason for not eating these foods has nothing to do with the quality of the supervision. There is no compromising of integrity," the Rebbe said.

The elder Rabbi Levy, who was also present, then asked, "Perhaps I should give up these hechsherim?"

The Rebbe responded: "You should not, because we could not be certain that those who would take over the supervision would be as reliable."

SOUR GRAPES

Rabbi Levy strode into the Michigan factory of the CJ Christoff and Sons Company, which produced horseradish, sauces and salad dressings. "He flung his arms wide, as if to encompass the whole world, and inhaled deeply," reported the *Grand Rapids Press* in March 1982. "He wears a black suit and shiny black shoes. Although his thick white beard reaches down to his stomach, Levy said, most of it is knotted up and shoved into an unruly nest of hair."

Rabbi Levy interrogated the president of the company, Wendell Christoff, about the factory and the ingredients, and the reporter followed the entire inspection, writing that Rabbi Levy "moved quickly through the Christoff plant, stopping to bend over and peer at labels on boxes and drums of ingredients. He sometimes took off his glasses, squinting at the tiny printing of the labels."

The salad dressings and sauces contained non-kosher ingredients, among them emulsifiers derived from animal products. "In order for me to certify," he told the reporter, "he [Mr. Christoff] will have to change to kosher suppliers for these things."

Rabbi Levy explained that the laws of kosher are complex. "It takes study to keep up with new applications of the law. Outside of Hebrew law, the only thing I read is a newspaper. I'll always have books of law with me. I'm always studying."

Rabbi Levy with a factory worker in India (circa 1985). People recalled feeling his strong presence when he walked into a factory. Courtesy of OK Kosher

The recipe for the horseradish included spices and vinegar, which immediately raised a red flag. The wrong vinegar could render the entire product not kosher. "The only vinegar that's not kosher is wine vinegar," Rabbi Levy said. "Any wine products are sacramental. They have religious connotations, and we're not allowed to have them mixed in food" unless they are approved kosher.

CJ Christoff's vinegar turned out to be kosher. But a few years later, Rabbi Levy would face the greatest challenge of his career over the issue of non-kosher vinegar.

Synthetic or Wine?

Rabbi Levy's statement that only wine vinegar is not kosher was a simplification of a more complicated issue. Vinegar is fermented using alcohol, and even if the vinegar itself is not made from wine, the alcohol that is used to produce it may be derived from grapes, which would render the finished product not kosher.

When Rabbi Levy was introduced to the Sofecia alcohol company in the early 1980s, they made it clear to him that their alcohol was derived from petroleum, not grapes. Alcohol is a common ingredient in many flavorings, and the company was requesting certification for Passover.

The Paris-based company first appeared in the *Jewish Homemaker*, although not by name, in February 1983. The article explained that since their alcohol was not derived from grains, "it should present no difficulty" for Passover use.

The OK arranged for a Paris rabbi to supervise the production of the alcohol and its transport to America. In New Jersey, the agency sent someone to inspect the tanks where the alcohol was stored. "Here we met head-on with a problem we never before knew existed," Rabbi Levy wrote in the 1983 article. The tanks were constructed as tanks within tanks. The inner tanks contained grain alcohol, and the outer tanks were to receive the synthetic alcohol.

Rabbi Levy presented the question to Rabbi Feinstein, who said that the synthetic alcohol was not permissible for Passover. "This meant, of course, that we could not and would not give the French company certification," Rabbi Levy wrote.

Two years later Sofecia once again turned to the OK to request certification. Rabbi Levy brought up several issues, including the dual tanks, that would have to be resolved, and the company promised to look into them. A week and a half later, Hans Van Der Klut of Sofecia wrote to Rabbi Levy, asserting that they no longer stored any alcohol produced from grains with their products, and that the shipping vessels were live–steam cleaned before loading.

The letter also stated explicitly that "Sofecia's ethyl alcohol is synthetically made from ethylene gas," confirming that no wine or grape products were used. The OK once again sent supervisors to oversee the alcohol's production, transport and storage, and Sofecia was certified as kosher for Passover and year-round use.

Vinegar Gate

In the 1980s the *Jewish Press* had been the only weekly newspaper in the Orthodox world for decades, but it seldom reported on scandals in the community. Cover stories were usually about Israel, and its pages were filled with press releases, op-eds, stories and an abundance of advertising. So when a story appeared on February 28, 1986, in a highlighted blue box with the headline "Kosher Food Inspectors Get Death Threats," it made waves.

The brief, rather cryptic article revealed that two employees of the now-defunct Kosher Law Enforcement Division of the New York State Department of Agriculture and Markets had received death threats because they "are on the brink of uncovering a kosher food scandal of major proportions."

Who made the threats and what happened with the actual charges was unclear, but that story thrust the brewing vinegar scandal into the public eye. Rumors began to spread, without any concrete information published on the topic, until the president of the National Council of Young Israel finally addressed the situation publicly. Harold Jacobs, who had been the president of the OU for six years, decried the secrecy adopted by many kosher agencies.

"In the wake of the nationwide kashruth scandal," reported the *Jewish Press* on June 13, 1986, "in which scores of products under a variety of supervisions were found to be using an unacceptable wine alcohol derived for a vinegar ingredient, the president of the international Young Israel movement, Harold M. Jacobs, has demanded that all kashruth supervision agencies make full disclosure to the public of their internal standards and operations."

Rabbi Levy gives an interview to an Israeli magazine (1984). Uncharacteristically, during the "vinegar crisis," he refused to talk about the problem for a long time.
Courtesy of Menachem Wolff Collection/Lubavitch Archives

To readers of the *Jewish Homemaker*, the request may have seemed absurd, since the OK regularly discussed its policies and how they differed from those of its competitors. In his very last article for the magazine, Rabbi Levy described the scandal as "a clash of personalities." What began as an unfortunate misunderstanding was blown into something much larger and more destructive.

The Switch

When Sofecia assured Rabbi Levy that their alcohol was synthetic, they were not lying. "It is not worth it for companies to lie about their basic operations," said Rabbi Blech, who was a leading figure at the OU when the vinegar scandal broke.

Sometime later, however, the Star-K called Rabbi Harvey Senter of the Kof-K to ask if their herring was kosher for Pesach. He replied that he had never certified it for Passover, but they could call the company and ask how it was made. Tracing each ingredient in the herring to its source eventually led Star-K to Sofecia, who produced the alcohol used in the vinegar. When a Star-K rabbi asked if there was any grain in the alcohol, the company representative said, "Rabbi, there is no issue. We do not make the alcohol with grain. We make it with grapes."

The alcohol was actually made with the residual skins and seeds that remained after pressing the grapes. Known as *marc* (pronounced "mahr"), the byproduct was sold cheaply by French wineries. In the 1980s, with the French wine market burgeoning, a process was developed to make marc into alcohol, raising its value. Like synthetic alcohol, marc alcohol could be used to make vinegar.

When exactly Sofecia had begun using marc instead of petroleum was not clear, but it likely wasn't long before it was discovered. In the June 1986 issue of *Kashrus Magazine*, Rabbi Yosef Wikler wrote, "This Spring, New York State passed a law requiring food producers to cease using synthetic alcohol, for health reasons. This precipitated a switch several months ago, to natural sources." This law was not widely publicized, and kosher agencies were not aware of it (shortly thereafter, the magazine reported, the law was overturned).

Sofecia failed to inform the OK about the change, perhaps not realizing that it was such a grave issue. In their reporting, *Kashrus Magazine* did not name the company who certified the alcohol, only noting that "recently it came to light that Sofecia has been using a grape-based alcohol."

When the truth came out, three of the leading agencies placed a joint ad listing the products under their supervision that contained Sofecia's alcohol. They excluded the OK, which placed a separate ad. This decision, as well as the text of the ad, made clear to consumers who the "culprit" was:

It was discovered through research done by the OU, Vaad of Baltimore [Star-K] and the Kof-K that an importer of alcohol under the kashruth certification of a widely known kashruth laboratory had in fact been importing for approximately a six-month period a non-acceptable, wine-derived alcohol. This alcohol was sold to many companies under various supervisions to be used to ferment into vinegar. The consumer should be aware that, especially within the Metropolitan New York area, many products that contain vinegar may have been derived from this wine alcohol…

By placing an ad, Rabbi Wikler said, Rabbi Levy explicitly acknowledged his mistake. "It is too bad that all the [kashruth] agencies did not list their products together in one ad," he said.

Kosher Symbol Monopoly

The animus that erupted publicly over the vinegar controversy had been brewing for several years. "This was their chance to do him in," said Rabbi Blech. "It was not done out of pure halachic interests." He added, however, that Rabbi Levy's behavior during the crisis exacerbated the situation.

As previously mentioned, Rabbi Levy had enjoyed good relationships with the other agencies from the time that he entered the world of kosher supervision. Rabbi Yacov Lipschutz, who headed the OU for several years in the 1970s, said that Rabbi Levy was to be admired for what he accomplished. "It was amazing to see how much he was doing," he said. "He was not lazy."

Describing Rabbi Levy as a "lively figure," Rabbi Lipschutz said he never had any clashes with him. Rabbi Berel Wein, who ran the OU in the early 1970s, concurred. "I didn't have angst against Berel Levy," he said. Issues between the two agencies just "didn't exist."

These good relationships were due, in part, to the fact that the OK

Rabbi Levy felt strongly about choosing his own supervisors. He is seen here in a manufacturing facility in the 1980s. Courtesy of OK Kosher

was still relatively small and did not pose a threat to the larger agencies. Rabbi Levy was like "many other *rabbanim* that had hechsherim," Rabbi Wein said. "We had nothing to do with the OK, and they had very little to do with us. They used our ingredients and we used theirs; that's all."

By the late 1970s, however, the OK was gaining national recognition. "He was a pioneer, truly was a pioneer," said Rabbi Senter. "Before Rabbi Levy came on the scene, the only recognized national hashgacha was the OU. What he really did popularize is that there is more than one show in town now. His hashgacha became one of the very well accepted and very, very well recognized [ones]."

Around this time, one high-ranking member of the OU leadership arrived at the OK's offices in Brooklyn and acted in a demeaning manner toward senior staff members, said one inside source at the OU. "They broke the glass ceiling," Rabbi Blech said, and "the OU did not like the competition from Levy."

Rabbi Levy's habit of pointing out problems in the way other agencies did things did not help to endear him to them. During that period, if he visited a factory under another agency's supervision and found something amiss, he would immediately call them, and the conversations sometimes grew heated. Though he never named the organizations he criticized in the *Homemaker*, many felt that he went too far in exposing his competitors to ridicule.

To many in the world of kosher supervision, it seemed that the OK held itself above its competitors, a feeling reinforced by Rabbi Levy's possessive attitude toward the letter K. "They found a way of grating on everyone's nerves with their feelings of superiority," Rabbi Blech said. "Though the OU also claimed that they adhered to the 'highest halachic standards,' not belonging to a private company or person."

Rabbi Wikler said that he believes that at the time the other agencies were upgrading to a higher standard, and that was the motivation behind what he called "Vinegar Gate." He acknowledged, however, that it does not explain their aggressive actions after the problem had been resolved.

Aftermath

In the issue of the *Jewish Homemaker* published after the scandal broke, Rabbi Levy's regular column was absent. In its place was this "important notice":

> The O.K. LABORATORIES has **NEVER** given a Hechsher on any wine alcohol. It has endorsed **ONLY** synthetic alcohol produced from ethylene gas.
>
> It is absurd to think that Rabbi Levy would permit the O.K. LABORATORIES to endorse an alcohol produced from non-Kosher wine.

Rabbi Levy inspecting a factory in Japan. Courtesy of OK Kosher

An article dealing in depth and in detail with all facets of this issue which is of grave concern to the Kosher Community—including the matter of unacceptable vinegar—is in preparation and will shortly be available to our readers and all other interested persons.

It was clearly a response to the attacks on the OK. Critics were quick to point out that it fell short of a real apology.

Rabbi Levy may have refrained from apologizing again in the belief that the situation might soon be resolved. After the alcohol was discovered and the realization hit of the enormity of the situation, a decision needed to be made what to do.

Kashrus Magazine wrote at the time that Sofecia alcohol "is used in mayonnaise, ketchups, pickles, salad dressings, mustards, barbecue sauces, Worcestershire sauce, relishes, sauerkraut, pickled herring, etc. It is also a common ingredient in commercial baking. Alcohol itself can be used in the making of flavorings (especially 'extracts')."

According to Rabbi Wikler, Jewish law clearly states that when such a situation arises with a liquid, and destroying the foods containing it would entail a large monetary loss, they would be permitted for consumption. Rabbi Feinstein also told Rabbi Levy that this was the case. However, the top three agencies decided that they were going to forgo the leniency and take the high road. "I never felt good about it," Rabbi Wikler said, noting that just after this story there were several other controversies in the kosher world that went by without an uproar. "I always felt guilty about it.… It is good when the kashrus world wants to be machmir [stringent], but machmir at whose expense?"

(The OK refused to accept Sofecia vinegar for many years after the scandal, having lost faith in the company. Shortly after the issue was resolved, however, Sofecia received offers of certification from agencies who had condemned the OK.)

Another kosher insider, who asked not to be named, found it abhorrent that agencies would level personal attacks against Rabbi Levy, "who was known to have dedicated his entire life to kosher and Yiddishkeit [Judaism] across the globe."

Their decision caused millions of dollars in damages, Rabbi Blech said. The agencies required items still in the factories to be destroyed and factories to be koshered. "There was never anything in the history [of the kosher agencies] that was a bigger loss than this case," said Rabbi Wikler.

Rabbi Blech said he believed that if the mistake had been made by any agency except the OK, the others would have looked for a way to resolve it without all the expense. "They were not terribly disturbed that they had this opportunity," he said.

At the encouragement of the other agencies, lawsuits against the OK ensued, as the companies tried to recover some of the money, and Rabbi Levy's lawyers guided him against further discussion. "Due to pending litigation," Rabbi Levy wrote in the June 1986 issue of the *Homemaker*, "our lawyer has advised us not to print, at this time, any article pertaining to 'the vinegar affair.'"

Thus Rabbi Levy became silent on the issue, though others continued to fight. Rabbi Levy was shunned; some suggested collectively banning him from kosher certification, while others boycotted OK products.

When his father died, Rabbi Don Yoel (above) did not want to take over the OK; however, at the urging of the Lubavitcher Rebbe, he accepted the responsibility. Courtesy of OK Kosher

"I was shocked when he was attacked," Rabbi Don Yoel wrote in 1987, "for a situation that was *beyond his control*. Who of those who so heartlessly attacked him could compare with my father's *mesiras nefesh*?... Three times, as far as I can recall, my father cried bitterly for what was being done to him and to Yiddishkeit. *Is there any question that this took its toll?*"

"Somehow this mistake was not forgiven," Rabbi Senter said regretfully. "He was very aggravated. It did hurt him deeply. It should not have turned out the way it did."

One result the agencies did not anticipate was the response of the Jewish community, which was deeply disturbed by both the crisis and its aftermath. "I don't think it played out well for anybody," Rabbi Wikler said.

The community demanded more transparency, and that the agencies work together for a general standard. "The incident revealed, on a massive scale, a basic design flaw in all kashruth supervisions," wrote Mr. Jacobs in the May issue of *Young Israel Viewpoint*, "and dramatically underlined the urgent need to establish a sense of collective responsibility and uniform standards among all kashruth supervisions.... The practice of kashruth agencies stonewalling inquiries from concerned consumers about obvious problems themselves, only to be told by the responsible kashruth authorities that what they saw with their own eyes didn't really happen, or to have their questions simply go unanswered."

In his last column for the *Homemaker*, Rabbi Levy asked for forgiveness. "We deeply regret our involvement with a company that has caused so much grief to the Kosher-keeping public and to so many plants under Kosher supervision," he wrote. He ended with a fervent plea for more goodwill and cooperation between agencies: "We feel that the time has come for mutual respect among all agencies who are sincerely interested in furthering the cause of Torah generally and Kashruth in particular.... Personality clashes are counterproductive: they sap our energies and leave us too weak to do our best in bringing our mission to fruition."

Rabbi Levy's plea and the demands of the Jewish community did not go unheeded. The other agencies altered their policies to make them more transparent, and began to cooperate with each other more actively. "Things are much better now, there is no question," Rabbi Blech said.

Even as he was being attacked, Rabbi Levy applied himself once again to the business of kosher certification. "If you've been brought up in that kind of work and you're happy with it, you don't want to look for anything else," he once said. "I'm working for people, serving people and trying to make the world a better place to live."

New Leadership

During the year after the scandal broke, at one point Rabbi Levy was battling three lawsuits. "The weight of responsibility and aggravation had to have taken their toll," Mr. Axelrod wrote.

On Shabbat afternoon, April 4, 1987, Rabbi Levy went to pray as usual. As he walked down 15th Avenue, he was not feeling well, and sat down on someone's steps. Another congregant noticed him as he passed and, sizing up the situation, ran to the synagogue and called Hatzalah. The volunteer medics took Rabbi Levy to the hospital. He had had a massive heart attack.

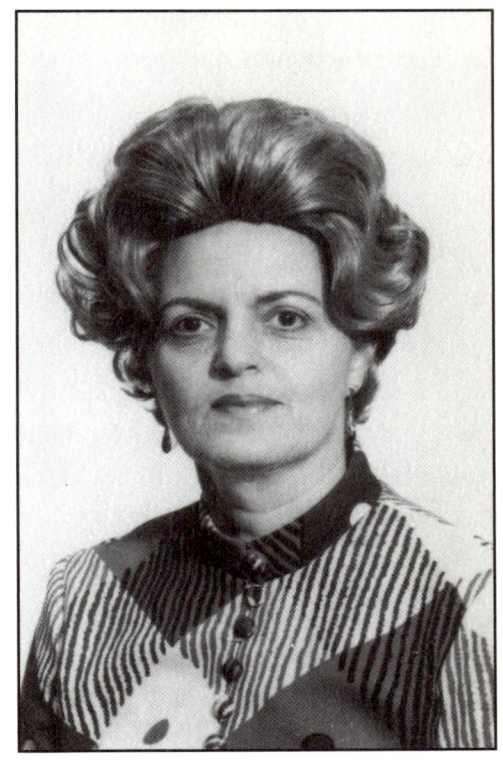

Rabbi Levy had a heart attack on the way to synagogue. By the time his wife, Thelma (above), arrived at the hospital, he had already died. Courtesy of Thelma Levy

After Shabbat someone rang the doorbell at the Levy home and told Mrs. Levy that she should come to the hospital immediately, because her husband "doesn't feel well." She threw her coat on, ran downstairs, and there on the street a police car was waiting to take her to the hospital.

By the time she arrived, Mrs. Levy said, "He was gone. That's all I know. They would not let me go into the hospital room."

"I couldn't talk," she said. "I couldn't say anything. I was ready to fall down, but they held me up. It was not easy, it was not easy."

When the Lubavitcher Rebbe heard what happened, his immediate reaction was to attribute the heart attack to the aggravation the scandal had caused Rabbi Levy.

After his father's passing, Rabbi Don Yoel was contemplating leaving the kosher agency. "I believed that I too could not stand up under this sort of pressure," he said.

His teachers from the Talmudical Yeshiva of Philadelphia came to convince him that he should not continue. "You should now take the OK and sell it," Rabbi Shmuel Kamenetsky told him. "Sell it to the OU. Sell it to somebody. Get rid of it." Rabbi Wikler was asked to broker a deal for millions of dollars.

"People felt that Don Yoel could not take over this operation," Amos Bunim recalled, "because it was very difficult. Because you were dealing with very difficult people in the kashrus world. Rabbi [Moshe] Tendler, who was very close to [Rabbi Berel Levy], felt that it was best for him to sell the business and not to continue."

The younger Rabbi Levy agreed. He sent a message to the Rebbe, stating that "kosher [supervision] killed my father, and I am afraid to continue." But the Rebbe would not hear of it, and shrugged off the entire worry. "He urged me very strongly to continue in kosher supervision," the younger Rabbi Levy recalled, "in spite of the tremendous pressure with which I was faced. This gave me strength, and helped the OK survive and prosper."

Mr. Axelrod was surprised when Rabbi Don Yoel decided to continue the agency. This, he wrote, shows how the father inspired the son. "The fact that, despite all of the problems, he was able to inspire his son to [follow in his footsteps] truly speaks volumes about his own sense of paternity to all of the Jewish people," he wrote.

Rabbi Don Yoel, who continues to lead the OK until today, took the organization to new heights, Mrs. Levy said. Mr. Bunim concluded that we must "give him tremendous credit."

In the April 1987 issue of the *Homemaker*, Rabbi Don Yoel wrote that he hoped to follow in his father's footsteps: "We hope that the Almighty will give us strength to continue with the devotion that he displayed, to service the kosher community in the tradition of my father… and strive untiringly to maintain and continually improve his standards of *Kashrus* and his standards of *Yiddishkeit*."

PART FOUR

AMBASSADOR OF JUDAISM

Sitting close to the Lubavitcher Rebbe as he spoke for hours at Chassidic gatherings, Rabbi Levy grew to share his desire to reach every Jew. The Rebbe wanted to strengthen Jewish observance in the most far-flung locations in the world, and Rabbi Levy's work took him to some of them. In an interview, he paraphrased a message he received from the Rebbe more than once: "There is no such thing as traveling somewhere only for whatever mission I have to do in the food world. Every trip also has to be utilized for spreading Torah and Judaism."

Rabbi Levy's grandson Rabbi Yosef Gartenhaus, principal of Yeshivas Torah Temimah in Lakewood, New Jersey, remembered how his grandfather used to emphasize the importance of reaching out to non-observant Jews. "We need to bring people closer to Yiddishkeit," Rabbi Levy would tell his grandchildren. "It is not only about us and our immediate community."

"He lived it," Rabbi Gartenhaus said. "We expected to always hear about his trips, and we knew that this [Jewish outreach] was what his life was really about."

Rabbi Levy's task as the Rebbe's "ambassador" was not usually stat-

Attending the gatherings presided over by the Lubavitcher Rebbe, Rabbi Menachem Mendel Schneerson, Rabbi Levy (top, center) was inspired to reach out to Jews across the globe (circa 1985). Courtesy of Rabbi Don Yoel Levy

ed explicitly, and sometimes came as a surprise. But Rabbi Levy always rose to the occasion. "Man never knows what the Almighty has in store for him when he travels around the world," he wrote in February 1985. "It's true that my work is a *melechet hakodesh*, a sacred mission in itself. However… it seems that G-d has other missions for us [as well]."

Before every trip, Rabbi Levy would write to inform the Rebbe where he was going. The Rebbe's responses varied greatly depending on Rabbi Levy's destination, but were always short and to the point. "I felt like I was living in the times of the Baal Shem Tov," Rabbi Levy said, referring to the cryptic instructions that the founder of Chassidism was known for giving his disciples.

"Speak Before the Community"

In the late 1970s, Rabbi Levy traveled to Manila, capital of the Philippines. When he wrote to the Rebbe about his upcoming trip, the Rebbe instructed him to "speak before the community," adding that he was sending them a donation of $180.

The Rebbe had heard about Jewish life in Manila from an army chaplain who was stationed at a U.S. base there. He subsequently sent Chabad representatives to visit and assess the community's needs.

Rabbi Levy arrived in Manila with no idea how to fulfill the Rebbe's directive: he didn't know anyone in the Jewish community. But it turned out that the owner of the banana chip factory he was visiting was very well connected. "My uncle is the president of the Jewish community," Eddy Moses told him. Rabbi Levy asked for an introduction, and a meeting was arranged.

Ezra Toeg had arrived in Manila from Shanghai in 1941. The Toegs were lumber merchants in China, and he and his mother came to the city to inspect a lumber concession. At the time the Philippines were controlled by the United States. Several hours after attacking Pearl Harbor on December 7 that year, the Japanese bombed U.S. bases in the Philippines. Returning to China, much of which was then occupied by Japan, became impossible.

The mother and son obtained asylum in the Philippines by hiding their Chinese citizenship and using instead Mrs. Toeg's Iraqi passport. They made a living selling coal from a cart. Mr. Toeg, a devoted, religious Jew, found life difficult on the island, where there was no community or infrastructure for observance. For the first time he put into practice the laws of ritual slaughter he had studied in Shanghai. He became the unofficial rabbi and president of the Jewish community.

"My father was the religious person in the community," said Hanna Toeg-Kuhr. "He personified what our sages say, 'In a place where there is no man, stand up and be a man.'" Mr. Toeg led the Jewish community's prayer services, read from the Torah and, when necessary, circumcised newborns.

Refusing to compromise on Jewish law, he would walk seven miles every Shabbat to and from the synagogue, which at the time was in downtown Manila. The community respected him greatly, and he in turn respected them, never chastising them for laxness in observance. "They recognized that he sincerely believed and acted with religious conviction, and not because he wanted to control anyone in the community," said his daughter, noting that he never sought an official position in the synagogue.

Rabbi Levy recalled that the Toegs received him very cordially and respected his decision not to eat with them because of his specific standards for kosher food. "He and his wife are very hospitable," he wrote in 1985. "All observant people who visit Manila are welcomed warmly to their home."

Mr. Toeg agreed immediately that Rabbi Levy should speak to the community on Shabbat afternoon. They arranged to meet on Friday evening and walk to synagogue together.

When Rabbi and Mrs. Levy arrived at the synagogue accompanied by Mr. Toeg, they found that Mrs. Levy was the only woman in attendance. She asked where the women's section was, but was told that there was none. "My eyes darkened when I heard there was no division between the men and women," wrote Rabbi Levy. "I knew that I could not pray there the next day, but I was slated to speak and had to go." He resolved to pray alone and go to the synagogue afterwards.

After services the next day, Rabbi Levy rose and stood before the community. "It is incumbent on me to ask forgiveness," he said, "and to explain why I did not pray with you."

He then told one of his favorite stories: A rich man lived on the Lower East Side of Manhattan. Over the years he became more affluent, and decided to move to Long Island. As a good Jew does, he looked for a synagogue in his new neighborhood to attend. It turned out that the only synagogue in his area was a Reform temple.

The man made an appointment with the president of the exclusive temple and asked how he could become a member. The president looked him up and down. Seeing the man's traditional dress and large skullcap, he wondered why such a person would want to join his temple. He gave the man a form to fill out and told him that he would receive an answer. But weeks and months passed, and no answer came.

One day the man met the president in the supermarket. "All these days I have been saddened that you have not accepted me as a member of the temple," the rich man said. "But last night I had a dream in which G-d came to me.

In the dream, G-d asked me, 'Why are you sad?' So I told G-d that I had not been accepted to the temple.

'There is nothing for you to be sad about,' G-d answered. 'They don't let Me in there either.'"

"The Torah says, 'They will make Me a sanctuary, and I will dwell among them,'" Rabbi Levy told the Manila community. The text lists in detail the materials from which the Tabernacle was made, and gives the measurements and design of each component. The question is: What difference does all this make to G-d?

"A person just wants to come and be closer to G-d," he told the crowd. "What difference does the size, material or design of the sanctuary make to the individual?" But the Torah makes it clear that it does matter. If you want your sacrifices, your prayers, to be accepted, they must be offered in a place where G-d can dwell, he said.

"Meat is good. Milk is good," said Rabbi Levy. "Women are good. Men are good. However, G-d does not want them to be mixed together,

As a result of Rabbi Levy's visits, the Jewish community in Manila, Philippines, raised their standards of Jewish observance. Here Rabbi Levy and the unofficial president of the community, Ezra Toeg, observe the construction of the ritual bath, which Rabbi Levy partially funded. Courtesy of the Jewish Homemaker/OK Kosher

not milk and meat, and not men and women.

"Surely you come here with all sincerity. The question is, to whom are you praying? G-d wants to be welcomed in this synagogue, so He can dwell among you."

Rabbi Levy told the congregation that the seed money for the *mechitza*, the divider between the sexes, had already been donated. "The Lubavitcher Rebbe sent you $180," he told them. "At first I did not understand why. Now I comprehend his intention. It is for you to erect a proper partition."

Inspired by Rabbi Levy's words, the congregation installed a *mechitza*.

Message from the Philippines

After the talk, a young man approached Rabbi Levy and told him that he was from New York; in fact, his parents lived not far from the Levys in Brooklyn. The young man had been raised in a religious home and attended a yeshivah his entire life. When he was not accepted into a medical school in the United States, he went to the Philippines to attend a school there.

"Please give my regards to my parents," he said. "Also, perhaps you could prepare them for some news: I am coming home in two months with my fiancée, a local Filipina woman." Rabbi Levy was grieved, and surprised that the young man thought he would be a fitting messenger for such a piece of news. During the 90-minute walk back to the hotel, he spoke to him about the negative effect that intermarriage would have on his life, his girlfriend and any children they might have together.

The young man was unmoved. "No matter what you say," he told Rabbi Levy, "however shocked my parents are going to be, I will do as I please."

Back in New York, Rabbi Levy contacted the parents and invited them to his home. When they arrived, he sadly told them, "When your son comes back, he will have some kind of present for you…"

The father fainted, and the mother began to wail in anguish. "You have to help us," she pleaded. "Please call him and try to convince him not to do this."

That night Rabbi Levy called the medical student. With a keen understanding of people, he knew that strong words would only make him more resistant to the message. So he took another route. Having appealed to the young man's intellect in Manila without success, he now spoke to his heart.

Rabbi Levy described the scene that had transpired in his home hours before. He emphasized the parents' deep distress and concern

The ritual bath in the Beit Yaacov Synagogue in Manila, Philippines, which Rabbi Levy helped inspire and build. Courtesy of Lee Blumenthal

for their son's future. They were not a wealthy family, and they had invested their life savings into their son's education. "Their love for you is so great," he said, "that their reaction to the news was extreme. You can imagine for yourself what will happen when you actually introduce her to them."

The young man listened in silence without responding or arguing, and Rabbi Levy went to sleep that night not knowing what was transpiring in his heart.

The next morning the mother called Rabbi Levy to tell him that her son had called early in the morning and told them that he had decided to sever his ties with his Filipina girlfriend. "I want to thank you from the bottom of my heart for helping our son come to his senses," she said.

Thank the Lubavitcher Rebbe, Rabbi Levy told her. If he had not asked me to speak for the community, I would never have been in the synagogue that Shabbat or met your son.

A few years after Rabbi Levy's visit, Mr. Toeg began to organize the community to build a new synagogue, and Rabbi Levy took it upon himself to fund the construction of a mikvah, a ritual bath.

In 1981, the Rebbe wrote to Mr. Toeg to encourage his efforts. "I was pleased to receive a personal report from our esteemed mutual friend Rabbi B. Levy," the Rebbe wrote. "Many, many thanks for the good news that the construction of the new synagogue and mikvah has been initiated.... May G-d grant that it be completed even sooner than the most optimistic expectations, and that both are well attended and fully made use of."

Because Jewish law gives many detailed specifications for the construction of a ritual bath, and the process is usually overseen by an expert, Rabbi Levy paid for someone to travel to Manila and oversee the building.

"First of all, I wish to tell the Rebbe that I sent [an expert] to inspect the mikvah in Manila," he wrote in a report after a trip to Europe. "I took care of all the expenses for the trip.... He found a leak in the mikvah, and they [fixed and] finished it. Now they are waiting for rain. The synagogue with the mechitza is also completed."

Today, Manila's magnificent synagogue and mikvah serve its Jewish community and vacationers from around the globe.

Manila to Kobe

When Rabbi Levy was scheduled to return to the Philippines, the Rebbe told him, "They built a *shul* [synagogue] and a mikvah. Now you need to find out what they do about the circumcision of newborns, education of children and Jewish burial."

Rabbi Levy arrived to find that in fact the community had recently

Rabbi Levy explained to the Jewish community of Kobe that the partition between the men's and women's sections at the Ohel Shlomo synagogue was not proper, and offered to fund the construction of a new one (pictured). Courtesy of Thelma Levy

hired a G-d-fearing man who led the services, slaughtered kosher meat and also served as the *mohel*, ritual circumciser. The man told Rabbi Levy that he had already circumcised several children.

During their conversation, the Manila rabbi mentioned in passing that not long ago he had received a telegram from an Israeli in Kobe, Japan. "The telegram asked that I come there to circumcise his son," he said. However, two days later he had received another telegram canceling the request. Knowing that there was no other mohel in Kobe, he inquired what happened, and learned that the family had decided to use a local surgeon for the circumcision.

"When I left Manila, I went to Japan to visit plants producing macrobiotic foods," Rabbi Levy wrote in the article from 1985. "My itinerary called for me to go to Tokyo, but I ended up in Osaka. When I discovered how near Osaka was to Kobe, I made arrangements to spend Shabbos in Kobe."

Such unexpected changes in his itinerary happened frequently, he wrote, and while he made every effort to return home to his family as soon as possible, "sometimes… I later discover that it was through *hashgacha pratis,* divine providence, and I end up in another city doing things that have no connection with *kashrus*."

The history of the synagogue in Kobe goes back to World War II, when the Americans bombed the city's old synagogue, leaving the community without a home. The Jews mourned and fasted, with the war raging and no one to turn to for help. A local businessman, Rahmo Sassoon, eventually offered to host the congregation in a warehouse he owned. He named the synagogue Ohel Shlomo in memory of his father. In 1964, when Mr. Sassoon moved to New York, he donated the warehouse to the Kobe Jewish community.

Repeat Performance

Rabbi Levy arrived at the synagogue in Kobe on Friday night only to discover that, once again, there was no divider between the sexes. Disappointed, he returned to his hotel and prayed alone. Several other religious Jews were also staying there, and together they discussed how to rectify the situation.

It was decided they would all pray early at the hotel and then walk to the synagogue, where someone would request that Rabbi Levy be allowed to speak after services. It was a peculiar situation. A bunch of Jews arrived on Shabbat morning and sat in the sanctuary without praying. The congregation offered Rabbi Levy the honor of being called up to the Torah, but he refused.

After the services, permission was granted for Rabbi Levy to speak. "I feel that I owe you an explanation," he told the assembled. "I am sure you noticed that we came to your *shul* but didn't participate in the service. Not only didn't I participate in the service, but I refused to take an *aliya*."

He proceeded to repeat the talk he had given in Manila years before. "You might think I refused to take the aliya because I didn't want to make a contribution," he added. "Tomorrow, please G-d, I will leave you a check of $180, and I want you to earmark it for building a partition."

Rabbi Levy then discussed the circumcision of the Israeli man's son. He became very emotional, describing the importance of a proper circumcision, which could not be performed by a surgeon, and ended by saying that the situation could still be rectified.

Rabbi Levy's insistence on building a proper ritual bath in Kobe, Japan, inspired locals and businesspeople from abroad to work together. Today, Chabad of Kobe is working on renovating it. Courtesy of Rabbi Shmuel Vishedsky

After his speech, the head of the company where the Israeli worked approached Rabbi Levy and thanked him for bringing the problem to his attention. "Tell me," he asked, "how did you know about the entire story?"

Rabbi Levy replied that it had all started with one request from the Lubavitcher Rebbe: to find out what was happening with circumcisions in Manila. "If so, there are no questions," the man said. "I will make sure that there will never be another case like this in Kobe." Soon after, Rabbi Levy received word from the rabbi in Manila that he had been called to Kobe to rectify the circumcision.

On his return to America, Rabbi Levy heard from Victor C. Moche, who owned an import-export firm in Kobe. The installation of the mechitza was being met with resistance, and Mr. Moche had taken the initiative, at the behest of the board, to meet with the congregants who opposed the partition.

"I want you to use the check!" Rabbi Levy said, adding that he would be more than happy to meet those who objected, to try to persuade them to change their view. Eventually, the mechitza was ordered and installed.

Having succeeded with the Kobe synagogue, Rabbi Levy turned to the mikvah, which was not constructed in accordance with Jewish law. "He went around and spoke to the community that they need a good mikvah," said Meir Plotkin, a Canadian jewelry dealer who often visited the city to buy pearls. "People were not interested in it, and it took a lot of pushing,"

Several Chabad businessmen who had ties to Kobe, including Mr. Plotkin, began to organize the construction of a new mikvah. They brought an expert, Rabbi Avraham Feigelstock from Vancouver, Canada, to see what could be done.

"When I arrived for the first time, it [the city's mikvah] looked like some kind of bathtub," Rabbi Feigelstock said. "It seems that they wanted to build a mikvah, went to see one, and built it without any experience."

Over three visits, Rabbi Feigelstock and a Vancouver architect, who donated his time, succeeded in building a mikvah in the small area that the synagogue designated for it. It was not beautiful, but it was a kosher mikvah, and remains so, still in use today.

His success with the Kobe community, Rabbi Levy concluded, "only proves that so much can be accomplished if one tries and becomes involved."

From then on, wherever he traveled, Rabbi Levy would inquire about the number of mikvahs and their kosher status. If there were not enough, he would strongly encourage the community to build more. After a visit to the Netherlands, he wrote a report to the Rebbe: "It seems that the only mikvah is in Amsterdam. The other communities have no mikvah.... The Rebbe gave some money to begin a new mikvah in one of the towns, but they never got off the ground. I spoke very strongly about this, and I do not know how much of an impression I made."

Cemeteries in China

Before Rabbi Levy's trip to visit the Hunt-Wesson plants in China, the Rebbe told him that there were Jewish cemeteries in China which were in danger of being demolished and used for real estate. To stop the desecration, the cemeteries needed to be identified.

The Rebbe also told Rabbi Levy to look out for Jews in the country. "How do you find Jews?" the Rebbe asked rhetorically. "Ask any professor. They won't admit that they don't know, and they'll work very hard to find Jews for you."

Rabbi Levy was not successful in locating the cemeteries. On a trip to Shanghai years later, Rabbi Don Yoel inquired about them and was told that, tragically, they had indeed been developed as real estate.

Check on the Mikvah

In the early 1970s, Rabbi Levy was scheduled to travel to Copenhagen, Denmark, to inspect some factories. While you are there, the Rebbe told him, take a look at the mikvah in the Great Synagogue.

For many years, the mikvah in Copenhagen's largest synagogue had been maintained by Chabad rabbis, who also served as leaders of the congregation Machzikei Hadas. By the time of Rabbi Levy's trip, however, the community had dwindled, and the Chabad rabbis were no longer there. That was why the Rebbe wanted to make sure the mikvah was still in working order.

Rabbi Levy was in the city for only one day, and was unable to reach the synagogue's caretaker. He went anyway but found the mikvah locked.

A year later he returned to the city, and the Rebbe again guided him to check the condition of the mikvah. This time Rabbi Levy resolved to do whatever was necessary to get access. He finally managed to locate someone with the keys and went in.

Sure enough, during his inspection, he found several problems that rendered the mikvah invalid according to Jewish law. Rabbi Levy spoke to the rabbi and caretaker, urging them to address the problems. He told them that the Lubavitcher Rebbe cared so much about their community that he had sent him to check the mikvah on two separate occasions.

On a subsequent stop in London, Rabbi Levy met the rabbi who had originally approved the Copenhagen mikvah for use and told him about the problems he had discovered. The rabbi was shocked and said that he had discussed these issues with the community, and they had promised to fix them. He was surprised to hear that the Rebbe, in New York, was concerned, because he had not reported any of the issues to him.

The rabbi made the trip to the city and oversaw the necessary repairs. A few years later, Machzikei Hadas built a new mikvah. It was renovated in 2014 by the Chabad representatives in Copenhagen.

Rabbi Levy visits a Japanese manufacturing plant (1980). Trips across the globe to visit food plants were also used to reach out to local Jews and encourage them in their observance. Courtesy of OK Kosher

UNDERCOVER IN THE USSR

"Would you give me a ride to the synagogue?" Rabbi Levy asked the occupants of the black car. "You are going there too, so why not just take me with you?"

The time for prayer services was approaching, but there were no taxis outside the Soviet hotel in Rostov. The Soviet secret police, the KGB, were following his every move. He knew that as soon as he found a ride, the car idling outside the hotel would make its way to the synagogue as well. But the two stone-faced men inside ignored his request.

"We finally got a taxi," Mrs. Levy recalled. "We get into the taxi, and of course the black car follows right behind us."

Rabbi Levy's extensive travel schedule and his willingness to take risks spurred one of the Chabad movement's most daring projects in the 20th century: sending Westerners to the Soviet Union with the goal of spreading Judaism, supplying Soviet Jews with ritual objects and assisting them in any way possible.

"Should I?"

While the Soviet government did not outlaw religious practice, they did everything they could to uproot it. Public Jewish gatherings were forbidden. Young people were ridiculed by their teachers for attending synagogue, and most Jewish schools and institutions were shuttered or

While American Jews protested the plight of Soviet Jewry, Rabbi Levy jumped into the lion's den and headed to the Soviet Union to help. Here he gives a lecture in Leningrad (today St. Petersburg) in 1981. On Rabbi Levy's left is Ilya Essas. Courtesy of Thelma Levy

requisitioned for other purposes. Ritual items became difficult to find as the older generation died out.

Throughout these years the Rebbe Rayatz and his successor, the Lubavitcher Rebbe, kept the flame of Judaism alive in the Soviet Union. Chabad's clandestine network of Jewish schools and institutions was in place from the time that the USSR began restricting religious practice, preceding the surge of American support for Soviet Jewry by decades.

"In the mid-1960s, I decided, with several of my friends, to dedicate myself to the Jews living in Russia," then Israeli Prime Minister Yitzchak Shamir said in a 1999 interview. He believed this was a forgotten cause at the time, but was surprised to find that someone was already working on it.

"The Lubavitcher Rebbe preceded us by many years," he said. "I was astonished… at how entrenched and encompassing their activities were. They supplied matzahs for Passover, religious books, ritual items, kosher slaughtering and every single other thing that the Jews needed there."

The Rebbe was a visionary who recognized that "the saving of Russian Jewry was a great deed and a must for the future of the survival of the Jewish nation," the prime minister said. He often told people that "there is a Jew living in the United States [who] is there to assist any Jew in need."

For many years the Rebbe sent ritual items to the Soviet Union through the Israeli diplomatic mission in the Soviet Union. But when diplomatic ties between the two countries were severed after the Six-Day War in 1967, he began to look for an alternate route.

Around the same time, American Jewish activists began to publicly protest on behalf of Soviet Jewry. As his work in kosher took him to the Far East frequently, Rabbi Levy wondered if he might be able to assist Jews in the USSR. In 1967 he wrote to the Rebbe asking advice about entering the Soviet Union.

It was a dangerous undertaking. Not long before, a fisherman in Prague had discovered the body of Charles Jordan, a high official with the Joint Distribution Committee, in the Vltava River. Mr. Jordan dedicated his life to helping Jews and other refugees to flee the Soviet Union. The murder remains unsolved until today, but at the time it was believed to have been orchestrated by the KGB.

The Rebbe discouraged Rabbi Levy, stating that it was too risky, and he dropped the idea.

In 1972, Rabbi Levy wrote to inform the Rebbe that he would be in Europe for several days, and from there would travel to the Far East. In between, he would have a break of several days. "Should I go to the Soviet Union to assist the Jews there?" he asked. The Rebbe crossed out the

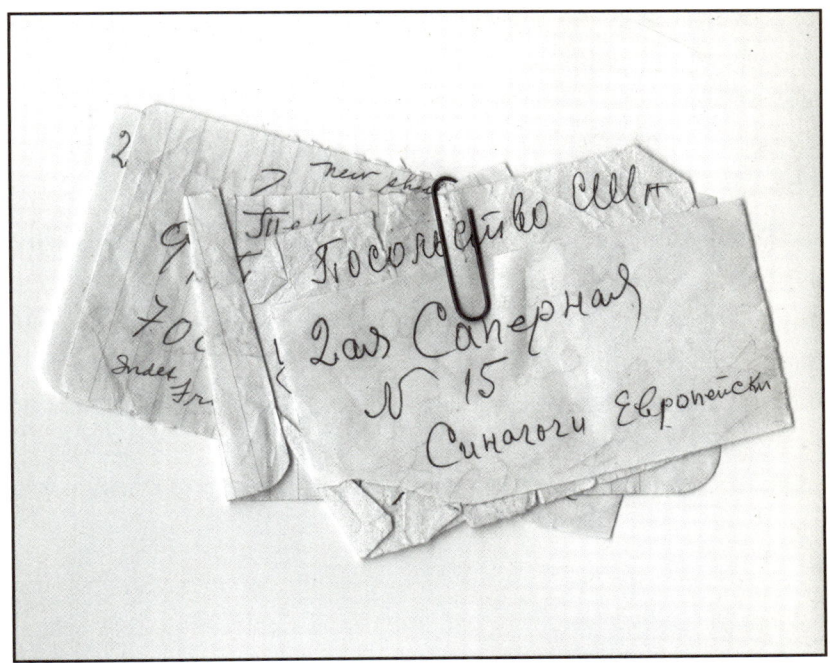

The Levys used small notes with the addresses of the United States embassy and synagogues they wanted to visit to get around the country. *Courtesy of Thelma Levy*

words "Should I," and returned the letter. The message was clear.

Rabbi Levy's trip to the Soviet Union that winter was the first of many. On five of them he was accompanied by his wife; once his son Don Yoel came with him; and three times he took his youngest son, Eliezer. Rabbi Levy did not write or speak much about these trips, fearing to endanger the Jews he met. "I am not ready to say even one word about my trips there," he once told a reporter who asked. However, he did make brief diary entries in order to be able to give the Rebbe a full accounting of everything that happened.

Once, Knesset member Menachem Hacohen was in the USSR at the same time as Rabbi Levy, and they participated in a farbrengen together with one of the Chabad activists. Afterwards, Mr. Hacohen wrote an article for *Yediot Achronot*, at the time Israel's largest newspaper, in which he described the gathering and those who attended. In a private audience the Rebbe told Rabbi Levy how much the story had pained him, and fervently hoped there would not be repercussions.

The Unexpected

On that first trip to the Soviet Union, the Levys did not know what to expect, or how to make contact with Jews in the country. In order to be granted visas, they were required to provide a detailed itinerary, with flights, hotels and tourist destinations scheduled to the minute. This itinerary had to be preapproved by the Soviet travel agency, Intourist. Founded by the infamous Joseph Stalin, the agency was staffed with secret police. It was said that "Intourist is to tourism what indigestion is to digestion."

The Levys decided to focus their itinerary on cities that were important in Chabad history or had a personal significance. They scheduled visits to such places as Ilya, the town where Rabbi Levy's maternal grandparents had resided, and Haditch, where the founder of the Chabad movement, Rabbi Schneur Zalman of Liadi, was interred. They hoped that in each city they would be able to visit the synagogues and meet local Jews.

They quickly discovered, however, that the Soviets were not easy to deal with. Their hotel rooms were never the right ones, and their flights were never scheduled at the times their tickets indicated. Intourist officials were constantly at their side—their every move was monitored. Changes to their itinerary, Mrs. Levy wrote, seemed to require "federal legislation from Moscow."

They went from Moscow to Kharkov, Ukraine. "We went sightseeing, [and] all you see all over are statues of Lenin and more statutes of Lenin," Mrs. Levy wrote in a letter to her daughter. They could not locate a synagogue in the city, and thus met no Jews. From Kharkov they traveled to Rostov-on-Don, where they finally found a functioning synagogue.

Their "guide" permitted them to attend morning services, but when they requested to return to the synagogue later in the day, he was not happy. "The driver refused, but we insisted, and finally he took us," Mrs. Levy wrote. "He drove like a maniac there and back. He was so angry."

Back in Moscow for Shabbat, they made their way to one of the main shuls, and there began to form a clearer picture of the state of Soviet Jewry. The services were well attended, but Mrs. Levy noted that most of the younger men seemed not to know how to pray, and would just "stand in the back and in the lobby."

Most of the Jews would not talk to the Levys, fearing that they were informers. Those who did talk would not give their last names.

Rabbi Mordechai Lifshitz, a Lubavitcher who was affectionately known as Reb Mottel the Shochet, was an integral part of the Chabad underground in Moscow, serving the community as a ritual slaughterer and performing clandestine circumcisions. He told Mrs. Levy that the most difficult part of life in the USSR was the lack of Jewish schools. "We have no jurisdiction over our children," he said. Under the influence of their Communist education, thousands of Jewish children abandoned the faith and traditions of their parents.

The Levys concluded their first trip by distributing the kosher salami they had brought with them. "[Rabbi Levy] even took off his *tzitzis* [four-cornered garment with fringes] and gave it away," Mrs. Levy wrote. They found that the demand for tzitzit, tefillin, *siddurim* and other Jewish basics was so great that "more of anything would not [even] have been enough."

The Danger

Few in the American Jewish community understood how dangerous religious observance had become in the Soviet Union. After a visit to the USSR, Senator James Buckley spoke publicly about his visit to a synagogue and the fear he had witnessed in the Jews he met there.

"Religious persecution is an important part of the strategy of the Soviet rulers to erase all forms of freedom," he wrote in a February 1975 statement. "In many ways [the Soviet Union today is] far more cruel and more oppressive than even the persecution under Stalin."

Mrs. Levy was blunt about the anxiety she felt during their trips. "Freedom!! At last," she began a letter to her daughter. "I have not slept one night yet since I left home. If I had to stay any longer, I don't think I'd have made it." Until they landed in the Rome airport, she wrote, she never believed they would make it out. "It's just an awful country, and we don't know how lucky we are to be living elsewhere."

Though Rabbi Levy himself seemed to think little of the risks involved in his expeditions, others thought of them often. "Rabbi Levy is in Russia," Rebbetzin Chaya Mushka Schneerson, the Rebbe's wife, once said to the man who helped her with household chores. "It is very dangerous there. He brought there Jewish books and other items. I think about him every day." The rebbetzin had first-hand experience, having lived in the Soviet Union with her father, the previous Lubavitcher Rebbe, who was arrested and sentenced to death for the crime of strengthening Jewish observance. Under international pressure, his sentence was commuted and he was expelled from the country.

When she did not accompany her husband on his trips, Mrs. Levy worried incessantly. To Rabbi Levy, however, they were simply an exciting challenge. "I am doing so much for these people," he told his wife. "You don't have to be so frightened."

Those who encountered him in the Soviet Union confirmed that he seemed utterly confident and unafraid. "He knew that he was an emissary of the Rebbe," said Rabbi Yitzchok Kogan, who was a leader of the Chabad underground in Leningrad, now St. Petersburg. "As an independent-minded person, he exhibited no fear in all of his doings and visits in the houses of the Chabad underground." Now the chief slaughterer of the Russian Jewish community, Rabbi Kogan recalled how Rabbi Levy,

Since the Levys' visas said that they were travelling to the Soviet Union as tourists, they spent their days visiting tourist attractions. In the early morning and at night, however, they engaged in clandestine Jewish activities. Here the couple pose outside of the Astoria Hotel, which had been confiscated by the Communists and was run by the Intourist organization (1979). Courtesy of Thelma Levy

on one of his trips, gave him the certification to be a shochet.

Persona Non Grata

On their second trip the Levys brought more supplies. They entered the country with *mezuzahs*, kosher food, many pairs of tzitzit and various Jewish books tucked as discreetly as possible between the clothes and personal items in their luggage. It was impossible to hide them, however, and when the Soviet customs officers realized they were attempting to conceal something, they emptied out every suitcase. "Eliezer was crying. I was just about hysterical," Mrs. Levy wrote in an unfinished letter after the trip.

One of the officers came over and told them to be quiet. "No one will tell me to be quiet," Mrs. Levy retorted. "I'll say what I want and when I want." He tried to shush them again, and she told him not to talk to her like that. When he threatened to call the police, she said, "Fine, I'll wait right here. But at the same time call the American consul." He never returned.

In the end they managed to retrieve much of what they brought, but clearly, Mrs. Levy wrote, they had made a mistake by hiding the items, thereby arousing the officials' suspicion that they were not for personal use. "[Rabbi Levy] made one mistake. When they asked him if he had anything to declare, he said 'No.' And we should have packed the 'literature' right on top, instead of scattered among the clothes," she wrote. "It was an aggravating, nerve-racking and most humiliating experience."

Rabbi Levy had learned his lesson: he had to declare every item he brought into the country and fabricate a reason why it was for his own personal use. Unfortunately for him, the Soviets were not going to give him another chance to get it right. His next application for a visa was declined.

He reported to the Rebbe that his visits to the USSR could not continue, but the Rebbe was not ready to give up. The Levys' second trip, he said, had been a great success, providing much-needed support to the Chabad underground, and this assistance must continue.

The Rebbe advised him to approach Senator Buckley, who had become an activist for freedom of religion in the Soviet Union. The Rebbe believed that Senator Buckley would understand how important Rabbi Levy's work in the country was, and would organize a visa.

In his letter to the senator, Rabbi Levy stressed that no mention of Chabad, Lubavitch or the Rebbe should be made to the Soviet embassy in Washington. "During our visit I spoke in several synagogues in Russia," he wrote. "I, of course, did not get involved in any politics." The official purpose of his trip was to visit the graves of his family and do some sightseeing.

Shortly thereafter the Levys made their way back to the Soviet Union, this time well prepared and with many direct instructions from the Rebbe.

No matter what time of year he traveled, Rabbi Levy always brought several pounds of *shmurah* matzah, made from wheat that had been guarded from the time of harvest to ensure it did not become wet. The preferred choice for use at the Pesach Seder, shmurah matzah was not available at all in the Soviet Union. He would also bring recordings of the Rebbe's talks and Jewish music.

Rabbi Levy was instructed to deliver all the goods to the point men in Moscow: Getzel "Getche" Vilensky and Gershon "Grisha" Rosenstein.

When Mrs. Levy accompanied her husband, the Rebbe guided her to speak to Jewish women about the laws of family purity and other observances, and to urge them to implement them in their daily lives. The Rebbe often gave Rabbi Levy personal messages to be relayed to individuals, and words of encouragement for everyone.

If the trip were close to Chanukah time, the Rebbe would provide Chanukah *gelt* to be exchanged for rubles and distributed to Jews in the Soviet Union. Once, after giving Rabbi Levy the money, the Rebbe said, "Surely you will sing *'Maoz tzur'* with them." Since the song is not part of the Chabad liturgy, the Rebbe asked, "Do you know the words?"

Rabbi Levy said he did, and the Rebbe asked him to sing it. He began to sing, but got stuck with the words partway through. The Rebbe said with a smile, "Good, that's enough."

The Jewish Women

By her own choice, Mrs. Levy remained in the hotel during most of her husband's meetings with Chabad operatives. When necessary, however, she knew how to stand up to the Soviet authorities.

When they arrived at the customs booth on one of their trips, an agent took Rabbi Levy to a side room to interrogate him. A tough, humorless female agent then turned to Mrs. Levy and asked if she was carrying any cash. Mrs. Levy produced an envelope, which the woman took and began to walk away. "Where are you going?" Mrs. Levy asked. The agent, who was fluent in English, explained that she was going to another room to count the money. "Count it in front of me!" Mrs. Levy bellowed. The woman turned around and, for some reason, returned the envelope without opening it.

The agent then began rummaging through their suitcases, at one point dumping all of their clothing and personal belongings on the floor. Most of the kosher food, besides for one of the salamis, was confiscated, and many of the ritual items met a similar fate. The agent spotted a wig box and was about to open it, when Mrs. Levy said sternly, "I want you to know I paid $50 to have that set, and if you mess it up you will have to pay for it." The box was left alone.

Having completed her search, down to removing the sole from one of Mrs. Levy's shoes, the agent instructed her to clean up the mess. Mrs. Levy's frustration was palpable. "I packed once," she said. "You made this mess, you scattered everything, you will repack my suitcases neatly."

The agent was outraged and started to shout, threatening to call the *politzei*, the police.

"Please call the American ambassador, too," Mrs. Levy said. "I'd like to ask who is responsible for packing this all up." Without another word the agent repacked the suitcases neatly.

Just then Rabbi Levy returned and told his wife what had happened in the interrogation room. The officer had asked him to undress.

"What for?" Rabbi Levy asked.

The guard responded, "Undress now."

Rabbi Levy was defiant: "You want to see what I have? I want to see what you have. It is the same."

A proudly observant woman, Mrs. Levy was a breath of fresh air for the Jewish women in the Soviet Union, who felt alone in their struggle. Here a group of women pose with Mrs. Levy (second from right) after a secret circumcision. Courtesy of Thelma Levy

At this the guard left him alone.

"In the Soviet Union you had to know how to handle the people," Mrs. Levy said years later.

She recalled attending weddings which Rabbi Levy conducted in secrecy. Newly religious couples who were already civilly married waited for him to come and perform their Jewish weddings. The entire ceremony would take place inside—no one dared to risk having the ceremony outdoors. Several couples would be married simultaneously, and everyone contributed to the festive meal as best they could. "It was heartbreaking to know that they had no one to marry them and had to wait for my husband to come and perform the wedding," she said.

One year, she said, they did seven weddings at once. Afterwards the meal was served on a makeshift table made out of a door that had been removed from its hinges and placed atop four chairs.

In her meetings with the women she learned of their great pain. "The few observant Jews there are have no Yiddishe *nachas* [satisfaction] from their children," she wrote. "[The children] know nothing!! [The parents] are thankful and grateful if the children marry someone whose mother was Jewish. More they don't even ask!" Some of the women observed Judaism based on such limited knowledge that they had never heard of Shabbat candles.

When the women asked her about her wig, she explained to them why married Jewish women cover their hair, and that a wig is the preferred way to do it. Five of the women expressed interest in wearing a wig, but there were no stylish wigs for women available in the Soviet Union. Mrs. Levy took samples of their hair, gave them to a wigmaker in New York, and on her next trip brought five wigs.

Movie Messages

Since Rabbi Levy entered the Soviet Union as a tourist, he always brought with him a good camera and a movie camera. When he wasn't meeting with Chabad operatives or teaching Torah classes, he would visit tourist attractions and take pictures. He had another mission, however: he wanted to document the Jewish community under Communism. He began filming the synagogues and secret gatherings he attended. To avoid detection, he would bring in new films, which did not raise any red flags with customs. Whenever he recorded an event that could put others in danger, he would begin in the middle of the reel. That way, when he returned the film to the box, it looked as if it were still brand-new. The Soviets never checked the center of the reel.

After each trip Rabbi Levy had a private audience with the Rebbe. Often these went on for hours, as the Rebbe asked him to repeat every detail of what he had heard and seen. He would also visit the Lubavitcher Rebbetzin, Mrs. Chaya Mushka Schneerson, to show her the films he made. One time she asked Rabbi Levy why he did not show the movies to the Rebbe. "Surely this would interest my husband," she said.

Rabbi Levy hesitated, saying he did not want to waste the Rebbe's precious time. "In my opinion it would surely be of interest to him," she said. "I will speak to him about it."

Immediately Rabbi Levy replied that if the Rebbetzin felt that way, he would bring it up with the Rebbe himself. When he did, it was clear that the Rebbe already knew about the films. He confirmed that he would like to see them.

As part of their tourist disguise, the Levys brought movie cameras to film Soviet tourist attractions. On later trips, they filmed the Jewish community as well. Here Mrs. Levy can be seen with her movie camera in Japan (1977). Courtesy of Thelma Levy

The Rebbe spent many hours watching the movies, listening to people's greetings and requests. At the first screening he wrote down the names of those in the film.

It became the custom that after Rabbi Levy showed the films to the Rebbe in his office, he would go directly to show them to the Rebbetzin, just a few blocks away. The Rebbetzin would stay up late in order to spend time with her husband when he finished his private audiences, usually in the early hours of the morning. Once, when Rabbi Levy's post-trip audience stretched until 2 a.m., the Rebbetzin, eager to see the films and hear about the trip as well, called the office at Lubavitch World Headquarters to ask what was taking so long.

Now that the Rebbe was watching the films, Rabbi Levy would encourage those who appeared in them to speak directly to him. They would immerse in a mikvah, get dressed in their finest clothing and make other spiritual preparations before addressing the camera.

The Rebbe took these long-distance audiences quite seriously. Rabbi Don Yoel Levy, who went with his father one time to show the films, recalled that "the Rebbe would sit for hours patiently responding to the requests."

The Rebbe's responses were delivered in various ways. Urgent requests were answered over the phone, others were sent by mail, without stationery and signed *"Zeide"* (Grandfather). To those who did not understand Hebrew or Yiddish, an aide would write in Russian, and the Rebbe would review the letter, signing it *"Dyedooshka,"* grandfather in Russian.

Anxious to hear the Rebbe's response to a question he had recorded during one of Rabbi Levy's trips, leading Chabad activist Grisha Rosenstein sent this cryptic postcard to Rabbi Levy:

> Dear Rabbi,
>
> Happy Pesach to you, your family and Grandfather [the Rebbe]. Till 120 of health and happy life. Our situation didn't change till now. What will happen? [I.e. what did the Rebbe guide us to do?] Don't forget us.
>
> With deep feeling to you and yours.
>
> Gregory

With Rabbi Levy's mixture of bravery and extensive knowledge of Jewish law, Jews in the Soviet Union began to look forward to his visits. Here Grisha Rosenstein (right), an activist in the Chabad underground, appears with Rabbi Levy. Courtesy of Thelma Levy

The messages people sent to the Rebbe through Rabbi Levy ranged from requests for spiritual guidance to inquiries about more mundane matters. One man, who was married to a convert, wanted to divorce her after he found out she had eaten a product during Pesach that he considered not kosher for the holiday. Rabbi Levy and others tried to talk him out of it, telling him that it was not such a grave issue and that in fact according to the letter of the law it was permissible.

The man was adamant, however, and Rabbi Levy spoke to the Rebbe about the issue. The Rebbe sent a message to the man: "Know that she is not just a good Jewish woman, she is one who chose out of self-sacrifice to be a Jew in a country where it is not an easy feat."

With the message in hand, Rabbi Levy arrived at the couple's home and reunited them.

Spiritual Worries

It was clear from watching the films how difficult life was in the Soviet Union. Yet the Jews Rabbi Levy recorded seemed to feel spiritual privation more deeply than physical suffering. In one, a ritual slaughterer's wife in Tashkent cried to the Rebbe that she had extraneous thoughts during prayers. In another, a concerned father asked whether he should wait to emigrate until his daughter became engaged; he hoped that as long as he remained, she would marry a Jew.

Hardship seemed to have intensified these people's thirst for Jewish knowledge. Rabbi Levy described one encounter in his diary:

> I never met Kalman before. He is a very warm man. He speaks Yiddish. He was complaining that he knows so little. He is a Jew who is apparently suffering very much in both material and spiritual pursuits.

In Alma-Ata, today Almaty, Rabbi Levy visited a pious elderly couple. The man was in his nineties, the woman in her eighties. Overjoyed to see a religious Jew, they served him their finest meal: a bowl of water and chicken bones. The old man lay in bed while Rabbi Levy filmed him relaying a message to his brother in Europe. With great effort he then got up so that he could speak with proper respect to the Rebbe.

"How Is the Rebbe?"

Like the old man in Alma-Ata, most of the Jews Rabbi Levy encountered had never seen the Rebbe. But they knew him through his followers and his emissaries, and they loved and revered him. Rabbi Levy was amazed at how anxious they were to hear even a few words of encouragement from the Rebbe.

In every city, Rabbi Levy would conduct *farbrengens,* Chassidic gatherings, in the homes of the local Jewish leaders. He would share stories and ideas of Chassidism, sing Jewish songs and make small toasts over a bottle of vodka the Rebbe had given him as a way of conferring his blessing and participating in the gatherings. Invariably, the farbrengens went late into the night and ended with Rabbi Levy speaking to individuals one by one for as long as they needed.

In 1977, shortly after the Rebbe had a heart attack, Rabbi Levy wrote:

> In the morning both the Bukharian and the Ashkenazic [Jews] were very happy to see me. They all hugged and kissed me. The first question they asked was how the Rebbe is. They all heard he wasn't feeling well.
>
> They wanted to know how he is and what regards I have from him. We first sat down, as I always do, and I learned with them a chapter of *Tanya* and briefly told them what is going on with the Rebbe.

The Beadle

As a rule, Rabbi Levy kept his diary entries short, but interspersed here and there are more detailed portraits of some of the memorable characters he encountered. In November 1978 he took the time to describe an old man who had preserved his Jewish observance at great cost:

> The house is very old. It only has two rooms and a yard. He has thousands of old books. The *seforim* [Torah books] mean everything to him. He has many pictures of the Rebbe around the house.
>
> He is the *gabbai* [beadle] in the *shul* [synagogue] and controls everything.
>
> He says that his children and everybody beg him to move to one of the large new apartment houses, but he refuses, because he has an enclosed yard and he builds a *sukkah* in the yard and everyone comes there to eat. He is able to make *chupahs* [Jewish

weddings] there without anyone knowing it. He is a Jew who feels strong ties to the Rebbe. He cries [and asks] why the Rebbe doesn't do anything to destroy the wicked Soviets....

He eats very little. He prepares his own food and is looking through the *seforim* all day. He doesn't have the strength to go to shul every day, but he does go every Shabbos. He came [to synagogue] the two days I was there.

The entry continues that there had been a debate among those in the synagogue whether to admit Rabbi Levy to their clandestine prayer services and risk discovery by the KGB. He didn't write what the final decision was, but it provides a glimpse of the constant fear in which people lived.

"If I Would Have Such a Pair!"

One Friday afternoon in Moscow, Rabbi Levy went to the mikvah, as was his custom before Shabbos. There Reb Getche, one of the leaders of the Chabad underground, saw his *tzitzit* and said loudly, "Oy, if I would have such a pair!"

Reb Getche was wearing his tattered pair that he had worn for years with self-sacrifice. To Rabbi Levy they were just as desirable as his pair appeared to Reb Getche, because he saw them as a symbol of a true chassid. They agreed to exchange garments. Unfortunately, Reb Getche's pair did not fit Rabbi Levy, and he had to wait until he arrived in Israel, where the first thing he did was purchase a new pair.

"It was more of a mitzvah to give him the tzitzis," he later said, "than for me to say no and wear them myself."

Rabbi Levy cherished Reb Getche's tzitzit. They remain a family heirloom until today.

Reb Getche was another person whom the Rebbe told not to leave the Soviet Union. When he received this message, Reb Getche gave up

When Getzel "Getche" Vilensky envied Rabbi Levy for his new tzitzit, Rabbi Levy readily gave them to him. Here Getche is seen after a gathering with Rabbi Levy in Moscow (1980). Courtesy of Thelma Levy

hope that he would ever make it to America. "*Rebbenu*, since I do not know if the Rebbe would permit me to leave Russia," he said, addressing the Rebbe through Rabbi Levy's movie camera, "and since I want to have from time to time *yechidus* [a private audience] with the Rebbe, I am asking that the Rebbe should give me a *nigun* [Chassidic melody], and when I want to go into yechidus, I should have a nigun to sing."

As he watched this film, Rabbi Levy later told Rabbi Hacohen, "The Rebbe cried like a baby."

In response the Rebbe told Rabbi Levy a story about the late president of Israel, Zalman Shazar. In 1948, when he first joined Israel's new government as the minister of education, at times he did not know what to do. "So I would go into a room," he told the Rebbe, "sing the nigun of the Alter Rebbe [the melody of four stanzas, known as *"Daled bavos,"* composed by the founder of Chabad, Rabbi Schneur Zalman of Liadi] and I knew what to do."

The Rebbe concluded, "This is what he should do, too."

The Shochet

Another memorable character Rabbi Levy encountered was Nachman Roisman, in Alma-Ata, Kazahkstan, who learned at the age of 60 how to be a shochet, and built a mikvah himself in the basement of his home.

After a trip in 1980, Rabbi Levy described Avrohom Aharon Geisinsky, a shochet and mohel in Tashkent, Uzbekistan:

> He is a strong believer in G-d, a Jew full of *mesiras nefesh* [self-sacrifice for Judaism]. He is the only one left in Tashkent who knows [how to lead the] *davening* [prayers].

> What he does [for business] is illegal [since he did not work on Saturday], and his wife is very frightened. He is very strong-minded and nothing fazes him. He would very much like to leave, but he realizes that there would be no [kosher] meat left in Tashkent if he leaves.

> He is convinced that he will come to America one day. The only reason he wants to come to America is to see the Rebbe. I have yet to see the simple faith of another Jew like Avrohom Aharon. I gave him a new pair of tzitzis, and he was so pleased.

When he returned to New York, Rabbi Levy told the Rebbe about Mr. Geisinsky's strong desire to leave the Soviet Union, but the Rebbe said that it was important for him to remain until he had trained a replacement shochet.

Mrs. Levy at the gravesite of the founder of Chassidism, Rabbi Israel Baal Shem Tov (1979). In the Soviet Union the Levys visited the graves of great Chassidic leaders, many of which had not been seen in decades. Courtesy of Thelma Levy

Years later, when Mr. Geisinsky informed the Rebbe that he had trained someone to replace him as the shochet, the Rebbe told him to ask permission from a rabbi before leaving the Soviet Union. He received it and moved to Israel.

Searching for Graves

Before each trip, the Rebbe asked Rabbi Levy to visit the gravesite of his father, Rabbi Levi Yitzchak Schneerson, in Alma-Ata, Kazakhstan. The Rebbe had already immigrated to the United States when his father passed away, and had never been to his gravesite. Rabbi Levy brought photos back from those visits, and the Rebbe was very appreciative.

Rabbi Levy felt that, as a "tourist," it behooved him to visit cemeteries where various Chassidic rebbes and other Jewish leaders were buried. In Samarkand he visited two cemeteries that had been vandalized. He reasoned that the government would take better care of the graves if they saw that tourists were interested in them.

Realizing that many of Russia's Jewish cemeteries had been neglected for decades, he hired Kalman Melech Tamarin to locate and photograph a whole list of holy gravesites that were in danger of being forgotten. The photos became the only documentation of these sites, until many of them were refurbished under the guidance of Chabad "tourists" in 1988, when the Communists were becoming much more lax about monitoring tourists' movement.

Kalman

Whoever met Mr. Tamarin was immediately struck by his sincerity. In the late 1970s the Rebbe called for all of his followers to don an additional pair of tefillin every day. This second pair is known as Rabbeinu Tam tefillin, because the parchment scrolls in the boxes are arranged in the order favored by that 12th-century authority in Jewish law. The Rebbe explained that adding a daily mitzvah would bring more light into a dark world.

When Mr. Tamarin heard about the Rebbe's directive, he had only one thought: he wanted a pair of Rabbeinu Tam tefillin. "With all the difficulties inherent in keeping religion," said Rabbi Don Yoel Levy, who accompanied his father on the visit in 1980, "Kalman Melech was determined to go beyond the letter of what is required according to Jewish law."

While they were at the Tamarin home, they noticed that Mr. Tamarin's son had a black eye. When asked about the cause of the injury, the boy proudly smiled and said it was "because I am Jewish."

When Mr. Tamarin spoke to the Rebbe through the camera, he requested one thing: success in studying Chassidism and Jewish law. He told the Rebbe that he desired that "not one minute of the day should

People like Kalman Melech Tamarin (right) found in Rabbi Levy (center) a fountain of information and inspiration. On the left is one of Mr. Tamarin's children.
Courtesy of Thelma Levy

go to waste."

The Great Blessing

Before that 1980 trip, the Rebbe had instructed Rabbi Levy and his son Rabbi Don Yoel to make a point of discussing the three mitzvahs specifically for women: lighting Shabbat and holiday candles, taking *challah* by separating a piece from the dough when baking bread, and observing the laws of family purity.

At every gathering, Rabbi Levy spoke about these observances, and his son described the great blessing of having many children. One night, a young couple who were becoming more observant approached them and said with great bitterness that because of fertility issues, they had given up on having children.

"Why don't you ask the Rebbe for a *brachah*?" Rabbi Don Yoel asked.

"Who am I to ask for a brachah from the Rebbe?" the man replied.

Rabbi Don Yoel asked for copies of their medical records, and when the Levys returned to New York, they sent them to the Rebbe and to several specialists in the field. The Rebbe gave his blessing and the doctors gave their advice, which the couple followed with success.

Remain There

The dangers Rabbi Levy encountered on his trips were nothing compared to those faced by the Soviet Jews who participated in and led Chabad underground activities. Most observant Jews wanted to emigrate. But, Rabbi Levy would tell them, the Rebbe insists that unless there is an imminent threat, you should remain here and continue to strengthen Jewish observance and knowledge.

This message was especially difficult for one family to hear. A wayward car had "accidentally" hit the mother as she exited a trolley in Leningrad. A short while later, her son was beaten up coming home from school. The family knew they had been targeted by the KGB because of their involvement with Chabad. They felt that to remain in the USSR was to risk their lives and the lives of their children.

Through secret channels, the Rebbe sent a message that they should not emigrate. Nevertheless, the father applied for visas for his family. "We were turned down," he told Rabbi Levy. "I attribute this to the Rebbe's insistence that we stay."

Rabbi Levy felt the man's pain, but also understood why the Rebbe wanted him to stay. Every time Rabbi Levy visited, a group of courageous Jews would gather in the family's house to hear him speak about Torah and ask questions. Their departure could have meant the collapse of the Chabad underground in Leningrad. In the end they remained there for many years, and no further harm came to them.

When the Levys began to travel to the Soviet Union, they found mostly elderly Jews in the synagogues. In the 1980s, however, younger Jews began to attend in large numbers. Here Rabbi Levy (extreme left) studies Talmud with the local Jewish community in Riga, Latvia (June 1975). Courtesy of Thelma Levy

Youth Movement

Over the years, with the assistance and encouragement of the Rebbe's "tourists," the Chabad network in the Soviet Union grew, and many Jewish young people began to participate and organize activities and classes themselves.

Rabbi Levy marveled that in 1972 there were few young men in the shuls, but by 1978 many new faces had appeared. In a diary entry from 1980 he described a group he had spoken to in Moscow:

> We had an interesting group come; only a few are religious, but the others are very interested in Judaism. I spoke quite a bit about Yiddishkeit and about becoming more religious themselves and bringing others closer.

Rabbi Levy with a Latvian Jew in 1975. The Levys were constantly under Soviet surveillance. Their hotel rooms were bugged, often with devices hidden in the televisions. They learned that in the hotel and synagogue no sensitive information could be discussed. Messages were written on paper and then flushed down the toilet. Courtesy of Thelma Levy

Of a 1981 visit to Leningrad, he wrote:

> There were many newly observant Jews there. We only ate vegetables and fish.... I spoke and they asked me many questions. We made them happy. We told them about... love and unity among Jews....
>
> There were more than a hundred people in shul. Many, many more than there were last year.... They asked me for a proper course of study in *Chumash* [the Pentateuch]. I told them to concentrate on the *Kitzur Shulchan Aruch* [the concise code of Jewish law].... I also promised them that I will see to it that the group from Moscow will come more often to Leningrad and learn with them. We sang, and it was very lively.

Smuggling Cash

In Samarkand, Uzbekistan, there were several underground Jewish schools run by Lubavitcher chassidim. Rabbi Levy visited them and began to fund them, bringing large amounts of cash with him on each trip, which he exchanged for rubles. Smuggling money into the Soviet Union carried a stiff punishment, which added an additional element of danger to his trips.

"If you got caught by the KGB," Mrs. Levy said, "you didn't need to know what you were being caught for. You needed to know what they were claiming you were caught for. They could say whatever they wanted."

On one of his journeys to Samarkand, Rabbi Levy noticed that he was being followed more closely than on previous trips. On him he had 10,000 rubles.

Realizing that his life was in danger, when he arrived at his hotel he immediately went into the bathroom, tore up the money and flushed it down the toilet.

Sure enough, a few minutes later KGB officers knocked on the door and searched the room. Finding nothing, they left him alone.

Smuggling Out Books

On several of his trips Rabbi Levy was able to smuggle rare books and valuable Chabad manuscripts out of the Soviet Union. These precious items he gave to the Rebbe. In December 1975, Soviet authorities confiscated several manuscripts and books as Rabbi Levy was about to board his departing flight.

He turned over every stone in the effort to get them back. "These were all religious items that I brought in from Amsterdam," he wrote to the State Department. "I neglected to declare these items because I read only the front of the declaration [form]. The book has no value to anyone but myself, because it is available today in print. It has much sentimental value to me because it was written by my grandfather."

The State Department informed him that they had hit a wall of resistance to the request from the Soviets. The Soviet embassy in Washington, D.C., was of little help. "We would like to inform you that we unfortunately are not in a position to help you on the matter you are interested in because such matters are out of our embassy's competence," they wrote.

While those books were never returned, Rabbi Levy was successful in bringing many others to the United States, which otherwise might have been lost forever.

Surveillance

Rabbi Levy's claim to be a tourist did not fool the Soviet authorities. They tracked all his movements closely. Ironically, it was in synagogues that he had to be most careful what he said and did. The official religious organizations were run and strictly monitored by the government with the cooperation of the "rabbis" and presidents of the shuls.

In 1975 he described the situation:

> In the morning we went to shul [synagogue]. I learned *Chassidus* [Chassidism] before davening [prayers], and the shul was full. The word got around that I was there… [a rabbi] was there, and they all sat and listened to my learning. After the services I spoke to the congregants about Chanukah, and I gave them all Chanukah *gelt*.
>
> I told them that this was from the Rebbe, and that they should give it to their children and grandchildren in order to remind them that today is Chanukah, and… to tell them the story of Chanukah and to emphasize self-sacrifice and not to despair.
>
> I distributed about 100 new rubles.… They all asked why I don't

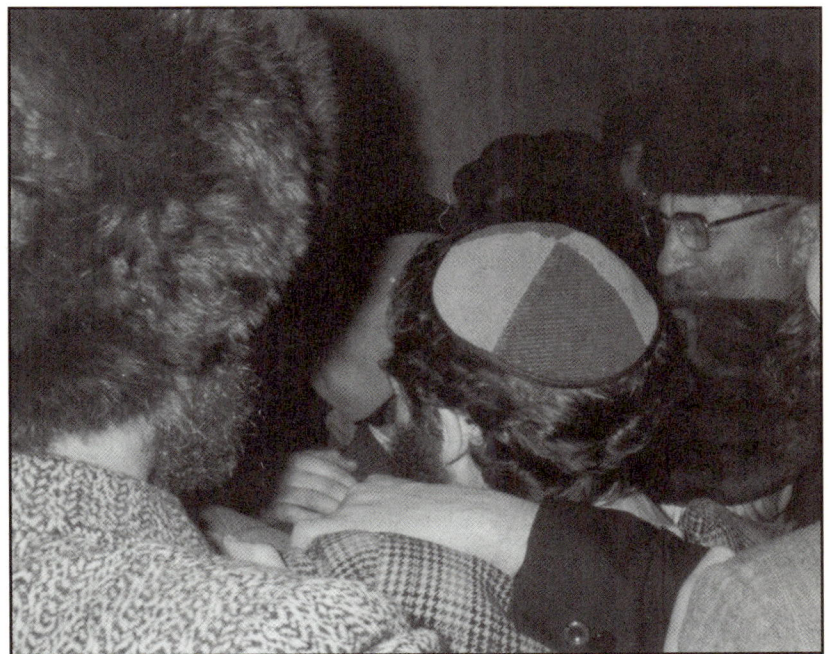

Rabbi Levy dances with young men in Tashkent, Uzbekistan (circa 1981). Courtesy of Thelma Levy

come more often.

Incidentally, [this rabbi], who has a very bad reputation as an informer, claims he was there to look at the mikvah, because he is going to rebuild the mikvah in Kiev.... I think they sent him to Leningrad to keep an eye on me.... [This rabbi] accompanied me the whole time I was in the shul.

On several occasions the government used his status as a tourist as an excuse to spy on him. Intourist, the official state travel agency of the Soviet Union, was staffed by KGB officers. In 1978 he recorded this incident:

When I arrived at the hotel, the KGB were waiting for me. A young fellow ran into the Intourist [office] and reported that I arrived, and another ran out to see me. I went up to the room.

As soon as I got into my room, an Intourist girl together with the fellow knocked on my door. They came in and they wanted to know where I was [that day].... How could I get around without knowing Russian? Is it true I have relatives in Alma-Ata? If I came to visit, why did I say I was a tourist? I am the guest of Intourist, and I had no business going around on my own.

I didn't answer them. Later I walked out of the hotel and took a walk. Two fellows, one of them was the one who ran into the Intourist to report I was there, followed me wherever I went. I turned around and walked over to them and told them to stop following me.

Rabbi Levy became aware that his hotel room was bugged when he privately complained about a problem with the room and it was fixed shortly afterward. Once, in Tashkent, when he had gone to synagogue and left Mrs. Levy and their son Eliezer at the hotel, two people knocked on the door and said they were there to fix the television. Eliezer said that no one ever complained about the device.

"Well somebody did, perhaps your father," one of the men replied.

The young boy knew that his father would not complain about the television, since he had no interest in watching it. But the people at the door were adamant. "It does not matter; we are here to fix it."

"Nobody complained, nobody said there was anything wrong," Eliezer retorted, and he closed the door.

"You know what they wanted to do?" Mrs. Levy said years later. "The bug, to eavesdrop, most probably was broken and they wanted to fix it."

In truth, Mrs. Levy said, it would not have made a difference, because the only place they spoke was in the street. Conversations in the room took place on paper, and every paper was flushed down the toilet.

Rabbi Don Yoel and his father were once walking on the street when they noticed someone following them. Rabbi Levy turned around and

Rabbi Levy brought with him ritual items like mezuzahs, which were difficult to obtain in the Soviet Union. Here he affixes a mezuzah on the new apartment of Zalman and Svetta Lifshitz in Tashkent, Uzbekistan (1975). Courtesy of Thelma Levy

stared at the person. The man realized that he was spotted and began to run away. Rabbi Levy ran after him, and the man disappeared into a large department store. Rabbi Levy went in and asked if anyone had seen him. As was typical in the Soviet Union, everybody made believe they saw nothing. "He must have run out a back door," Rabbi Levy told his son.

Once, after KGB officers followed Rabbi Levy to a wine factory in Samarkand, where he had gone to see if it would be possible to produce kosher wine there, he was called into the Intourist office. "Why did you want to go to a wine factory?" they asked. Just out of curiosity, he told them.

"For hours they questioned him," Mrs. Levy recalled. "Over and over again, with the same question, hoping to trip him and that he would slip in one of his answers. But they didn't know who they were dealing with." In the end they just let him go.

No Shadow?

When the Levys were in Moscow in 1980 they stayed at the Rossiya Hotel, which was run by the Russian government. For the Friday night services they went to the Moscow Choral Synagogue, known as Archipova. For Shabbat morning, Rabbi Don Yoel planned on walking to the Marina Roscha Synagogue, which was over an hour's walk from the hotel, while his father would return to the Choral Synagogue.

Early the next morning Rabbi Don Yoel met Sasha, one of the Chabad operatives in the city, who worked in the Moscow post office, and the two walked to synagogue. Strangely, the streets were deserted. "To my shock," Rabbi Don Yoel recalled, "I did not see any 'shadows' following us."

During their debriefing in the Rebbe's office back in New York, the younger Rabbi Levy mentioned the incident. "There is no such situation like that," the Rebbe said. "Surely the KGB knew your every step. The way they work is that they do not follow every time; rather, they have moles planted in the Jewish community. You speak to a few people, one of them tells the other, and then to another, until it reaches one of the KGB agents, who reports it to a higher official."

Visits Expand

For a long time, Rabbi Levy was alone in his work to aid Soviet Jews. "There was no one going there during those years," said Rabbi Shmuel Lew, a Chabad leader in London, who in the 1980s traveled to the Soviet Union several times and helped arrange for others to go as well. "Whoever would go would never stop hearing about Rabbi Levy, whom they all considered to be their rabbi and mentor."

Svetta Lifshitz remembers Rabbi Levy's visits vividly. It was 11 p.m.

when the Levys first knocked on the Lifshitzes' door. "Knocks on the doors at night usually meant trouble," she recalled. They said they had a message from Zalman's mother, Genya, who was living in the United States. Mrs. Lifshitz and her husband invited them into the small apartment, and from there grew a friendship spanning close to a decade. "I could not understand what he was doing there," she said. "That is the first time I saw a foreigner, and an observant one. It was a miracle to see him at the door."

In a letter from Tashkent, Uzbekistan, Mr. Lifshitz expressed his joy upon hearing that the Levys would be returning to the Soviet Union. "We were very happy to get to know that your wife and you are going to make a tour of Russia," he wrote. "We always recollect with pleasure the hours you spent with us, and we'll be very happy to meet again with your wife after a long interruption."

At the time of Rabbi Levy's visits there were no longer any qualified rabbis in Moscow or Leningrad. Jews throughout Russia waited until he came to ask their questions in Jewish law; he once wrote that he was "bombarded" with questions.

Baking matzah for Pesach was one of the few public traditions that Soviet Jews managed to maintain. In 1981, Rabbi Levy described the process in his diary:

> When I came into the shul, they were baking matzahs, and they invited me in to see the baking. There were several things wrong with the baking. After the davening [prayers], I took [one man] into the bakery and I showed him [the proper way to bake]; he promised me he would take care of it.

As the leader of the Jewish underground, Chabad was the group most hated by Communist officials. A known connection to Chabad put operatives at greater risk. The organization Lishkas Ezras Achim (the Bureau to Aid Brethren) was not officially affiliated with Chabad, though it was run under the Rebbe's direction. In the late 1970s they began sending many individuals to the Soviet Union for the purpose of aiding Jews there. Most of the "tourists" were sent in groups through the organization, and had no direct contact with the Rebbe before their trips, though afterwards they would submit lengthy reports to him.

Rabbi Levy, on the other hand, the Rebbe trusted not to reveal his affiliation. He always received direct instructions from the Rebbe and messages to bring back to the Soviet Union. Thus, many people would confer with Rabbi Levy before they traveled to the USSR. He was always happy to assist anyone interested in the cause, including those not affiliated with Chabad.

Working Together

"After seeing my father's success," said Rabbi Don Yoel, "other groups came to ask how they too could be involved in helping Russian Jewry." Rabbi Levy welcomed the help. The plight of Soviet Jews was such that there could never be enough done to aid them. In the late 1980s, however, one of the groups began actively competing with Chabad.

Rabbi Mordechai Neustadt of the Perfect Travel agency arrived in the Soviet Union in the mid-1970s intent on helping Jews. But without any Chabad connections, he had little success. "During that time no one really went to Russia," he recalled. "The few who wanted to go, and were connected, found out about others who went."

Rabbi Neustadt quickly learned that he could not speak to just anyone in the shul, and that he needed to be constantly on the lookout for KGB agents. He approached Rabbi Levy, who spent many hours painstakingly describing his methods, and provided contacts Rabbi Neustadt could trust.

"I wanted to hear from him who I could talk to," Rabbi Neustadt said. "We discussed the names of those in Russia that I have nothing to worry about being in contact with. Every piece of knowledge was important for our future work."

A large crowd listens to a class by Rabbi Levy, 1981. Courtesy of Thelma Levy

One of the names Rabbi Levy gave Rabbi Neustadt was Ilya Essas, a refusenik with whom Rabbi Levy had a special connection. He had met Mr. Essas when he was just becoming interested in Judaism and had convinced him to begin observing Shabbat and the laws of family purity. Mr. Essas eventually became involved in Chabad activities.

Rabbi Neustadt went on to establish the Vaad L'Hatzolas Nidchei Yisroel. In the 1980s the Vaad, as it became known, began sending groups to the Soviet Union for the purpose of teaching Torah and strengthening Jewish observance.

Around this time Mr. Essas began to organize Torah classes in his city on behalf of the Vaad, which were competing with similar Chabad events. Things became contentious, and the Chabad operatives felt that the two organizations should work together, rather than against each other. In a diary entry from 1981, Rabbi Levy described a farbrengen Mr.

Essas attended in Moscow:

> Essas came to the farbrengen. I spoke about love of fellow Jews and unity and spreading Judaism. That everyone should work together for one cause… to bring close as many people as possible. We also spoke about going to other cities, and [I urged them] to do what they can. I told them that all the money they need for all this is available, and whenever they need money they should speak to Getcha.
>
> I left Getcha 10,000 rubles for this purpose, and [told them that] whenever they need more they should contact me. Essas agreed to work with our group on the projects.

With the average salary in the Soviet Union around 160 rubles a week at the time, the sums Rabbi Levy provided were a huge relief for the Jewish community.

Rabbi Levy Disappears

Knowing how closely Rabbi Levy was watched, Mrs. Levy worried continuously when he traveled to the USSR alone. Rabbi Levy made an effort to keep her updated on his whereabouts, but communication was sometimes difficult. Once he was delayed in the USSR, and asked a tourist who was on his way to Paris to notify Mrs. Levy that he would be late. "I want to thank you for making arrangements to notify my wife about my delay in Russia," he wrote in a January 1979 letter.

One year he was scheduled to visit a food plant in Europe and then fly to the Soviet Union. After his visit he planned to fly to Israel, as he had done often in the past.

At the time Rabbi Don Yoel was living in Israel with his wife, Malka, and their children. He went to the airport to greet his father and bring him to his home in the city of Kiryat Malachi, but Rabbi Levy was not on the plane.

"I was petrified," Mrs. Levy said. "He was missing in the Soviet Union. This was an emergency." She immediately called Rabbi Levy's close friend Amos Bunim, who told her to call the State Department. It was December 25, however, and the United States consulate in New York was closed. When she called the consulate in Washington, DC, the machine stated that the office was closed until Tuesday.

For the Levy family, "the entire Shabbos was literally hell."

After Shabbat, Rabbi Levy called and told them that he was in Paris and was okay.

He had been arrested at the airport in Moscow on the grounds that he was smuggling ritual items out of the Soviet Union. In his possession were various manuscripts and a set of candlesticks belonging to a family that was emigrating. They had asked Rabbi Levy to take them, on the assumption that the authorities would be more lenient with a tourist.

In the end he was cleared of any crime, and the government offered to put him on a plane the next day, which was Shabbat. "You will not put me on a plane, because I will not go," he told them.

Instead he took the last plane to Paris on Friday. He arrived shortly before Shabbat started in the city, checked into a hotel near the airport, and for the next 24 hours lived on an apple and one matzah that he had left over from his trip.

Learning to Push

In 1981 the Levys' youngest son, Eliezer Yitzchak, was 15 years old and already an enthusiastic Lubavitcher. He made every effort to attend the Rebbe's Shabbat farbrengens, the Chassidic gatherings at Chabad headquarters, despite the fact that the family lived in Borough Park, a long walk from 770. When a farbrengen was announced ahead of time, the Levys would spend Shabbat in Crown Heights with Rabbi Don Yoel so that Rabbi Levy and his son could attend.

Eliezer, however, would spend every Shabbat there, in case a last-minute farbrengen would be announced on Shabbat morning, as often happened. Before their 1981 Chanukah trip to the Soviet Union, the Levys wanted to remain home together with their son, but Eliezer wanted to be in Crown Heights as usual.

Early Thursday morning Mrs. Levy made her way to Chabad headquarters and waited for the Rebbe to arrive. When he got there he greeted her warmly, and she asked if there would be a farbrengen that Shabbat. Yes, he said, there would be.

The Rebbe, surprised at the question, asked her, "Would you be attending?" No, she responded, she did not come to the farbrengens (the question was for her son's benefit). The Rebbe asked if perhaps it was too difficult to hear from the women's section, but she said the reason was that she "did not like the pushing."

With a broad smile, the Rebbe said, "So many years in Lubavitch, and you have not learned how to push?" He told her that she should come, adding, "I hope that over the next few days you learn how to push."

That Shabbat she vied for a seat up front, and made a point of attending farbrengens from then on.

Chanukah Trip

In a private audience before they left, the Rebbe gave Rabbi Levy money and told him to exchange it for rubles and distribute it to Soviet Jews on the Rebbe's behalf as Chanukah gelt. "The Rebbe does not need to give. I could give from my own money," Rabbi Levy said. "People entrust me with their money to give it to Jews in the Soviet Union," the Rebbe responded.

The Rebbe also asked the Levys to collect names of Jewish children in the Soviet Union so that they could participate in the children's Torah scroll being written in Jerusalem. Rabbi Levy's son Eliezer collected 1,047 names, and each child had a letter dedicated in their merit.

As the Soviet oppression lessened, the Jewish community gained courage. In 1981 the Chabad underground staged a play for the Levys. Courtesy of Thelma Levy

During the Chanukah trip Rabbi and Mrs. Levy visited an illegal Jewish kindergarten in Moscow. Mrs. Levy recalled how the children were absolutely fearless, and lit the menorah in the window.

For many years Muscovites recalled Rabbi Levy standing on the podium in the center of the synagogue, giving out Chanukah gelt from the Rebbe.

Visa Denied

By the 1980s, Rabbi Levy had become a prime suspect of the KGB, and he began to rely on others to smuggle ritual items into the country. He continued to visit as a tourist, however, teaching Torah and encouraging Jews in their observance. A diary entry from this period describes

Even after he was banned from the USSR, Rabbi Levy maintained a close connection to the Jews he knew there. Here he greets Rabbi Yitzchak Kogan (sitting, second from right), who left the Soviet Union in 1987, upon his arrival in Vienna.
Courtesy of Thelma Levy

his arrival in the Moscow airport:

> Things haven't changed any. I brought very few religious articles, for my own use only. They still searched us thoroughly. They took me into a room and had me empty my pockets. They found nothing. Nevertheless, one young man threatened me that if I bring any more of these religious items they will not allow me into the country again. There must be superiors who can reprimand these youngsters for their behavior.

"The later trips were more exciting," Mrs. Levy recalled. "It was obvious they were on to us. It was obvious that they were aware. You didn't know who was an informer, who was a government man, even… people who came to daven [pray] three times a day."

On a subsequent visit Rabbi Levy was in Tashkent, when he was brought into the local KGB office:

> Just before we got ready to leave Tashkent, the KGB called me in to tell me I didn't behave in Tashkent.
>
> They have a declaration from the Jews in the shul that I spoke against the government. [They told me that] I said that the government is oppressing the Jews, and that Russian children know nothing about their religion.
>
> I laughed; they asked me why I was laughing. I said, "The youngest Jew was 75 years old, and that was hardly the place for me to stir up a revolution. Whoever wrote the declaration didn't know what I was talking about. He must be senile."
>
> They said, "We have a declaration."
>
> I told them, "Then tell me who he is and I will prove to you that he is senile. If you want, I can give you a declaration to that effect."
>
> They said, "Next time you speak, speak so they can't make any mistakes."
>
> We left back for Leningrad. The group knew I was coming, so several of them came to say goodbye. They all begged us to come back soon. Many of them cried.... They repeated several times to me that we should come back soon. Everybody asked for the Rebbe's blessing that the redemption should be very soon.

"When Rabbi Levy interacted with us quietly, the KGB kept their angst to themselves," said Rabbi Nachman Tamarin, Kalman's son, who today is a rabbi in Zhitomer, Ukraine. "However, when there was an open display of interaction, they were not too happy."

Rabbi Levy's next application for a visa to the Soviet Union was denied. As in the past, he reached out to politicians who he thought could

After the Soviet Union collapsed, Rabbi Don Yoel Levy traveled to Russia to see what he could do to aid the production of kosher food there. Here Rabbi Don Yoel (standing, left) reviews the matzah-making process in St. Petersburg (1994).
Courtesy of OK Kosher

intercede on his behalf, but this time all efforts were fruitless. In a May 1986 letter he wrote, "I have personally made several applications for visas to visit Russia and have been refused. It's been many years since I had the opportunity to visit the beautiful city of Leningrad and the wonderful people who live there."

Though Rabbi Levy was deeply disappointed that his trips could not continue, the Rebbe saw the situation in a positive light. "The fact that they don't let you in [to the Soviet Union] is not because anything is lacking by you," he told Rabbi Levy at a farbrengen. "On the contrary, it is because of your virtues and what you accomplished there."

Quiet Diplomacy

Rabbi Levy kept in contact with the Jews he had met in the Soviet Union and closely followed all the efforts to aid them. Many would send him greetings and questions through the Chabad emissaries who continued his work.

"He knew how to deal with the people. He had great success; he gave focus to these Jews' search for Yiddishkeit," Rabbi Lew said. "He was like a father to all those people there. They were not an organized community with a support system. They were under severe pressure, without someone that could unite them from inside.... He was the one that kept them together. He was their leader."

In 1986, the Rebbe sent a "tourist" to build a mikvah in Moscow's Marina Roscha Synagogue, one of the centers of Chabad clandestine activities. With the help of some 15 members of the Chabad underground, the mikvah was dug and, within a short 16 days, completed.

It did not take long for the KGB to discover it, however. They immediately filled the mikvah with sand and then poured a layer of cement over the entire room, using the excuse that it did not meet the government standards for hygiene.

When Rabbi Levy heard about the closing of the mikvah, he was furious. He wrote to the Rebbe that he wanted to get the story written up in all the newspapers, hoping that an international uproar would convince the Soviets to capitulate and reopen the mikvah.

The Rebbe's response was based on years of experience with the Communist authorities. Quiet diplomacy will be more effective, he told Rabbi Levy: "Stand strong that it should not be closed; however, do not do so aggressively or the like. Rather, stress to them that they enhanced its hygiene (cleanliness and the like), since the authorities demand this for the good of the users."

Rabbi Levy followed the Rebbe's advice. Permission was eventually granted, and the authorities re-dug the mikvah.

When Rabbi Yitzchak Kogan was granted permission to leave the Soviet Union (he later returned after the fall of Communism), the Rebbe asked Rabbi Levy to go meet him in Vienna, Austria. Rabbi Levy demurred, however, saying he had already scheduled a trip to Asia during that time. "Even so, I ask that he should cancel his trip," the Rebbe told his aide. "I want him to represent me at Kogan's welcoming." Rabbi Levy canceled the trip and went to Vienna.

The Last Word

When the Soviet Union dissolved in 1991, the underground study groups and synagogues established by Rabbi Levy and those who followed his lead were still in place. In the new atmosphere of religious freedom they grew and blossomed into the extensive Jewish infrastructure that exists in these countries today.

Russia's Chief Rabbi Berel Lazar said that Rabbi Levy had a great impact on Soviet Jewry in the two decades before Communism fell. "He was very attached to the people," he said. "They felt that they had with him a personal connection."

This connection was made possible because Rabbi Levy kept returning to the country, while others came once and never returned, the rabbi said. "He kept up with the people and always followed up with them. This made an incredible impression."

Not long after the Iron Curtain fell, Rabbi Don Yoel Levy went to Russia to assist in kosher food production. "The training I received from the Rebbe and my father is that love of our fellow Jews is utmost in our minds," he said at the time. "That should be the guiding light—not to go to Russia to see how much vodka we can import with the OK name on the bottles, but to see how we can help the Jews there."

On Rabbi Don Yoel's first visit, he went to the matzah bakery in St. Petersburg. He told Rabbi Yefim Levitis, the city's chief rabbi since 1980, what corrections needed to be made in the baking process. "I know, I know," Rabbi Levitis replied. "Ten years ago when your father was here, he also told me these exact issues needed to be corrected."

EPILOGUE

DETERMINED TO THE END

By Rabbi Menachem Hacohen

At the end of 1959, I was planning a trip to the United States, and my brother asked his friend Rabbi Berel Levy if he would host me during my stay. He readily and happily agreed.

My views on Israel and Zionism could not have been more different than my host's. I was the rabbi of the Histadrut, Israel's organization of trade unions, which was affiliated with Mapai, the country's center-left party. Mapai was then the dominant political force in Israel [it later merged with the Labor Party] and was utterly opposed to the agenda of the religious parties.

Berel, as we called him, was the nephew of Rabbi Chaim Avraham Dov Ber Levine, known as the Malach, the Angel, and had imbibed his uncle's passionate views on religion and aversion to Zionism from an early age. Yet, despite our differences he greeted me warmly, with open arms. Over our years of friendship I saw how his good heart led him to seek the positive in others. It was our first meeting, yet after an hour we felt like long-lost friends.

Berel was naturally a people's person, but there was more to it than that. He had absorbed the unconditional love for every Jew that his rebbe, Rabbi Menachem Mendel Schneerson, was so famous for. When he picked me up at Idlewild

Rabbi Menachem Hacohen recalls Rabbi Levy (above) as a man who had strong opinions, but never held hatred in his heart. Courtesy of OK Kosher

Airport [later known as JFK] he proudly told me, "I arranged for you to have an audience with the Rebbe at two in the morning." He dropped me off at 770 Eastern Parkway, and promised to pick me up when I was done.

Suffice it to say that the Rebbe received me courteously, was well prepared for the audience and took great interest in my work. On the desk were some twenty *Machanayim* magazines (I was an editor of the publication). The Rebbe commented on the various articles and the pictures used. He shared his thoughts on Israeli life with me, some of which I agreed with and some of which I didn't.

Toward the end of our audience the Rebbe asked me why I had come to the United States. At the time – and to a certain extent until today – everything in Israel was connected to political parties. That was the way it was also with the newly founded *moshavim*, agricultural cooperative villages, across Israel.

I explained to the Rebbe that in Israel there were two kinds of villages. Two hundred and forty-two were affiliated with Mapai, and sixty with the religious Hapoel HaMizrachi party. The Hapoel HaMizrachi villages had synagogues and Torah scrolls but not much livelihood. The Mapai villages had livelihood but no synagogues. This was because the minister of religion was Hapoel HaMizrachi and the minister of agriculture was affiliated with Mapai.

"I've heard that in America many synagogues are shuttered or on the verge of closing," I told the Rebbe, "and I wanted to see if I could bring Torah scrolls to be used on the moshavim that do not have any."

Without a moment's hesitation the Rebbe asked his aide to give me four Torah scrolls. There was no ceremony, no publicity. I understood then that the Rebbe did not recognize political divisions.

When he heard that I had received four Torahs from the Rebbe, Berel immediately donated another four scrolls from a synagogue in Brooklyn where he had served as rabbi for a short period of time. I had just arrived in the country and I was already well on my way to achieving my goal.

Though on a personal level he was warm and accepting, Berel was unbending in his religious beliefs. During my visit he made no effort to hide his disgust for the secular culture of the Jewish state. He ticked off a list of transgressions: Israelis were not keeping kosher, observing Shabbat, etc. It was clear that his uncle had influenced him deeply.

I told him that he did not have a right to such strong opinions without first visiting Israel. He agreed, and when he came to Israel he fell in love with the land and its inhabitants, though he remained unhappy about the lack of observance.

Though we disagreed, I respected Berel's convictions and his fearlessness in expressing them. His experience leaving home at a young age to live with his uncle had taught him to stand up for what he believed, even in the face of overwhelming pressure (in that case, his parents' displeasure).

That experience had also hardened him against physical discomfort. He knew how to live on very little and to be happy with what he had. It was my feeling that he didn't like money. If he had any in his pocket, by the time he came home he had already given it away. His wife had to keep an eye on their bank account, otherwise they might have been paupers.

Berel had always been very careful about the kashrus of his food, which made his entrance into the field of kosher supervision seem natural to me. As described in the book, he began by purchasing the supervision of my uncle, Rabbi Hersch Kohn.

It turned out that Berel's character and life experiences were perfectly suited to the business. His exacting standards, his outspokenness and his willingness to endure inconvenience and discomfort all helped him build the OK into an enormously successful enterprise.

His personal warmth and kindness aided him as well. The companies he certified loved him, but they also knew he was not a pushover. When problems arose, he was not hesitant to pick up the phone and deal with them head-on. If that did not work, he would use the OK's publication to inform the public.

When I asked him why he found it necessary to travel all over the world personally inspecting factories—he could have easily employed someone else to do it—he said, "I want to see the places myself. It is my approval. I need to make

It was said that Rabbi Levy never arrived home with money in his pocket, having given a donation to anyone who asked. He was especially fond of supporting Jewish education, and, in addition to funding schools from Cleveland to Lakewood, helped purchase the land for the Beth Rivkah day school. Here, Rabbi Levy is honored by the Educational Institute Oholei Torah in Brooklyn. Courtesy of Educational Institute Oholei Torah

sure that it is kosher." He devoted himself to the supervision heart and soul.

Berel brought that same devotion and courage to his missions in the Soviet Union. I was part of an Israeli delegation to the Soviet Union in 1982, during a period when there were no official diplomatic relations between the two countries. Whom did I meet? There was Berel, in the synagogue, proudly speaking to people and distributing gifts of money in honor of Chanukah. If you understood how dangerous that was at the time, you would not be able to comprehend how it was possible. It was an act of bravery, of self-sacrifice.

Even in that hostile environment Berel maintained his zeal for Jewish observance. With me in the delegation was a left-wing Knesset member. She decided to take some photos in the synagogue we visited on Shabbat. Seeing her, Berel could not understand how an Israeli official could publicly desecrate the Sabbath. He admonished her on her blatant disregard for Jewish tradition in a synagogue where people had self-sacrifice to come and congregate on the holy day.

Unfortunately, Berel's success became a liability. Seeing that his supervision was trusted by a larger segment of the Jewish community, companies began to choose the OK over the OU and other certifiers. This created a lot of resentment among Berel's competitors, which found expression in the "vinegar scandal." It is my belief that the episode took an enormous toll on him and ultimately hastened his death.

Berel and I came from different worlds, yet we shared a very special friendship. Throughout my tenure in public life I met few people like him. I miss him greatly.

Rabbi Menachem Hacohen is the rabbi of Israel's moshavim. He was a member of the Israeli Knesset for fourteen years, and was the chief rabbi of Romania from 1997 to 2011. He has authored nine books. Today, he serves as vice-chair of the Conference for Jewish Material Claims against Germany, and is on the board of the American Jewish Joint Distribution Committee (JDC). He lives in Jerusalem.

APPENDIX I

RABBI LEVY EXPLAINS

Bernard Levy

Is Dairy Bread Permissible?

The Jewish Homemaker, April-May 1981

The Gemorah says in Pesachim 36a, "It was taught, dough must not be kneaded with milk, and if one does knead it with milk, the whole loaf is forbidden, because it leads to sin. (One may come to eat it with meat). Rabina said, '[When made] like the eye of an ox, it is permitted.'" Rashi comments: When it is very small like the eye of an ox, it is eaten at one time and not kept for later, and one does not have time to forget that it was cooked with milk.

Shulchan Aruch Yoreh Deah devoted a complete *siman* [chapter] with three *s'ifim* [paragraphs] to this subject. The title is Shelo Lalush Issah B'chalav – One should not knead dough with milk. I wish to quote the Bais Yosef, "One should not knead dough with milk, and perhaps he might come to eat it with meat. If he kneads it with milk, the bread is forbidden even to be eaten alone. If only a small piece was baked, where it is eaten all at one time, or if the form of the bread was changed so that it is recognizable and one will not eat it with meat, it is permissible."

The Pischei Tshuva III on the siman states, quoting the Tshuvos Mahrit: "Changing the form of the bread only helps when a private individual bakes for himself, but not a commercial baker." A change in the bread only helps, he continues, when the change is made at the time of baking, where the bread was not *assur* (forbidden). Once the bread is forbidden, a change coming later does not remove the *issur* (prohibition). The Gilyon Marsha states that it does not help to make a change after the baking even to cut out the word "milk" on the bread.

One can easily deduce from all this that if the word *dairy* is printed on the package, it is useless and certainly forbidden. If the word *dairy* on the bread doesn't help, the word *dairy* on the package certainly doesn't help.

In recent years more and more *machshirim* are giving supervision on bread baked with milk and are ignoring an explicit Halacha in Shulchan Aruch. It seems that nothing can be done about the machshirim; the customers, however, should be aware of the law. If anyone tells you that a renowned rabbi says it is permissible, ask them for this in writing from the renowned rabbi and let us see how he can refute the above.

A rabbinical organization which is trying very hard to give *hechsherim* once thought of giving a hechsher on dairy bread. Hagaon Rabbi Moshe Feinstein, *shlita*, personally contacted them and told them that this would be the wrong thing to do.

One must be familiar with this law so that he may be careful to do everything in accordance with Jewish law.

What Is Glatt Kosher?

The Jewish Homemaker, January-February 1970

I am asked repeatedly by observant and non-observant Jews to explain the significance of glatt kosher and how it is different from "regular" kosher meats. Why, in recent years, has glatt kosher become so popular? Hotels and caterers no longer advertise just "kosher," but they advertise glatt kosher. Most of the butcher stores in the religious sections of New York display signs that say "glatt kosher" and do not display the name of the rabbi who supervises the store.

This matter has brought about much confusion in Orthodox Jewish life. Many religious Jews will not eat in the homes of other religious Jews because of the meats and chicken used in these homes. It is my intention to clarify this matter as much as possible, and for you, the reader, to draw your own conclusions.

In this article, I will attempt as much as possible to restrict my remarks to facts rather than to opinion. First, allow me to explain the meaning of glatt kosher. Kosher meat is slaughtered by a *shochet* who is ordained by a rabbi and trained by another shochet. Besides knowing the laws of kosher slaughtering and having the practical knowledge, a shochet must be a G-d-fearing individual in his private and public life. This should be noticeable by his conduct and appearance.

When slaughtering animals, in addition to properly slaughtering the animal, the shochet inspects the lungs of the animal to make sure it has no adhesions or other blemishes, which, according to Jewish law, may be non-kosher. When an adhesion is removed, and the lung is not punctured, the animal is kosher. According to other opinions in *halacha* (Jewish law), the animal is not kosher. If someone wishes to be more stringent in his observances, he will not accept any meat from animals with adhesions; he will use only glatt-kosher meat. This means meat which according to *all* opinions is kosher.

Forty years ago, glatt kosher was practically unheard of in America. Religious observant Jews were careful to buy meat from observant butchers upon whom they felt they could rely completely. The butcher was particular in his purchase of meat. He made sure that the meat came from a slaughterhouse where all the *shochtim* fulfilled all the requirements that I mentioned above. Others, who were not as particular, relied upon any kosher butcher who had rabbinic supervision. In those years there were very few butcher stores operated by strictly religious Jews. I don't think that there were any butcher shops who sold only glatt-kosher meats.

A few years later, a shochet from New Jersey opened a butcher shop in Williamsburg, and he was the pioneer of glatt kosher meat. He slaughtered the animals in a slaughterhouse in New Jersey. The animals belonged to the slaughterhouse so there was no problem of one person being the shochet and the butcher. This is questionable according to halacha only if the shochet owns the animal. Torah-observant Jews began purchasing this meat for two reasons. First and foremost, because they knew the shochet to be a G-d-fearing individual, though they were not particularly interested in the meat being glatt. Secondly, to a smaller measure, because one had an opportunity to be stricter in his observance and eat meat which is kosher according to all opinions.

After the Second World War, when many immigrants came from Romania, Hungary and Czechoslovakia together with their *rebbeim*, and also with the increase in the numbers of American Torah-observant Jews because of the growth of *yeshivos* and *mesivtos* in America, glatt kosher became more popular.

At the beginning, all glatt was restricted to particular groups. There were three or four groups, the Zehlemer, the Lubavitcher and the Satmar. The shochtim were chassidim or disciples of the above-mentioned rebbeim and were under their jurisdiction of a rav designated by them. Of course, shochtim of this caliber are noticeably G-d-fearing individuals.

In recent years, owners of slaughterhouses who never before marked their meat glatt began doing so. The shochtim slaughtering in these slaughterhouses are not under the jurisdiction of the groups mentioned above. As previously stated, the majority who purchase glatt do so because of the status of the shochtim more so than because the meat is glatt kosher. It seems to me that the above-mentioned groups of rebbeim and rabbonim have made a mistake by popularizing their products as glatt, but should have sold their products as Zehlemer shechita or Lubavitcher shechita, so that the customer who is interested would know where his meat is coming from.

I recommend therefore for those who are interested in glatt kosher that when they make a reservation in a glatt kosher hotel or buy meat in a glatt kosher butcher shop, they should inquire as to whose shechita they are purchasing.

You occasionally hear somebody saying, "We use only glatt kosher chickens." This is ridiculous because there is no such thing. A shochet does not inspect the lungs of a chicken for adhesions as he does cattle. One does, however, need a shochet for chickens as well; and the qualifications of a shochet for chickens are the same as the qualifications of a shochet for meat. Therefore the above-mentioned groups have their shochtim slaughtering chickens as well.

Most chickens today are slaughtered in "mass production" by large companies. Several of these companies have the chickens slaughtered and made kosher so that the customer has only to cook it. In the New York area there are two large and well-known processors who sell eviscerated and kosher-made chickens. In both of these places, there are two types of shechita, regular shechita and one of the above-mentioned shechitos, namely the Satmar and one called the Margarettener. Most of the glatt-kosher butchers sell chickens from these shechitos. I hope that this gives some clarification to this matter.

[Addition from the *Jewish Homemaker*, February-March 1975]

Again, I wish to remark that there are many butcher stores, restaurants and hotels who advertise glatt kosher and have no reliable supervision, or no supervision at all. In many cases, the proprietors of these establishments are not even observant in their own private lives; and still many customers are satisfied to purchase products from these stores. I therefore again state that one should be extremely cautious before purchasing meat, and should make certain that the owner of the store is a

G-d-fearing individual or that there is very reliable supervision. Do not be blinded by the low prices!

[Addition from the *Jewish Homemaker*, September-October 1977]

I wish to mention one more fact pertaining to glatt kosher. The law is that meat must be koshered within three days of shechita. If it is kept, for some reason, more than three days, it must be soaked in water within three days; and it must be soaked again after the three days before salting the meat.

Those who are strict about eating only glatt-kosher meat eat only meat that is koshered within the three days of shechita. I am stating this fact because there is much meat and sausage in America being sold as glatt although the meat is not salted within the three days of shechita.

Bishul Akum – Cooking by Non-Jews

The Jewish Homemaker, November-December 1972

The rules of *bishul akum*, the cooking of foods by a non-Jew or idolater, are little known. Bishul akum is a complicated area of kashruth, and rabbinical authorities have gone to great lengths to soften the extent of the prohibitions involved.

Stated simply, the basis for the prohibition is social: maintenance of the integrity and purity of our people. For though all the ingredients in a food may be kosher, it may not be eaten because it was prepared or served by a non-Jew. Our sages were ever aware that the stomach has been the cause of many Jewish households being lost to Judaism. Eating foods prepared by non-Jews or in their homes too often leads to eating and drinking with them, and eventually could lead to intermarriage.

With wine there was the added fear of *yayin nesech* – wines used for libation purposes (and the intent of the *akum* may be to dedicate the wine with his touch).

The Shulchan Aruch discusses various foods of gentile origin or foods handled by non-Jews. With wine we are most strict. Not only can gentile wine not be drunk, but it cannot be utilized in any fashion. Jewish wine that is touched by an idolater is forbidden because of *yayin nesech*. Non-Jews may handle sealed bottles of wine, but a bottle that was opened but is now closed cannot be handled by them. Note that a Jew who has willfully desecrated the Sabbath is considered an idolater, and his touch makes wine forbidden.

Non-intoxicating drinks and beverages like apple cider or pomegranate wine may be drunk in the company of gentiles. Beer, however, should not be drunk in gentile homes or taverns because of the danger that conviviality will lead to closer relations. Non-Jewish beer may be bought and drunk in the Jewish household.

Non-Jewish oil or honey, even if prepared in *treifa* utensils, may be used, since the flavor of meat spoils their taste rather than improves it. Milk of non-Jewish farms, unless the milking has been supervised by a Jew, should be avoided because of the fear that it has been adulterated with unclean milk. Jewish cattle may be milked by non-Jews. In the U.S. and other countries where adulteration with unclean milk is rare and illegal, non-Jewish milk is used by many. Gentile cheeses are on the disapproved list due to the use of treifa rennet. If there has been hashgacha from the outset, it may be eaten. Non-Jewish butter is permissible.

Bread baked by a gentile householder is forbidden; if produced by a non-Jewish professional baker it may be eaten in the Jewish home but not in the home of the baker. In towns where gentile and Jewish bread of equal quality are available, preference should be given to Jewish bread; in communities where there is no baker, it is permitted to use the bread of a gentile householder. Bread is considered baked by a Jew when he assists with its baking – even if the assistance is as nominal as lighting the pilot light. Of course, if the bread has non-kosher substances in it, it is not permissible in any case.

As a general rule, foods that cannot be eaten raw may not be eaten if cooked by a non-Jew. If they are not fit to be served at the "table of kings," they are permissible. Again, if the Jew helps at all with the cooking, even by putting the pot on the stove or lighting the fire, the non-Jewish domestic may do the actual cooking.

Eggs boiled by non-Jews may not be eaten; fish salted or smoked by them are allowed.

Here we have only some of the laws as outlined in the Yoreh Deah and Maimonides. They are being presented to acquaint our readers with the problem and what one must watch out for.

We have often been asked about canned fruit. Fruits that are edible raw may be eaten canned. Vegetables such as maize—corn on the cob—and potatoes are considered "not fit to be served on the table of kings" and are permissible in the aspect of *bishul akum*. However, there may be other questions involved, such as non-kosher equipment.

There is an accepted opinion that foods that are cooked by steam are permitted, and so all canned foods that are cooked in the can would be permitted. This applies to most dried cereals.

Incidentally, if you eat Grape-Nuts or any bran cereal, you should wash and make [the blessing] *Hamotzee*. Bran cereals are baked like bread, then dried and ground to tiny pieces.

This article includes corrections from the February-March 1973 issue.

Trumos and Maasros on Foods from Israel

The Jewish Homemaker, September-October 1972

I am writing this article in Israel while making arrangements for the preparation of Mazel Tov products for the coming year 5733, which is *Shmita*, the Sabbatical year. It requires special care to see that everything is done according to *halacha*.

Last year, during one of my many visits to the Holy Land, the following occurred. One of the companies under our supervision was interested in importing agricultural products from a non-religious kibbutz which grows its own olives, cucumbers and other vegetables. This kibbutz has a cannery as well, and does its own canning. In the diaspora there is not much of a problem with produce such as cucumbers and olives; in Israel, however, with food products, we must be concerned with the separation of tithes – *terumos* and *maasros*—in addition to making certain that all ingredients are kosher.

Before visiting the kibbutz, I dropped in on the local rabbi, a man in his late eighties or early nineties, and asked him if he had given the kibbutz products his hechsher. He claimed that he had not, and said that he supervised them only for Pesach. But when I visited the kibbutz I found that they had a current certification bearing the signature of the rabbi. I was never able to resolve this conflict of facts. In any event, after thorough investigation I found that no terumah or maaser had been separated.

The companies under my supervision do not purchase any of the produce of this kibbutz, which exports many of its products to the U.S. under various names. All are sold as Kosher and Kosher for Passover! They also sell pickles and olives to kosher caterers.

I am relating this to you to make you aware that if you are not sure that terumah or maaser has been set aside from Israel fruits, you are obligated to do so yourself. Let me quote from the Kashruth Directory Guide published by the Chief Rabbinate in Israel for the year 5732:

The Tithing of Israeli Fruit that Is Exported

A) When I was abroad last summer, I was often asked if in Israel they set aside trumos and maasros from agricultural products – including oranges and grapefruits – that are exported. I replied that to the best of my knowledge it is not done for all exports, which reach millions of crates and are not for only Jewish consumption, so proper tithing would be impossible. This is not a new question and it has been discussed by many. In our office we have been bombarded for a practical and legal solution to this problem. The following encompassing inquiry came from the head of an important Orthodox body in England: "With the notable increase in the quantity of fruits and vegetables from Israel reaching European markets, the question of tithing becomes more acute. Many of our constituents want to know what procedure they must follow with Israel products."

These points are thus being raised:

> a) Is it a fact that the Israeli Rabbinate does not tithe the fruit for export?
>
> b) Even if it does not, is it necessary for persons in the diaspora to tithe Israeli fruit?
>
> c) In any case, should the blessing be recited?

To all these questions, I clearly answered:

> a) The Israeli Rabbinate does not tithe its fresh fruits and vegetables which are scheduled for export. Of course it is different with preserved fruits and vegetables processed under rabbinical supervision under brand names listed in our Kashruth Guide.
>
> b) The majority of poskim say it is necessary to tithe Israeli fruit in the diaspora.
>
> c) The blessing on tithing is no deterrent to tithing itself.
>
> d) I have explained that with tithing in the diaspora, there is really not much of a problem or expense, since we follow the procedure of tithing not from the good for the bad, and that even peels could be used for tithing: anyone who peels an orange can say even without a blessing – "I hereby set aside from this my tithes as written in the order of tithing." This

is according to the Chazon Ish. Naturally, the peels must be treated as truma and should not be thrown into the garbage can, but kept together till they rot.

B) In the U.S. I was told that official Israeli government agencies claimed that all fruits and vegetables for export to the U.S. are tithed. On inquiring from these agencies I received a positive reply: that they have documents to the effect that Israel does indeed tithe all foods for export. On closer inquiry I found that the agencies were not authorized to make this statement, and sent a full report to the Institute of Citrus Marketing for full clarification. This was their reply: "…it seems that the Marketing Institute sets aside trumos and maasros only for the fruit that remains in Israel, that is, fruit that is sold to be eaten in Israel or to be processed, preserved or squeezed for juice in Israel, when most of these by-products are to be sent out of the land. The Institute does not tithe fresh fruits that are exported."

C) We have made an effort with various agencies to arrange for the tithing of fruits that are marked for export, especially when this is so inexpensive (since we do not tithe on the principle of from the good for the bad). But we got nowhere, and the fresh fruits that are sent from Israel to other lands are not tithed at all.

Products with the OK and OU have been checked and have had trumos and maasros separated from them. However, if you want to make sure, it is not too difficult to follow the procedure in the quoted excerpt above.

Blood Spots in Eggs

The Jewish Homemaker, November-December 1976

Eggs and milk produced by non-kosher fowl or animals are forbidden. When purchasing eggs from a market, you do not have to suspect that the eggs are not kosher, because most eggs come from kosher fowl. Unless of course you have genuine cause to be suspicious, you must be completely convinced that the eggs are kosher. For instance, eggs that are imported from countries that market non-kosher eggs, or eggs that are not rounded on one side and pointed on the other. Although the latter is not a definite indication of a kosher egg, if an egg is equally rounded on both sides it is definitely not kosher.

An egg must be laid naturally. If a chicken loses an egg in an unnatural way, such as a knock on the back and the egg is still connected with the ovary, it is considered *ever min hachai* – a limb cut off a living animal.

Eggs found in chickens, whether they have a shell or not, are considered meat and must be salted after soaking, just like chicken. This is, of course, only if it is produced from a kosher slaughtered chicken. If it is found in a non-slaughtered chicken, it is *treif*. Needless to say, such eggs should not be eaten together with dairy. These eggs are called "ova." When koshering such eggs, they should not come in contact with meat or its juice, and should be put on the topmost part of the salting board.

According to the Torah, blood in an egg is prohibited if the blood is found on the *kesher* – knot within the egg. According to our sages, all blood spots on eggs are forbidden. In practice, therefore, any blood spot found on an egg makes the egg not kosher. The spot must be red. If a yellowish spot is found, the egg is permissible. If the speck is brown, the egg should be shown to an experienced person. An egg may not be eaten even if the blood spot is removed.

A person is permitted to eat a raw egg and sip it from the shell. He may also cook an egg in its shell without examining it first, because most eggs contain no blood spots. However, when taking a raw egg from its shell for frying, cooking or baking, or even eating it raw, examination of the egg is necessary. If you do not examine the egg, it amounts to deliberately ignoring the possibility of a blood spot. In other words, where examining it is impossible or where one forgot to examine the egg, one may rely upon the fact that the majority of eggs do not contain blood spots. Where possible, one must examine eggs.

If one finds a blood spot while eating eggs, he must stop eating them immediately and remove whatever remains in his mouth and ask a *shailah* [halachic query] about the utensils he used for the egg. If a person has cooked an egg with a blood spot, the pot in which he cooked the egg is not kosher. If two or more kosher eggs are cooked together with the egg which has the blood spot, and cold water was added to the pot before removing any egg so that your hands can be put into the water to remove the eggs, the pot and the other eggs are kosher. Therefore, it is advisable to cook three or more eggs together and to cool the boiled eggs by adding cold water to the egg pan until the original water turns cold or lukewarm before taking out the eggs.

Today, eggs are sold frozen or dried, commercially. All eggs are USDA government inspected. The government does not allow the use of blood spots. They do permit the use of the egg if the blood spot has been removed. In order to remove a spot from an egg, special equipment is required. Since most factories do not have this equipment, they therefore reject the whole egg rather than remove the blood spot. The government also permits the use of ova eggs, but these eggs must be marked OVA. The Kashruth supervision of eggs in most cases relies upon government inspection, and certification is given to those companies which reject the entire egg.

Challah

The Jewish Homemaker, February-March 1979

Three pillars of a blessed Jewish home and family, *challah*, *niddah*, and *hadlakas haner* – the separation of dough, the holiness of Jewish married life and the kindling of candles for the Sabbath – are the duties and privileges of a Jewish life. "Because of three transgressions women die in childbirth," says the Mishna: "Because they are negligent in the observance of menstrual uncleanliness, in the separation of the dough portions, and the kindling of the Sabbath candles."

According to the law of the Torah, the responsibility of [the mitzvah to separate] challah applies only in the Holy Land. This is learned from the words of the Scriptural text: "When you come into *the land* where I bring you, and when you eat of the bread of the land." The Talmud interprets this scriptural text as meaning that the obligation of challah only applies when the whole Jewish nation, and not only part of it, dwells in the land of Israel. Today, outside the land of Israel, our rabbis have ordained that the duty of challah serves as a reminder "so that the teaching of challah should not be lost from the House of Israel."

One is, therefore, obliged, according to rabbinic law, today in exile, to separate challah from the dough on the basis of the following rules. Challah must be separated from dough made of one of the following five kinds of grain: wheat, barley, spelt, oats, and rye. One of these kinds of grains comes under the obligation of challah only if so much dough is kneaded as will suffice for one man's daily sustenance, that is, a measure of one *omer*, which corresponds to the volume of $43^1/_5$ eggs. A minimum of three pounds of flour must be used in baking in order to oblige one to separate challah.

If three pounds of flour are used, one separates challah without a *brocha*. If five pounds or more are used, one is obliged to make a blessing over the separation of the challah. When dough has been kneaded with eggs or with any kind of fruit juice, there is doubt whether challah has to be separated. In such cases, it is necessary to mix the dough with a little water, milk, honey, wine or olive oil while kneading it, in order to make it come within the obligation of challah with recitation of a brocha, provided the necessary measure of flour has been used with it. If the dough is prepared for cooking or frying purposes, challah should be separated without pronouncing the blessing. However, if even a small part of the dough is prepared for baking, challah must be taken and then a brocha said.

If one purchases bread or cake and is in doubt whether challah portion has been separated, he should separate it from the bakery bread or cake without a benediction. When one separates challah from dough, a piece of dough the size of an olive is taken and burnt. After the benediction is made, the custom is to burn it in the same oven where the bread is being baked. If one forgets to separate the challah on the eve of the Sabbath, in countries other than Israel, the bread can be eaten on the Sabbath and a portion of it be left over, and at the termination of the Sabbath, the challah portion is to be taken therefrom. The portion thus left over should be large enough for challah to be separated therefrom and still have something left over, as it is necessary that after the challah has been separated, the remainder be substantial.

There are many breads being sold on the market today with kosher supervision for which no arrangements are being made for the separation of challah. No mention is made on the bread or on the packages or elsewhere notifying the public that challah was not removed from these breads. There are many bakeries that are not under kosher supervision, but are owned by religious Jews, where they do not know that one is obligated to remove challah from cake as well.

In many cases we have been asked to give supervision for products baked by Jewish bakers who are obligated to separate challah. We were unable to make arrangements to remove challah, and therefore refused supervision.

Kitniyos on Pesach

The Jewish Homemaker, February-March 1980

Erev Pesach we published an ad that the OK does not allow the use of *kitniyos* (legumes) in any of its products. I wish to go into some detail about the halacha and the history of the use of the products derived from kitniyos such as corn syrup, soya or corn oil, lecithin and corn sweeteners.

In Shulchan Aruch Chapter 453 we find that, actually, legumes are not considered grains that are forbidden on Pesach, and are not *chometz* (leavened). According to the halacha it should be permitted to prepare Passover food containing kitniyos. It is however the custom in Ashkenazic countries not to eat foods on Pesach that contain rice, buckwheat, peas, beans, sesame or other kitniyos, even on the last day of Passover. The reason the Shulchan Aruch gives is because in our generation there are many who are observant yet ignorant of the laws pertaining to *heter* (permitted foods) and *issur* (prohibited foods), and they will not know which are considered grain and which are considered legumes, according to the Torah. For instance, bread is baked from corn and wheat. One must of course differentiate between these two and know that wheat is considered grain according to the Torah and corn is not considered grain and therefore cannot become *chometzdig*. In order not to confuse the public, rabbis in the Ashkenazic communities prohibited the use of kitniyos.

Another reason given was that grain usually grows in the same fields that legumes grow. It therefore becomes necessary that legumes be completely inspected to make sure that not a speck of grain is found amongst the legumes. This is very difficult, and the rabbis feared that this would not be done properly.

There were and are rabbis of esteem who said that it is true that we Ashkenazim are not permitted to eat legumes on Pesach and we must be very strict about this. However, they state that products derived from legumes before Pesach, such as oils, corn syrup or corn sweeteners, are permitted to be used before Pesach.

For instance, the Chief Rabbi of Kovno, the Gaon Rabbi Isaac Elchanan, in his famous book Be'er Yitzchak, says that these products are permissible. He, however states that legumes must be well sifted before the products are manufactured. There are several other great rabbis who also permit these products.

Many rabbis, however, refute this decision and say that these products are not permissible. The Chaye Adorn and Zemech Zedeck are among the many others who say that these products are not permissible.

For many years in the United States, practically all the rabbis who gave *hechsherim* allowed the use of corn syrup in their products. Barton candies, for instance, originally allowed the use of corn syrup in their candies. As a matter of fact, Rabbi Nuchim N. Kornmehl, who supervises Barton candies to this day and is a renowned Talmudic scholar and author, in his Code of Jewish Law and Responsa Tifereth Zvi, permits the use of corn products and derivatives such as corn syrup.

Several years ago, Rabbi Yosef Ber Soloveitchik, at one of his famous lectures, stated that it was absolutely forbidden to use corn syrups or corn derivatives. As a result of this, Bartons and many other companies stopped using corn syrup. It came to such a point that even companies that were using kitniyos derivatives as recently as three years ago stopped using kitniyos.

Chocolate, for instance, used lecithin derived from soya in amounts of less than one percent, and most companies stopped this as well. In Europe until two years ago they had lecithin in all their chocolates, even the Cholov Yisroel chocolate. Because the U.S. market would not accept it, they also refrained from using it.

In the last two years, the price of cane sugar has been much higher than corn sweeteners. One of the major ingredients in soft drinks such as sodas is sugar. Because the price differentiation is so great, all soda producers switched to corn sweeteners. On Pesach all these companies must go back to using cane sugar. This is very costly to them. They threaten that they will either discontinue the hechsher of Pesach drinks or will look for rabbis who will allow the use of corn sweeteners. As a result of this, there are rabbis giving kosher supervision who are looking to go back to the old system and again permit the use of the above-mentioned products so that they do not lose their hechsherim. I bring this to the attention of readers, hoping that they will maintain their strong stand in this matter.

Rennet Kosher Cheese and Lactic Acid

The Jewish Homemaker, June-July 1972

Insofar as Kashruth is concerned, dairy products present their own set of problems. Let us start with cheese: specifically, hard cheese such as cheddar, commonly known as American cheese, Swiss, and the like.

In order to produce these cheeses, it is necessary to use a coagulating agent. Historically, veal rennet, extracted from calves slaughtered when 10–30 days of age, was the sole milk-clotting enzyme used in the manufacture of cheese. Relatively few stomachs of this age specification are available in the U.S. We estimate the average age of stomachs in supply at 2–3 months, and the average is steadily increasing.

There is a single large pool of high-quality 10-day-old calf stomachs in the world: in New Zealand. There the meat industry slaughters approximately 2 million 10-day-old calves each year. According to USDA statistics, the slaughter of milk-fed calves declined from 12 million in 1945 to approximately 4.5 million in 1970. In 1971 it is estimated that fewer than 4 million calves were slaughtered.

At the same time, USDA statistics reveal that in the 20 years between 1949 and 1969 cheese production almost doubled, increasing from 1.2 billion pounds to 2 billion pounds. Swine pepsin was introduced to the cheese industry in 1960, when the rennet shortage first became acute. Pepsin is obtained from the linings of hog stomachs. It is available in ample supply, and is the most economical animal source of milk-clotting enzyme. Pepsin is a very satisfactory milk-clotting enzyme when combined with veal rennet or other milk-clotting enzymes. These blends are the dominant type of milk-clotting enzyme system utilized in the United States cheese industry.

From the halachic point of view, pepsin is accepted as *not* being kosher by almost all authorities. There are a few who are of the opinion that rennet, if dried properly, is kosher even if it is extracted from non-kosher stomachs. However, if rennet is being used in any of the products that the OK certifies, be assured that only rennet extracted from kosher stomachs is used. This rennet is imported from Israel. No such rennet is produced in the United States.

Research-minded companies have long been seeking sources of milk-clotting enzyme which do not depend upon the animal byproduct industries. Their research has centered on microbial fermentation. Microorganisms can be propagated in unlimited quantities at low cost. The OK Laboratories now certifies two such clotting agents. One is distributed by Dairyland Food Laboratories and is called Emporase; the other is produced by Miles Laboratorie and is named Marzyme. These products have been tested and proved to be effective. Producers of kosher cheeses are already using these products.

There is another enzyme used today which has become popular. I am sure that there are many people in orthodox circles who have never heard of it. I am referring to Lipase Modified Milk Fat Products. This enzyme is extracted from meat and is used to enhance and improve the dairy flavor in fat products, baked goods, confections, sauces, dressings and other foods in which a dairy flavor is desired. There are many milk chocolates using this product, and it is not listed as an ingredient. It is also used in margarine, coffee whiteners, potato flakes, noodles and buttermilk.

Lactic acid is used in many sodas. We have been receiving many calls asking if this lactic acid is *milchig* (dairy). The answer is emphatically *no*: the lactic acid used in sodas is not milchig. There is lactic acid that is milchig, and this is used in processing cheeses and other dairy products, but the lactic acid used in sodas and olives is derived from fermenting starches, and neutralizes the acid as soon as formed with calcium or carbonate. It is also derived synthetically from sulfite pulp liquor. Do not mistake lactic acid for lactose. Lactose is only derived from milk. Lactose is milk sugar; it is crystallized from whey.

Cholov Yisroel and Dark Chocolate

The Jewish Homemaker, February-March 1977

Cholov yisroel is milk that is supervised by a Jew from the time of milking until the milk is bottled. All foods that pass through the hands of persons who are not obligated to keep the Kosher Dietary Laws must have proof of kashruth.

For this reason, milking and bottling in a non-Jewish dairy require Jewish supervision. In *halacha* there are differences of opinion as to whether this regulation applies only where the farmers in question keep *treifa* animals as well, or even where they do not.

Many hold that in cases where there is government control over milk, one is permitted to drink milk that has not been supervised. Then, of course, there are those who maintain that under all conditions one must drink only supervised milk. But the majority opinion seems to be that where cholov yisroel is available, one must drink cholov yisroel.

In a case where equipment has been used for cooking of non-Jewish milk, according to those who subscribe to the ruling that non-Jewish milk is prohibited under all circumstances, the halacha is that this equipment must be kosherized before it may be used again. But for those who maintain that where there is government control milk is permissible without supervision, if a product has been cooked in equipment which has been contaminated by non-Jewish milk it is Kosher.

With chocolate, briefly, this is the story. We know there are two types of chocolate: dark chocolate and milk. To classify a product as milk chocolate, the law requires a company to use at least 12% milk in their product. In the event that they use a lesser amount, they are forbidden to call it milk chocolate, and are not required to list milk as an ingredient.

The same applies to creamery butter. In many cases companies use small percentages of milk or butter to make the chocolate "bloom resistant," and do *not* list milk or butter as an ingredient. "Bloom resistant" means to keep the chocolate from turning gray. This chocolate is produced in the dark chocolate equipment, which means that the *pareve* chocolate would be produced in the same equipment as the milk chocolate.

The usual procedure for a changeover from milk to pareve is to flush the equipment with cocoa butter or plain chocolate, and then produce the pareve chocolate. Since certain equipment would be ruined if it were flushed with water, it is impossible to kosherize this equipment with water, so another method must be employed.

For those who go according to the opinion that nowadays one does not need kosherizing where there is government control, a purge of chocolate or cocoa butter would be sufficient as far as calling the chocolate pareve is concerned.

Those who wish to eat chocolate produced according to *all* halachic opinions would eat only chocolate manufactured in a company that has *separate* equipment for pareve chocolate and *separate* equipment for milk chocolate. There are very few such companies, and their chocolate is substantially costlier.

APPENDIX II

THE FINAL ARTICLE

Bernard Levy

Alcohol, Vinegar and a Personality Clash

The Jewish Homemaker, February-March 1987

The Jewish Homemaker, February-March 1987

The following article was written some time ago. We have withheld its publication in the hope that the three organizations which had used the "vinegar incident" for personal benefit and vendetta would consider and reconsider the ramifications of their actions, would have a change of heart and do T'shuva. But Rosh Hashannah and Yom Kippur have come and gone, and signs of T'shuva have not been forthcoming. There has been no letup: these Kashruth organizations persist in publishing and publicizing false statements in an effort to discredit us and gain entry into our companies to solicit them for certifications and attempt to pirate our Hechsherim. THEY HAVE DIRECTLY SOLICITED OUR COMPANIES. They have created chaos and perpetrated a disgraceful Chillul Hashem in the field of Kashruth. We are now publishing this article: our companies and readers insist that we break our silence and present the facts.

For the past fifty years, the O.K. Laboratories (OK) has enjoyed one of the best reputations in the field of Kashruth supervision. We take pride that in all that time we have done our utmost not to permit our standards to be compromised one iota. We have sought continuously to raise the level of Kashruth observance wherever possible, and feel we have been successful. We stand proud on our accomplishment.

It is distressing that in spite of all we have done, we are being subjected to campaigns of vilification by misguided and misinformed persons. It is a campaign that can only tarnish the name of O.K. Laboratories, and ultimately undermine the credibility of all Kashruth agencies. It is based on an absurdity: that the OK has been negligent in giving its endorsement to a patently non-Kosher product. The OK's scrupulous selectivity in awarding its Hashgacha is its benchmark. Many, many food processors have been turned down or terminated by us because they refused to or could not adhere to halachic requirements we insisted on – even when they were minor ones. In matters of Halacha we refused to act alone, but consulted with the sainted Reb Moshe, z"l, and Harav Dworkin, z"l, among others, to get a true Psak. Our dear friend Reb Moshe Feinstein knew the extent of our dedication to Kashruth and our sense of mission. Yes, we removed our OK symbol from many products, gave up numerous Hashgachos, and often watched others on the sidelines rush to give their own Hashgacha within a matter of days on the product that we rejected because of what we considered infractions. We would not solicit clients – and certainly not anyone who was under someone else's supervision, considering this unethical and degrading – since this places the client in a position of dictating terms and parameters.

If the OK terminated relations with a client because of relatively minor deviations, how much more so when the infraction was serious! So let us say categorically that in the matter at hand:

- The OK have never endorsed or certified any alcohol manufactured from non-Kosher wine.

- The OK has never endorsed or certified any vinegar companies using alcohol manufactured from wine.

Now, some particulars regarding the supervision of alcohol and vinegar. Wine alcohol on the food marketplace is a very recent phenomenon: Kashruth agencies had simply not run across it and not been aware of its possible use in foods. All alcohols used in the U.S.A. have been produced from grain, corn, molasses or petroleum. The only concern for Hashgacha was whether the alcohol was Kosher for Passover or not. To this day most Kashruth agencies use alcohol without any supervision at all; a mere phone call to the manufacturer ascertains the source, which may be an Arab land. Flavor companies use ethyl alcohol among their ingredients: it comes from worldwide lands that defy any possibility of supervision. The matter of wine alcohol was discovered by accident when someone visiting a food processing plant was curious as to the derivation of the alcohol they used, since, at the time, New York was not allowing vinegar companies to use synthetic alcohol. He was told that it came from a grape source. Which gave birth to the rumor that from the moment that OK gave its supervision to Sofecia, that company began selling wine alcohol to the vinegar companies. THIS WAS NOT TRUE. KOSHER VINEGAR COMPANIES HAVE BEEN BUYING WINE ALCOHOL SINCE 1984. (WE FIRST GAVE SOFECIA SUPERVISION IN SEPTEMBER 1985!) WE HAVE PROOF OF THIS AND OF THE FACT THAT KOSHER-SUPERVISED VINEGAR COMPANIES HAD BEEN BUYING ALCOHOL FROM SOFECIA SINCE 1980 WHEN IT HAD NO SUPERVISION AT ALL. But no one was concerned with wine alcohol then. Who knew of such a thing?

But let us review our relationship or non-relationship with Sofecia, a French company which has an office in New York. In 1983, a representative of Sofecia came to OK for certification of synthetic alcohol produced from petroleum. We refused to give certification. The following reprint from the March 1983 issue of *The Jewish Homemaker* spells out the details.

```
P.O. Box 10324
Stamford, CT 06904-2324
TEL: 203-323-2376
TELEX: ITT 4750057
```

September 9, 1985

Rabbi Bernard Levy
OK LABORATORIES
1430 57th Street
Brooklyn, NY 11219

RE: KOSHER FOR PASSOVER CERTIFICATION

Dear Rabbi:

Further to our meeting of August 30, 1985, we would like to confirm the following points:

1. Sofecia's ethyl alcohol is synthetically made from ethylene gas.

2. The grain alcohol we previously stored was produced by Grain Processing Corporation.

3. We do not store any other alcohol that is produced from grain nutrients.

4. The vessels we are transporting the alcohol from Europe to Perth Amboy are life-steam-cleaned before loading.

We hope that the above answers will enable you to certify our alcohol as soon as possible.

Please give me a call if you have any other questions.

Sincerely,

Hans van der Kloot

HVDK/jg

Several weeks ago, a French company contacted us and asked for our endorsement of ethyl alcohol that they produced synthetically in France, from petroleum. They would ship the alcohol by tanker to the United States: we would receive it here and it would be stored in tanks in New Jersey. We agreed: It should present no difficulty... Or so we thought.

We arranged for a highly respected responsible Orthodox Rabbi in Paris to supervise the production and shipping from France. And, in the meantime, we took a short trip to New Jersey to inspect the storage tanks where the alcohol would be stored. Here we met head-on with a problem we never before knew existed: the tanks were a tank within a tank. The inner tank contained grain alcohol, and the outer tank was to receive the synthetic alcohol.

According to Halacha, anything that soaks for 24 hours is considered the same as if it had been cooked. A *davar chariff* – a sharp food product – needs only to soak for a short while – the time it takes to cook it by fire – to be considered the same as if it had been cooked. Alcohol certainly is a *davar chariff*, which means that in a short while the wall of the inner tank is chometz-dik – not Kosher for Passover – and the synthetic alcohol would automatically be prohibited for Pesach use.

I presented this question to Hagaon Rabbi Moshe Feinstein Shlita and to Rabbi Zalman Dworkin Shlita of Lubavitch. They both concurred that the synthetic alcohol was not permissible. This meant, of course, that we could not and would not give the French company certification. (We trust that the agencies who give certification to alcohols for Pesach will look into this problem area.)

Another problem of which we were not altogether aware had to do with condensed and evaporated milk. The procedure for condensing and evaporating milk is to remove the water in the milk by applying strong heat to the milk. Only recently we discovered that many of the companies that condense milk add whey in order to increase the solids, and add shortening to increase the fat content. It is easy to see that this can present many questions as to the ultimate Kashruth of the product.

By the way, vinegar may be produced from alcohol derived from milk as well as vodka.

Note that even in 1983 Sofecia approached us specifically for synthetic alcohol produced from petroleum: even then we were told that Sofecia sells only synthetic alcohol. This was given to us in writing in 1985, in the Sofecia memo which appears herewith. Even with their assurances in 1983 we refused them because of a question of the permissibility of their equipment, as ruled by the Torah authorities on consultation with them.

The above letter assures us that Sofecia synthetic alcohol is manufactured from petroleum. It does not read *"one* of Sofecia's ethyl alcohols is made synthetically from gas." When we announced that we were giving supervision on this basis, it did not mean that we forfeited the requirement to visit their installations: it meant merely that Sofecia led us to believe that Sofecia sold only synthetic alcohol and that other tanks stored in its depot were not Sofecia ethyl alcohol. As a matter of fact, when Sofecia placed ads in Jewish periodicals, they stated "To our knowledge the OK never visited the facilities." It maligned the OK. We *did* visit and inspect the facilities: the words "to our knowledge" were inserted in order to protect one of the signers of the ad who knew that we had indeed visited the facilities.

The telex below, dated January 21, 1986, was sent to an alcohol company in Florida. It states that the alcohol involved in the shipment was under the supervision of Rabbi Frankfurter. According to information supplied to us by Florida Distillers, this shipment was wine alcohol. We were assured by Rabbi Frankfurter that he DID NOT give supervision on wine alcohol. Rabbi Frankfurter is a most respectable and respected rabbi.

TO: FLORIDA DISTILLERS LAKE ALFORT USA
FM: SESOS PARIS 611234F - 21101186 - SOFECIA - 348 -
ATTN: MR ARNOLD BEINSTEIN
RE l. 1000MTONS INDUSTRIAL l 90PF

WE HEREWITH NOMINATE VESSEL SHOUW FICTORIA LOADING FEB 1-15 FOR ARRIVAL MARCH 1-15 PORT MANATEE (FL)

PSE OPEN UC ACCORDINGLY

RE 2. KOSHER CERTIFICATE

WE HEREWITH CONFIRM OUR ALCOHOL WAS DECLARED

> KOSHER BY RABBI FRANKFURTER PARIS WILL CONFIRM BY LETTER
>
> RE 3. SAMPLE 1 90PF FOR UPGRADING
>
> WILL SEND YOU SAMPLE SOONEST. ARE EXPECTING SAMPLES ANY DAY HERE
>
> WILL REVERT
>
> REGARDS
>
> CHRIS PENNING

The statement which follows was made in a letter we received from a very large Kosher vinegar company. This company has been under the supervision of the largest Kashruth supervising agency in the U.S.A.

We quote:

> Rabbi,
>
> I know you are familiar with the saying that people who live in glass houses should not throw stones. It applies to this discussion.
>
> With fourteen years in the food industry, I have had the opportunity to deal with numerous organizations and individuals. None of them, with a rare exception or two, has displayed the devotion to kashruth and the knowledge that you exhibit. So I cannot understand how some of the Rabbis in the same field dare to question your dedication to Kashruth when your inspection is so thorough and theirs so shallow-to-non-existent. Our current Hashgacha has only recently begun to investigate who our suppliers are. Until a few months ago, no one took the trouble to investigate who these suppliers were. Furthermore, before the vinegar incident, we were permitted to buy alcohol *from any source we wished*! That went for both varieties – synthetic and ferment alcohol!

It seems to me that many have tried to shift their responsibilities and their shortcomings to you. To me it is very obvious that some organizations have been using the OK as a scapegoat and have attempted to besmirch your reputation and the OK symbol.

The fact is, dear Rabbi, that you and your OK were in no way to blame for our using wine alcohol in our products.

We have much more evidence vindicating the OK and incriminating the other agencies, but we do not think it is necessary or wise to continue the "battle." We hope that we can put an end to the matter here and now!

Not long ago we dropped in on a Rabbi in Israel who represents one of the above organizations here and abroad. He told us that he, together with a Rabbi from Chicago, visited many factories throughout Europe. Wherever they came in, at almost every factory, they were told that Rabbi Levy had already been there. And we had, because we make it our duty to be there in person as often as possible. They were happy to have proof positive of the fact that we DO NOT give supervision "over the telephone" or through inexperienced persons… in all parts of the world. He has seen what has been going on in the field and is upset by the Chillul Hashem. He has made valiant attempts to put a stop to it, but thus far has had no success…

We deeply regret our involvement with a company that has caused so much grief to the Kosher-keeping public and to so many plants under Kosher supervision. On our part, we pledge ourselves to continue to maintain the highest standards of Kashruth, as always.

In summary, we offer for our readers' examination a letter from Rabbi Mendel Feldman, a well-known and respected personage in Baltimore and an ex-president of the Igud Harabbonim, who was invited as an impartial witness at a meeting held at the Vaad Hakashrut of Baltimore.

"May He who makes peace in His Heaven make peace for us and for all Israel. And let us say Amen…"

We truly endorse Rabbi Feldman's sentiments. We are and have always been ready for peace. We feel that the time has come for mutual respect among all agencies who are sincerely interested in furthering the cause of Torah generally and Kashruth in particular. The Bais Hamikdash [Holy Temple in Jerusalem] was destroyed because of *sinnas chinam* [causeless hatred]. There is need for hearing two sides of a story… and of being open and aboveboard. Personality clashes are counterproductive: they sap our energies and leave us too weak to do our best in bringing our mission to fruition.

There are many other facts pertaining to the vinegar incident, but it is not my intention to malign or impugn the reputation of the agencies involved. In future articles, I hope to bring our readers up to date on what is happening in alcohol and vinegar companies today, since many investigations have been made recently in the methods used to give supervision on alcohol and vinegar. Many things have been discovered, and I am sure our readers are interested in finding out what these new discoveries are.

We hope to write more about the effect the solicitation of Hechsherim is having on Kashruth, and to publicize some of the letters we have received from companies who have been solicited and harassed.

SHEARITH ISRAEL CONGREGATION
PARK HEIGHTS & GLEN AVENUES
BALTIMORE, MD. 21215
466-3060

בס"ד

May 18, 1986

Rabbi Beryl Levy
1430 57th Street
Brooklyn, New York 11219

Dear Rabbi Levy:

I am writing to you to record my impressions of the meeting that was held on Iyar 6, 5746 (May 15th, 1986) in the offices of the Vaad HaKashrus. Present were Rabbis Heineman, you, your son, Shuman, Dr. Pollack and I. The following facts were brought out clearly.

1. Sofecia, on September 9, 1985, issued a letter to you stating "Sofecia's ethyl alcohol is synthetically made from ethylene gas", upon which basis OK Laboratories issued their certification. This letter states specifically that the Sofecia ethyl alcohol is synthetically made from ethylene gas. A copy of this letter was sent to the OU, but it was never shown to Rabbi Heineman or to any members of the Baltimore Vaad Hakashrus. The letter was never shown at any of the Rabbinic meetings attended by Rabbi Heineman.

2. Rabbi Shuman, administrator of the Baltimore Vaad HaKashrus admitted that the same procedure of Kashrus investigation used by the OK Laboratories in determining the Kashrus of this alcohol is used by the Baltimore Vaad HaKashrus and by all Kashrus organizations. As a matter of fact, all agencies use alcohol from companies who have no Kashrus supervision.

3. Rabbi Heineman stated that the text of the advertisement which appeared in the Jewish Press on May 9, 1986, co-signed by the Vaad HaKashrus did not in any way intend to discredit the OK. Also, the Vaad HaKashrus had no knowledge that the ad would be circulated among the members of the RCA to discredit the OK.

4. It was evident from the discussion that you were never contacted personally to discuss this serious matter at any meetings that were held by the organizations concerned. On the other hand, Rabbi Heineman did admit that when you found fault with or had questions for the Vaad HaKashrus, that you did, indeed, contact them personally to discuss the matter with the Vaad. It was also evident that this underlying problem was not a Kashrus problem, but rather it is the result of a personality clash between the OU and OK. They hoped that you and the OU could come to some agreement to resolve this problem.

I do hope that this issue that can have a detrimental effect on the Kashrus structure of our communities be resolved amicably in the true sense of

שלום מדרכיה דרכי נועם אלה יקר אלה על ב' יקראו ישראל את.

Sincerely yours,

Rabbi Mendel Feldman

APPENDIX III

T.U. CORRESPONDENCE

A selection of solicitation letters from the Torah Umesorah archives.

February 27, 1962

Dear Mr. Emerson:

I have just arrived from an extended trip, and was pleasantly surprised to find some correspondence from you, I heard from you sooner than I expected.

On behalf of the Staff and Board of Directors of Torah Umesorah, I wish to express my sincerest thanks to you to you for your contribution. You now have a share in this sacred work of strengthening and spreading Torah throughout the country.

I hope that we merit your support for many years to come.

With kindest personal regards,

Sincerely yours,

Rabbi Bernard Levy

March 5, 1962

About two months ago, we sent you a letter to remind you about a pledge for the year 1962.

We realize that you must be very busy and did not have the opportunity to take care of this.

Torah Umesorah is in desperate need of funds at this time in order to carry on our activities for spreading and strengthening Torah throughout the country. There are many communities waiting for us to contact them, but we are being hampered in our work because of a shortage of funds.

We would greatly appreciate your cooperation in this matter.

Best wishes.

Sincerely yours,

Rabbi Bernard Levy

P.S. Just for the record, your last year's contribution was $18. Would you kindly try to increase it?

March 5, 1962

Just a few words to thank you for the kind reception you gave me when I visited your office yesterday.

I was happy to see that you understand the work of Torah Umesorah, and I am sure you will respond accordingly.

My kindest personal regards to your father on his return, and best wishes to you.

Sincerely yours,

Rabbi Bernard Levy

April 6, 1962

Dear Mr. Engelberg:

Have just returned to the office to find the financial situation to be a very critical one. I do not think it is necessary for me to tell you how important it is for the Parent Organization of the Day School movement to operate smoothly in order to be able to help the many problems of the individual Day Schools.

As one who is keenly interested and concerned with the future of the movement, l am sure that I can call upon you to help us at this time.

When I spoke to you, I indicated that we would very much like to have you as a Life Member at $250 annually. If you would do this, it would alleviate our burden considerably, and you will have a vital share in the sacred cause of spreading and strengthening Torah through[out] the country.

Please do let us hear from you.

Kind personal regards from Dr. Kaminetsky, and all good wishes to you and yours for a Happy and Kosher Pesach.

Sincerely yours,

Rabbi Bernard Levy

January 3, 1961

Dear Mr. and Mrs. Schvatt:

As always, I enjoyed my visit with you last night, and I hope the Almighty sends Mrs. Schvatt a speedy recovery to her arm.

My wife and I enjoyed the apples immensely, and we wish to thank you very much for them.

As you requested, I am enclosing a return envelope for Torah Umesorah, and I am certain that you will be very generous to us. May G-d bless you both with many happy and healthy years.

Sincerely yours,

Rabbi Bernard Levy
Director of Development

PS Under separate cover, I am sending you a few copies of our children's magazine for your "aineklach" [grandchildren]. If you would send me their names and addresses, I will enter them as subscribers. I am sure they will enjoy these magazines very much.

March 28, 1961

Dear Eddie:

G-d bless you – you are a sweet guy. You were the first in Elizabeth to respond to the Torah Umesorah Pesach mailing. Following your contribution, I received several others from Elizabeth – so you see, yours was 'mazeldik' [auspicious].

The Almighty should be good to you and your family – you are all wonderful.

Best wishes for a happy and kosher Pesach.

Sincerely yours,

Rabbi Bernard Levy
Director of Development

November 20, 1961

Dear Mr. Berger:

We are in receipt of your most generous contribution to Torah Umesorah through your Rabbi, who is a member of our Executive Committee.

I know that you will feel an inner satisfaction that by virtue of your support you are helping us in disseminating Torah throughout the width and breadth of the United States and Canada.

We are proud of the fact that our organization has been instrumental in establishing more than 150 Yeshivas and Day Schools in the most far-flung communities of America. I am sure you will appreciate how vital is this work in insuring the spiritual and cultural survival and growth of the Jewish community.

May G-d grant you and yours health and vigor so that you may continue to serve our people through the strengthening of our Torah and traditions.

Sincerely yours,

Rabbi Bernard Levy

December 26, 1961

Dear Mrs. Barricini:

We missed you at our Dinner. Several people asked for you. I wish to report that it was an outstanding, successful affair and you would have certainly enjoyed it if you had been able to attend.

Torah Umesorah, now more than ever, is in need of your assistance. The growth of the Day School movement has made greater demands upon us, and our budget has increased substantially. As one who has always been interested in Jewish education for our youth, you will certainly appreciate this.

In the past you have always made a token contribution to our cause. We sincerely hope that this year, with our needs being what they are, you will make a substantial increase in your contribution.

Please let me hear from you.

Best wishes to you and your family, and kind personal regards.

Sincerely yours,

Rabbi Bernard Levy

February 13, 1962

Dear Moshe Chaim:

Do hope this letter finds you and the family in the best of health and the Hotel filled to the gills. At the outset, I wish to thank you for the wonderful reception you accorded me, and also for your warm hospitality.

Before I left, I wanted to say goodbye to you and also, incidentally, to pick up the check that the Hotel promised, but I was unable to locate you.

As you know, we work very close, and if you could send this money in to us, it will be greatly appreciated.

Kindest personal regards to Rabbi Kohler and all the others.

Sincerely yours,

Rabbi Bernard Levy

P.S. I am going to take care of the Rambams and Shulchan Aruchs today. I was unable to do so because of the Convention.

Please send me the address of Nathan Lehman of Montreal. I must send him a receipt.

BL

Dear Mr. A[...]:

Following the interesting discussion Dr. Kaminetsky and I had with you during our "shpatzier" [stroll] on Broadway, I wish to assure you that measures have already been taken to rectify the wrong perpetrated against you.

We are sure you realize that in a good business you try your utmost to satisfy your old customers – in addition to recruiting new ones, – and we certainly cannot afford to forfeit the support of as devoted a Torah Umesorah friend as Mr. A[…].

Please G-d, Torah Umesorah, this year, is embarking upon a tremendous program of activities which will necessitate that assistance, loyalty, and dedication of all its supporters. We would, therefore, greatly appreciate it if you would kindly help us meet our current expenditures by sending your generous contribution…

Thank you very kindly for your interest.

With Torah greetings, I remain,

Most sincerely,

Rabbi Bernard Levy
Director of Development

August 17, 1962

Dear Mr. Adler:

Just a few words of thank you for the encouragement you gave me when I solicited your contribution on the plane.

We are really desperate for funds and being seriously hampered in the progress of our work of building and strengthening Torah.

Because of the serious lack of teachers, we plan to open a Teachers' Seminary this Fall. We hope that our financial crisis will not hold this most necessary project.

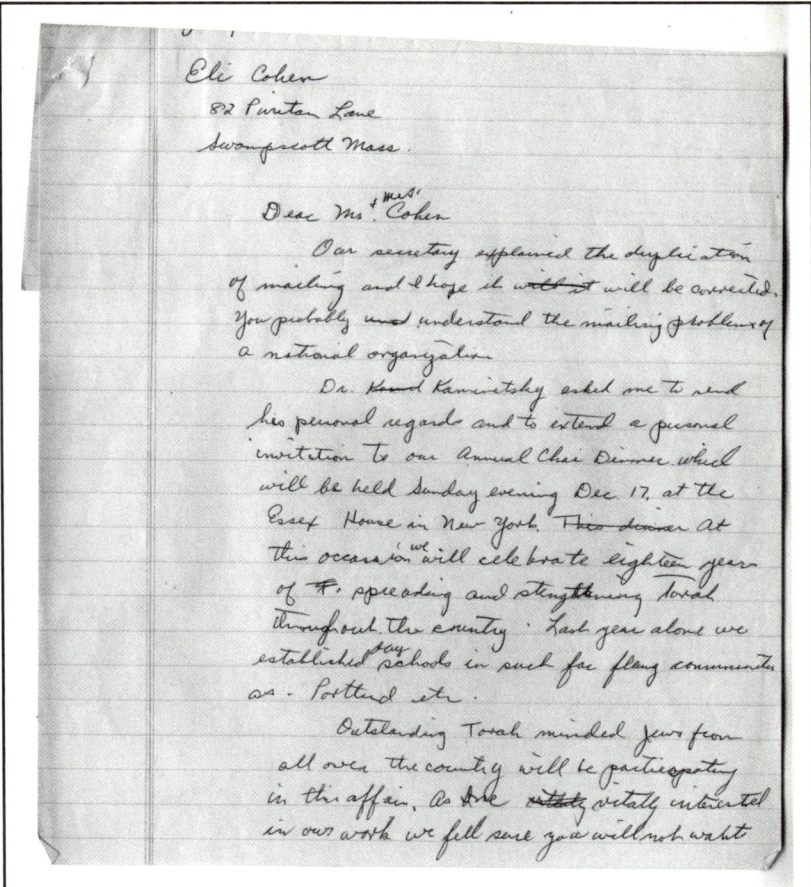

A draft of a letter by Rabbi Levy. Courtesy of Torah Umesorah.

In the past you were very generous to us. Please allow us to enjoy this generosity again.

Kindest personal regards.

Sincerely yours,

Rabbi Bernard Levy
Director of Development

SELECTED BIBLIOGRAPHY

Bunim, Amos. *A Fire in His Soul: Irving M. Bunim, 1901–1980: The Man and His Impact on American Orthodox Jewry*. Feldheim Publications, 1989.

Feinstein, R. Moshe. *Igros Moshe, Orach Chayim, chelek revii* (Vol. 6). Privately printed, 1982.

Feinstein, R. Moshe. *Igros Moshe, Yoreh Deah, chelek beis* (Vol. 5). Privately printed, 1973.

Fishkoff, Sue. *Kosher Nation: Why More and More of America's Food Answers to a Higher Authority*. Schocken Books, 2010.

Fitzgerald, Tom. "A Question of Kosher: Rabbi says 'yes' to Lowell firm's horseradish, 'no' to its salad dressings." *Grand Rapids Press*, March 18, 1982.

Freedman, Seymour. *The Book of Kashruth: A Treasury of Kosher Facts and Frauds*. Bloch Publishing Company, 1970.

Gastwirt, Harold P. *Fraud, Corruption, and Holiness: The Controversy Over the Supervision of Jewish Dietary Practice in New York City, 1881–1940*. Kennikat Press, 1974.

Goldstein, Abraham. *Kosher Food Guide*. Organized Kashruth, 1935–1944.

Goldstein, George. *Kosher Food Guide.* Organized Kashruth, 1944–1968.

Grinstein, Hyman. *The Rise of the Jewish Community of New York, 1654-1860.* The Jewish Publication Society of America, 1945.

Hecht, Avraham. *My Spiritual Journey.* Avraham Hecht, 2006.

Hershkowitz, Yitzchok. *Hamalach: Shaarei Hasagos.* Y. Hershkowitz, 2017.

Horowitz, Roger. *Kosher USA: How Coke Became Kosher and Other Tales of Modern Food.* Columbia University Press, 2016.

Jacobson, Yisroel. *Zikoroin L'Beis Yisroel: Zichronot Shel Harav Yisroel Jacobson, 5666–5699.* Kehot Publications, 1996.

Kaminetsky, Joseph. *Memorable Encounters: A Torah Pioneer's Glimpses of Great Men and Years of Challenge.* Mesorah Publications, 1995.

Kaminetsky, Joseph. *Torah Umesorah, Dynamic Force for Torah: A Brief History.* Torah Umesorah, 1963.

Kaminetsky, Joseph. *Hebrew Day School Education: An Overview.* Torah Umesorah, 1970.

Kraemer, David. *Jewish Eating and Identity Through the Ages.* Routledge Advances in Sociology, 2012.

Kramer, Doniel Zvi. *The Day Schools and Torah Umesorah: The Seeding of Traditional Judaism in America.* Yeshiva University Press, 1984.

Lamm, Norman. *Conversations with the Rebbe, Menachem Mendel Schneerson: Interviews with 14 Leading Figures About the Rebbe.* JEC Publishing Company, 1996.

Levin, Berel. *Toldos Chabad B'artzos Habris.* Kehot Publications, 1988.

Levin, Berel. *Toldos Chabad B'Polin, Lita, V'Latvia B'Shanim 5550–5706*. Kehot Publications, 2011.

Levy, Berel. *The Jewish Homemaker*. Organized Kashrus Laboratories, 1969–2005.

Lewis, Theodore. "Mashgiachs Form AFL Union." *Jewish Post*, December 14, 1945.

Lytton, Timothy D. *Kosher: Private Regulation in the Age of Industrial Food*. Harvard University Press, 2013.

Rosenblum, Yonoson. *Reb Shraga Feivel: The Life and Times of Rabbi Shraga Feivel Mendlowitz, the Architect of Torah in America*. Mesorah Publications, 2001.

Rosenwein, Rifka. "Making Things Kosher: Passover Means Lots of Work for Many Food Processors." *Wall Street Journal*, April 23, 1986.

Schachter, Zalman. *My Life in Jewish Renewal: A Memoir*. Rowman & Littlefield Publishers, 2012.

Schneerson, R. Menachem Mendel (Lubavitcher Rebbe). *Igros Kodesh 5722–5723* (Vol. 22). Kehot Publications, 1994.

Shenker, Israel. "With Them, It's Always Strictly Kosher." *New York Times*, April 15, 1979.

Sloane, Leonard. "Calling It Kosher: How to and Why." *New York Times*, May 18, 1975.

Sobel, Bernard. *The M'Lochim: A Study of Religious Community*. New School for Social Research, 1956.

Surasky, Aharon. *Shlucha D'Rachmana*. Feldheim, 1992.

Wolf, Zushe. *Dedushka: Harebi V'Yahadut Roosya*. Vaad Hashluchim L'Medinat Chever Haamim, 2006.

Yoskowitz, Jeffrey. "The Kosher Chocolate Wars." *Atlantic*, April 15, 2009.

Zaklikowski, Dovid. *Footprints: Colorful Lives, Huge Impact*. Hasidic Archives, 2017.

Zaklikowski, Dovid. *Kaleidoscope: Uplifting Views on Daily Life*. Hasidic Archives, 2017.

ACKNOWLEDGMENTS

When I was growing up, Rabbi Berel Levy was a frequent subject of conversation. His name often elicited strong emotions, as stories about him and his work in kosher supervision were told and repeated. Still, when I embarked on this project, I doubted whether I could scratch together more than a few dozen pages. After some preliminary research, however, I quickly realized that Rabbi Levy's story provided enough color and suspense for a full-length book. I met with Rabbi Eli Lando, executive manager at OK Kosher headquarters, who agreed to cooperate and provided my initial contacts in the organization.

I then conducted extensive interviews with Mrs. Thelma Levy. A gracious woman with an incredible memory, Mrs. Levy was a fountain of information, recalling in minute detail stories that happened over seven decades earlier. Every visit to her home opened new avenues for me to explore.

In four interviews, Rabbi Don Yoel Levy spoke frankly about his father's accomplishments and challenges. I came to appreciate that honesty was paramount to the Levys. They wanted the book to present Rabbi Levy as he was. They also asked that individuals who played a negative role in his life should not be named, a request I have honored throughout.

At first I wondered how it was possible for the family to remember events that transpired decades earlier in such detail. As I gained access to more documents and interviews with Rabbi Berel Levy himself, however, I found every detail was corroborated. When the Levys did not have an answer to a question, they were not afraid to admit it.

Rabbi Levy's granddaughter Devorah Leah Chein helped me to navigate the family archive. She took time out of her busy schedule to spend hours rummaging through her grandfather's papers, which had been kept untouched for decades. She also assisted in obtaining many of the photos used in the book.

Fifteen years ago Rabbi Levy's granddaughter Esty Scheiner, and her husband, Rabbi Dovi Scheiner, conducted several important interviews with people who had known Rabbi Levy, including Amos Bunim. I used these interviews extensively, as well as Dr. Ruth Benjamin's interviews with Rabbis Yosef Wineberg and Avraham Hecht. Many of the subjects have since passed on, and it is thanks to the interviewers' efforts that their words were included.

Locating the Torah Umesorah archive pertaining to Rabbi Levy was a difficult job that required assistance from many individuals. Mrs. Goldy Goldberger, director of the Brooklyn Teachers' Center, helped me access part of the archive; however, I found that many documents were missing. Numerous efforts to find the rest of the archive went nowhere, until Dr. Zev Eleff directed me to Rabbi Zev Dunner. Rabbi Dunner opened the most precious archive of Torah Umesorah, where I found eight hundred documents pertaining to Rabbi Levy's time there. While there were still many gaps and lost papers, this treasure trove formed the basis of the chapter on that period of Rabbi's Levy's life.

I owe a debt of gratitude to the staff of the Dorot Jewish Division at the New York Public Library, to Alyse Hennig and Astrid Emel at the St. John's University archives, and to Yaacov Greenwald, assistant controller at the *Jewish Press*.

Numerous individuals assisted me in my research. Among those not mentioned in the book are Rabbi Eli Bloch, Lee Blumenthal, Rabbi

Moshe Bogomilsky, Rabbi Chaim Shaul Brook, Rabbi Shlomo Gartenhaus, Yitzy Goldberg, Avi Goldstein, Baruch Gorin, Rabbi Moshe Herson, Yitzchak Yehudah Holtzman, Dr. Roger Horowitz, Rabbi Doniel Zvi Kramer, Rabbi Yitzchok Loewenthal, Rabbi Sholom Ber Levine, Bezalel Lesches, Malka Levy, Rabbi Josh Metzger, Rabbi Avraham Osdoba, Rabbi Aaron Raskin, Dr. Efrayim Rosenstein, Rabbi Shalom Ber Schuchat, Rabbi Naftali Silberberg, Rabbi Elazar Teitz, Rabbi Moshe Tendler, Chaimke Twersky, Rabbi Shmuel Vishedsky and Rabbi Kalman Weinfeld. Without them, Rabbi Levy's story would lack many colorful details.

The legendary Rabbi Menachem Hacohen spoke with me for over four hours about his memories of Rabbi Levy, and ultimately agreed to write the epilogue. His contributions were invaluable.

In addition to those contributed by the OK archives and the Levy family, many of the photos come from the files of the Library of Agudas Chasidei Chabad and from Lubavitch Archives, the largest digital archive of Chabad-Lubavitch documents and photos.

I thank Sarah Ogince for editing the book, Alexander Heppenheimer for proofreading, and Bentzion Groner and Elana Rudnik for contributing to the design.

This book would not have been possible without Rabbi Chaim Fogelman, director of consumer marketing and education at the OK, who opened doors, came up with leads and was always there to make sure that I received the information I needed.

As always, the credit for this work goes to my wife, Chana Raizel, who willingly stepped in at home on the many days that I disappeared doing research.

Dovid Zaklikowski

INDEX

adult education 100
Ahavas Achim Tzemach Tzedek 8
Altein, R. Mordechai 65
Althaus, R. Elya Chaim 48
American Jewish Joint Distribution Committee 45
Anshei Babroisk 16
Antitrust Law Journal 142
Asbury Park Press 73
Axelrod, Ira 122, 130, 131, 136, 173

Barnetsky, Avraham 22, 25, 30, 37, 40
Barricini 10, 112, 139–140
Bartons 113, 139–140
Baumgarten, Mendel 27
Beth Medrash Govoha 84
Beth Rivkah (day school) 242
bishul akum 249–251
Blech, Zushe 130, 164, 166, 168
Block, Irving 23
bread 244–245, 256–258
Bridgeport Telegram 36
Brownsville 16
Buckley, James 197–198, 200
Bunim, Amos 82, 83, 84, 88, 108–112, 114–115, 175

Cantor, Gilbert 73
Carvel 1, 140–142
catfish 133
Chabad-Lubavitch 12
 farbrengen 26, 77, 176
 Merkos L'inyonei Chinuch 97
 Outreach 78, 157, 176–236
 prayers 25, 29
 Tanya 21, 86
 teachings 17, 29
chalav yisroel 158
Chanukah 201
Cheder Bnei Torah 72
cheese 261–263
Chenovsky, Buddy 55
chicken 133–134
chocolate 263–264
City College of New York 59
CJ Christoff and Sons Company 160
coconut oil 125
Congregation Adath Israel 74
Connecticut Jewish Ledger 69
Congregation Kehilath Israel 55
Crown Heights 10

Dial-Clock Magazine 116
Di Yiddishe Heim 38
Dolly Madison 151
Don Yoel 70, 174
Dr. Pepper 116–117
Dworkin, R. Zalman 270

Eber, R. Yehudah 50
Educational Institute Oholei Torah 242
eggs 254–256
Elizabeth, New Jersey 36
Emanuel Synagogue 70
Essas, Ilya 193, 227–228

Fair Packaging and Labeling Act (FPLA) 118
fats 143
Feigelstock, Avraham 128, 188
Feigin, Chatche 22, 27
Feinstein, R. Moshe 114–115, 128–129, 170, 270
Fisher, Mordechai 38
Fishkoff, Sue 120
Fishman, R. Joshua 65

Gartenhaus, Fruma 14, 70, 75, 76
Gartenhaus, R. Yosef 176
Gartenhaus, Zvi 70
gefilte fish 131
General Mills 1
Gifter, R. Mordechai 96
Glace 151–153
Glatt Kosher 245–248
Goldstein, Abraham 4–5
Goldstein, George 6–7
Goldstein, Herbert S. 5
Goldzweig, Chaim 154
Grinstein, Hyman 60
Grodzinski, R. Chaim Ozer 50, 96
Groner, Leibel 98
Gurary, Dovber 31
Gurary, R. Shmaryahu (Rashag) 61, 94, 100

Hacohen, R. Menachem 77, 195
Hapoel Hamizrachi 3, 55
Hapoel HaMizrachi 240
Hartford Yeshivah 69
Hecht, R. Avraham 38, 41, 43, 61
Hecht, R. Shlomo Zalman 20, 22, 27, 47
Heifetz, Mottel 42, 47
Heineman, R. Shlomo 50
Heinz 5
Henkin, R. Hillel 70
Hillel Academy (Denver, Colorado) 103
Hino Yakuhin 137
Histadrut 238
Hodakov, R. Chaim 94, 97, 100
Hoffman, Yair 137
Horowitz, Sarah 55–59
Horowitz, Yitzchak 55
hotels 144–146

Hudson Pharmaceutical Corporation 151
Hunt-Wesson 122
Hurwitz, R. Chaim Yehudah 1–2

Ilya, Belarus 12
intermarriage 182–184
Israel 3, 238
  Tithing 251–254

Jacobson, R. Yisroel 16–21, 27, 29, 37, 46
Jewish Educational Center 73
Jewish Press 163
Jewish Telegraphic Agency 87
Jolly Time Microwave Popcorn 150
Jordan, Charles 194
Junket Company 6

Kamenetsky, R. Yaakov 88, 96
Kaminetsky, Joseph 64, 81, 82, 83, 84, 88, 90, 94, 99
Kaminetsky, R. Shmuel 174
Kaminetz Yeshiva 32
Kashrus Magazine 165, 169
Klein, Stephen 113–114
Kof-K 165
Kogan, Yitzchok 198
Kohn, R. Hersch 4, 112, 241
Kotler, R. Aaron 72, 84, 85, 86, 90, 96
Kovetz Lubavitch 67
Kraft 10, 140

Lakewood Hebrew Day School 71
Lamm, Norman 99
Lazar, Berel 236
Leibowitz, R. Boruch Ber 32–33
Levine, R. Avraham Dov Ber (The Malach) 13–14, 22, 24, 33, 238
Levitin, R. Shmuel 47
Levitis, R. Yefim 236
Levy, Eliezer 109, 129, 222, 229
Levy, Lillian 12, 35, 49
Levy, Louis 12, 35, 50
Levy, Malka 228
Levy, R. Don Yoel 10, 29, 46, 75, 76, 98, 156–158, 171, 224, 226, 228, 236
Levy, Thelma 3, 55–58, 65–67, 68, 90, 173, 196–205, 219, 222, 229
Liebenstein, R. Dov 105
Lifchetz, Sholom 74, 136

Lifshitz, Mordechai 197
Lifshitz, Svetta 224–225
Lipschutz, Yacov 166
Loose-Wiles Sunshine Biscuit 5
Lubavitch Yeshivah (Tomchei Tmimim) 93, 99
  New Haven 65–69
  New York 52–53
  Otwock 22, 27, 50
Lytton, Timothy D. 120

Malachim 19, 50
Marriage 203
Mashgiach Union 1
matzah 201, 225, 236
Maxwell House 4, 5, 10
McCormick (spice) 138
mechitza 181, 186
Mendlowitz, R. Shraga Feivel 15–18. 63
mikvah 184, 189, 235
Moche, Victor C. 188
mohel 185
Mordechai Fisher 47
Moses, Eddy 178
Mrs. Levy sai 80

National Education 80–113
Ner Israel Rabbinical College 87
Neustadt, Mordechai 226–227
New York Magazine 152
New York Times 10, 32, 116, 118, 120, 125, 128, 142

oil 125
OK 1–3, 6–10, 116–174
  Jewish Homemaker 8–9, 11, 118, 129
  Kosher Food Guide 7–8, 8–9, 130
Oneg Shabbos Synagogue 52
Orthodox Union 5–6, 112, 125, 130, 149, 155, 167, 243
  Kosher Certification Service (KCS) 5

Pardes, R. Shmuel Aaron 6
Paris, Avraham 27
pas yisroel 158
Peli, Pinchas Hacohen 3–4
Pesach 258–261
Pesach food 134
Philadelphia (cream cheese) 10

Pillsbury 140
Plotkin, Meir 188
Popack, Shmuel 54
Posner, Leibel 19, 104
Posner, Zalman 19
Poupko, R. Baruch 102

Queen Mary 25

Rabbinical Alliance of America 113
Rockefeller, Nelson 2
Roisman, Nachman 212–213
Rosenstein, Grisha 201, 206–207

Sam's (knishes) 10
Sassoon, Rahmo 186
Schachter, Zalman 67, 68
Schacter, Herschel 27
Schildkraut, R. Velvl 66
Schildkraut, Velvl 68
Schneersohn, R. Shalom Dovber (Rebbe Rashab) 29, 96
Schneersohn, R. Shterna Sarah 41
Schneersohn, R. Yosef Yitzchak (Rebbe Rayatz) 17, 20, 22, 24, 26, 28, 31, 32, 35, 37, 38, 49, 51, 52, 58, 60–63, 69, 77, 94, 96, 193, 198
Schneerson, R. Chaya Mushka 198, 205
Schneerson, R. Levy Yitzchak 213
Schneerson, R. Menachem Mendel (Lubavitcher Rebbe) 29, 65–66, 77–78, 85, 94–95, 110–111, 139, 156–158, 174, 176–178, 181, 187, 189, 193–196, 200, 204–207, 208–209, 225, 230, 235, 240
Selmar, Arthur 91
Senter, R. Harvey 164, 167
Shabbat 43, 56, 57, 243
Shamir, Yitzchak 193
Sofecia 162–175, 266–274
Soloveitchik, Chaim (Reb Chaim Brisker) 33, 34
Soloveitchik, R. Zev (Velvel Brisker) 34, 39
Soviet Union 192–236, 243
S.S. Mormaxport 48
Stasz, Clarice 153
Stone, Irving 90

Sussman, Berel 12

Talmudical Yeshiva of Philadelphia 174
Tamarin, Kalman Melech 214–215, 233
Tamarin, Nachman 233
tefillin 25
Teitelbaum, R. Yoel (Satmar Rebbe) 90
Teitz, R. Pinchas 73, 77
Telshe Yeshiva in Cleveland 74
Tendler, Moshe 174
Tenenbaum, R. Mendel 29
Toeg, Ezra 178–179, 181
tofu 152
Torah Umesorah 4, 63–64, 68, 70, 276–283
  Aish Dos 84, 89
  Hamenahel 97
  Jewish Parent (magazine) 96, 108
  National Association of PTA 73, 81, 101
  National Torah Fund 82
  Olomeinu 105–107
Torah Vodaath 14–19, 15, 19, 38, 50, 61, 87
Tuna 132

2 Alarm Chili Company 153
tzitzit 54, 197

Union of Orthodox Rabbis 113

Vaad L'Hatzolas Nidchei Yisroel 227
Vanderbilt, Gloria 151–152
Vilensky, Getzel 201, 210–212

Wasserman, R. Simcha 92
Wein, Berel 166
Wikler 172
Wikler, R. Yosef 125, 130, 166, 168, 170
Wineberg, R. Yosef 28, 39, 52
Wrigley's 145
WWII 40–51
  U-Boats 48

Yediot Achronot 195
Yeshiva University 81
Young Israel Viewpoint 172

Zembe, R. Menachem 44
Zuber, Israel 48

Photo: Marc Asnin

About the Author

Dovid Zaklikowski was born in the Crown Heights neighborhood of Brooklyn, New York. He began his writing career at the age of 16 while studying at the Rabbinical College of America. Since then he has written thousands of articles, with a focus on Jewish history.

His articles have appeared in, among others, *Mishpacha Magazine*, *Hamodia*, *Ami Magazine* and the *Jewish Standard*.

He is the author of twelve books, including *Footprints: Colorful Lives, Huge Impact* and *Kaleidoscope: Uplifting Views on Daily Life*.

Dovid lives in Brooklyn with his wife, Chana Raizel, and their five children, Motti, Meir, Shaina, Benny and Mendel. Today, Dovid is a freelance journalist. He can be reached at DovidZak@gmail.com.